HIGH STAKES: science

Gwen Gordon

Anita Haley, Technical Editor

THOMSON

PETERSON'S

Australia • Canada • Mexico • Singapore • Spain • United Kingdom • United States

About The Thomson Corporation and Peterson's
With revenues of US$7.2 billion, The Thomson Corporation (www.thomson.com) is a leading global provider of integrated information solutions for business, education, and professional customers. Its Learning businesses and brands (www.thomsonlearning.com) serve the needs of individuals, learning institutions, and corporations with products and services for both traditional and distributed learning.

Peterson's, part of The Thomson Corporation, is one of the nation's most respected providers of lifelong learning online resources, software, reference guides, and books. The Education Supersite^{SM} at www.petersons.com—the Internet's most heavily traveled education resource—has searchable databases and interactive tools for contacting U.S.-accredited institutions and programs. In addition, Peterson's serves more than 105 million education consumers annually.

For more information, contact Peterson's, 2000 Lenox Drive, lawrenceville, NJ 08648; 800-338-3282; or find us on the World Wide Web at: www.petersons.com/about

ISBN: 0-7689-1072-2

Printed in the United States of America
10 9 8 7 6 5 4 3 2 1   04 03 02

CONTENTS

CONTENTS

BEFORE YOU GET STARTED

Directions: Choose from (A), (B), (C), or (D) the words that make the completed sentence most accurate.

High Stakes tests are

(A) performed by supermarkets to ensure the highest quality beef for their customers.

(B) administered by vampire slayers to ensure the demise of their enemies.

(C) very tall poles.

(D) taken by students to determine whether they are ready to graduate from high school.

We're going to take a wild guess that you chose (D) as the correct answer.

All kidding aside, we refer to the exit-level proficiency exams as **"high stakes"** tests because your high school diploma is *at stake*. Your diploma is probably the most valuable piece of paper you'll ever have in your hands. Without it, you may be limited in the kind of work you can do as an adult, and you also won't earn as much money as people who have diplomas. So, unless you're the next Britney Spears or one of those lucky people who wins the million-dollar lottery, these tests *are* high stakes for you.

We're not going to lie to you. Most of the test questions on your exit-level exams will not be as easy to answer as the question above. We're sure you already know that. But we'd bet that you *don't* know what kind of questions will pop up on these exams. And this is one case where what you don't know *can* hurt you.

But not to worry. We have diligently studied the standards for **math, reading, writing,** and **science** skills set by the state educational professionals, as well as the test questions that appear on these exams. We're not only going to tell you what you will be tested *on* but also *how* you will be tested. So, whether your state is going to use multiple-choice questions, essays, or open-ended response, if you've got a *High Stakes* skill book in your hands, we've got you covered.

So that's the good news . . .

But here's even better news! Unlike the SAT, which tests "critical thinking," the state proficiency exams test only what you've learned in school. It's actually pretty hard to study for something as vague as *critical thinking,* which is why you'll find that most SAT test-prep books are full of tricks on how to squeeze out a couple of hundred more points on the test. But the exit-level proficiency exams test **real subject knowledge.** That's not vague, that's simple! And if you've bought this book, we're going to assume you're prepared for some review. So, the bottom line is that if you study the material we give you in this book (which is not that big, right?), you can do more than just pass these exams—you can score high!

Let's Get Organized

The organization of this book is really straightforward. The book is divided into three parts:

Part I provides a short guide to the state exit-level exams and a chapter on strategies and tips to help you plan your study and alleviate test anxiety.

Part II reviews all the topics that will be covered on your state exam.

Part III contains lots of practice questions to help you get comfortable answering the test questions on high stakes exams. We also give you answers and explanations to make sure you understand everything.

Now that you know you can rely on us to help you succeed, we hope we've reduced your stress level. So . . . sit down, take a deep breath, and . . . *relax.* We're going to take you step-by-step through everything you need to know for test day.

CHAPTER 1

ALPHABET CITY

Have you checked out the shaded bands on the top of the pages in this book? You'll see some pretty odd combinations of letters, such as TAAS, BST, FCAT, OGT, CAHSEE, and MEAP.

> MEAP? What the heck is that? Sounds like Martian for salad or something.

More likely you've recognized some of the letters because they are *acronyms,* which means they are letters that stand for the name of your state exam. MEAP, by the way, stands for Michigan Educational Assessment Program. You have to admit that *Meap* rolls off the tongue a bit more easily.

In this chapter, we list all sixteen states that require exams for graduating high school. Each of the high-stakes states (can you say that 5 times fast?) sets its own rules for the exams, and you'll find some students may appear to have it easier than others. North Carolina tests its students in reading and math only, and the question types are multiple choice only. Students in Minnesota, however, are tested in reading, math, *and* writing, and the question types include multiple choice, short answer, *and* essays! But don't worry, beginning in 2005, students in North Carolina will be tested in reading, math, science, social studies, English, *and* grammar. Perhaps that's why the official state beverage of North Carolina is milk . . . those students will need their strength!

The point is that you should look carefully at the rules for your own state. For example, if you're one of those lucky North Carolinians taking the test in 2003 or 2004, you can skip any practice question that is not multiple choice. As we said earlier, it's our job to make sure we cover all the bases for everyone, but you only have to study what you're actually being tested on.

You may have to take other subject tests in high school, which are not required for graduation. Some tests are for advanced diplomas (such as the Regents Math B). Other tests are actually testing your teachers and your school system. We're here to help you graduate, and we focus only on the tests where the stakes are high for *you*.

Log on to www.petersons.com/highstakes for your Graduation Checklist, which will highlight information you need to have on your state's scoring, test dates, required topics of study, and more!

The following list of states is in alphabetical order.

Alabama

Exit-Level Exam: Alabama High School Graduation Exam (**AHSGE**)

State Education Department Website: www.alsde.edu

Students take the AHSGE in eleventh grade. Beginning with the graduating class of 2003, students must pass all subject-area tests in order to graduate. Students have six opportunities to take these exams.

Test	# Questions	Time	Question Type
Reading	84	approx. 3 hrs.	multiple choice
Language	100	approx. 3 hrs.	multiple choice
Science	100	approx. 3 hrs.	multiple choice
Math	100	approx. 3 hrs.	multiple choice
Social Studies	100	approx. 3 hrs.	multiple choice

California

Exit-Level Exam: California High School Exit Exam (**CAHSEE**)

State Education Department Website: www.cde.ca.gov

Students take the CAHSEE in tenth grade. As of the 2003–04 school year, students are required to pass both parts of the CAHSEE. Students have multiple opportunities to retake one or both portions of the exam.

Test	# Questions	Time	Question Type
English-Language	82	untimed	multiple choice
English-Language	2	untimed	short essays (includes written response to text and prompt)
Math	80	untimed	multiple choice

Florida

Exit-Level Exam: Florida Comprehensive Assessment Test (**FCAT**)

State Education Department Website: www.firn.edu/doe/sas/fcat

Students take the FCAT in tenth grade and must pass the reading and math parts of the exam in order to graduate. Students have multiple opportunities to retake the exams.

High Stakes: Science

Test	# Questions	Time	Question Type
Reading	105	untimed	multiple choice
Math	100	untimed	multiple choice

Georgia

Exit-Level Exam: Georgia High School Graduation Tests (GHSGT)

State Education Department Website: www.doe.k12.ga.us/sla/ret/ghsgt.asp

Students take the GHSGT in eleventh grade and must pass each of the 5 tests in order to graduate. Students have five opportunities to take each of the tests before the end of twelfth grade.

Test	# Questions	Time	Question Type
English/ Language Arts	50	3 hrs. max	multiple choice
Math	60	3 hrs. max.	multiple choice
Social Studies	80	3 hrs. max.	multiple choice
Science	70	3 hrs. max.	multiple choice
Writing	1	90 mins.	essay

Louisiana

Exit-Level Exam: Graduation Exit Examination for the 21st Century (GEE 21)

State Education Department Website: www.doe.state.la.us

Students take the GEE 21 in the tenth grade (English language arts *and* mathematics) and must pass them both to graduate. Students also take the GEE 21 in the eleventh grade (science *or* social studies) and must pass one of these to graduate. Students have multiple opportunities to retake each portion of the exam.

Test	# Questions	Time	Question Type
English / Language Arts	61	untimed	multiple choice and essay

Math	60	untimed	multiple choice and short answer
Science	44	untimed	multiple choice and short answer
Social Studies	64	untimed	multiple choice and short answer

Massachusetts

Exit-Level Exam: Massachusetts Comprehensive Assessment System (**MCAS**)

State Education Department Website: www.doe.mass.edu/mcas

Students take the MCAS in the tenth grade and must pass the English Language Arts and Math portions of the exam in order to graduate. Students have multiple opportunities to retake both portions of the test.

Test	# Questions	Time	Question Type
Math	51	untimed	multiple choice, short answer, and open response
English/ Language Arts	55	untimed	multiple choice and writing prompt

Michigan

Exit-Level Exam: Michigan Educational Assessment Program High School Tests (**MEAP HST**)

State Education Department Website: www.meritaward.state.mi.us/mma/meap.htm

Students take the MEAP HST in eleventh grade and must pass all parts of the exam in order to graduate. Students have the opportunity to retake portions of the exam in the twelfth grade.

HSPT/HSPA, FCAT, MEAP HST, GEE21, Regents Exams, SOL, NCCT ... GHSGT, BST ...
CCT, AHSGE, GHSGT, BST, BSAP, WASL, CAHSEE, TAAS, OGT, HSPT ... A ... GE, GHSGT, BST, BS
, HSPT/HSPA, FCAT, MEAP HST, GEE21, Regents Exams, SOL, NCCT ... GE, GHSGT, BST, BS

CHAPTER
1

Test	# Questions	Time	Question Type
Math	43	100 min.	multiple choice and open response
Reading*	29	80 min.	multiple choice and open response
Science	50	90 min.	multiple choice and open response
Social Studies	42	80 min.	multiple choice and open response
Writing*	2	120 min.	open response

As of the 2003–04 school year, Reading and Writing will be combined into an English Language Arts test along with a Listening test.

Minnesota

Exit-Level Exam: Basic Skills Test (BST)

State Education Department Website: http://cflapp.state.mn.us/CLASS/stds/ assessments/bst/index.jsp

Students take the math and reading portions of the BST in eighth grade and the writing portion in tenth grade and must pass all portions of the exam in order to graduate. Students have multiple opportunities to retake each section of the exam.

Test	# Questions	Time	Question Type
Reading	40	120–150 min.	multiple choice and short answer
Writing	several	90–120 min.	short essays
Math	68	120–150 min.	multiple choice and short answer

High Stakes: Science

HIGH STAKES

New Jersey

Exit-Level Exam: High School Proficiency Assessment (**HSPA**)

State Education Department Website: www.state.nj.us/education

Students take the HSPA in eleventh grade and must pass both sections in order to graduate. In 2004–05, a social studies assessment will be phased in, and in March 2005, science will be added. Students have two additional opportunities to retake each portion of the exam in their senior year.

Test	# Questions	Time	Question Type
Language Arts/ Literacy	55	4 hrs.	multiple choice and open ended
Mathematics	48	2 hrs.	multiple choice and open ended

New York

Exit-Level Exam: Regents Exams

State Education Department Website: www.emsc.nysed.gov/deputy/Documents/ alternassess.htm

Students take the Regents in tenth and eleventh grades and must pass the five Regents Examinations listed below to graduate. In general, students in the tenth grade are tested in science, math, and global history and geography. Students in the eleventh grade are tested in English language arts, and U.S. history and government. Students who fail portions of the exam twice are required to pass a component test for that portion in order to graduate.

Test	# Questions	Time	Question Type
English	29	3 hrs.	multiple choice and essay
Math	35	3 hrs.	multiple choice and open ended

Global History and Geography	60–62	3 hrs.	multiple choice and open ended
U.S. History and Government	60–62	3 hrs.	multiple choice and open ended
Science	62–94	3 hrs.	multiple choice and open ended

North Carolina

Exit-Level Exam: North Carolina Competency Tests (**NCCT**)

State Education Department Website: www.ncpublicschools.org/accountability/testing/policies/

Students take the NCCT in eighth grade. Students who do not pass may retake portions of the test three times each year in grades 9–11 and four times in twelfth grade in order to graduate. Passing scores in both portions of the exam are needed in order to graduate.

Test	# Questions	Time	Question Type
Reading	156	1 hr. 40 mins.	multiple choice
Math	165	1 hr. 40 mins.	multiple choice

Ohio

Exit-Level Exam: Ninth Grade Proficiency Tests and Ohio Graduation Tests (**OGT**)

State Education Department Website: www.ode.state.oh.us

Students take the Ninth Grade Proficiency Tests and must pass all of the portions to graduate. Beginning in the 2003–04 school year, students will take the exams (to be renamed OGT) in the tenth grade and are also required to pass all portions of the exam to graduate. Students have multiple opportunities to retake portions of both the Ninth Grade Proficiency Tests and the OGT.

Test	# Questions	Time	Question Type
Writing	2	2.5 hrs.	essay
Reading	49	2.5 hrs.	multiple choice and open response
Math	50	2.5 hrs.	multiple choice and open response
Science	50	2.5 hrs.	multiple choice and open response
Citizenship	52	2.5 hrs.	multiple choice and open response

South Carolina

Exit-Level Exam: Basic Skills Assessment Program (**BSAP**) and Palmetto Achievement Challenge Tests (**PACT**)

State Education Department Website: www.myscschools.com/offices/assessment

Students take the BSAP in tenth grade and must pass all portions to graduate. Students may retake portions of the test once in eleventh grade and twice in the twelfth grade. The PACT will be given to tenth graders in the spring of 2004 and will test in English language arts, mathematics, and social studies.

Test	# Questions	Time	Question Type
BSAP Reading	60	untimed	multiple choice
BSAP Math	50	untimed	multiple choice
BSAP Writing	1	untimed	essay

Texas

Exit-Level Exam: Texas Assessment of Academic Skills (**TAAS**)

State Education Department Website: www.tea.state.tx.us

Students take the TAAS in tenth grade and must pass all three portions to graduate. Students have multiple opportunities to retake each portion of the exam.

Note that students who will be in the eleventh grade in spring 2004 or later and plan to graduate in spring 2005 or later will take a new test: the Texas Assessment of Knowledge and Skills (TAKS). This will cover English language arts, mathematics, science, and social studies.

Test	# Questions	Time	Question Type
Reading	40	untimed	multiple choice/essay
Writing	48	untimed	multiple choice/essay
Mathematics	60	untimed	multiple choice

Virginia

Exit-Level Exam: Standards of Learning (**SOL**)

State Education Department Website: www.pen.k12.va.us

Students must pass two SOL end-of-course English tests and any other four SOL end-of-course tests to graduate. Students entering ninth grade in 2003–04 must pass two English tests, one math test, one history test, one science test, and one test of their choosing in order to graduate. Students have multiple opportunities to retake portions of the exam.

The SOL tests are different from other exit-level exams in that there is no specific test for each subject area. Instead, numerous tests are offered in the required disciplines (i.e., biology and physics are tests offered in the science discipline). Listed below are the discipline areas where passing test scores are required for graduation.

Discipline Area	Time	Question Type
English	untimed	multiple choice and short answer
Math	untimed	multiple choice and short answer
Science	untimed	multiple choice and short answer
History & Social Sciences	untimed	multiple choice and short answer
Fine or Practical Arts	untimed	multiple choice and short answer
Health & Physical Education		
Electives		
Student Selected Test		

Washington

Exit-Level Exam: Washington Assessment of Student Learning (**WASL-10**)

State Education Department Website: www.k12.wa.us/assessment

Students take the WASL-10 in the tenth grade and are required to pass all subject-area tests to graduate. Students have multiple opportunities to retake portions of the exam. As of the 2003–04 school year, science will also be a required test.

Test	# Questions	Time	Question Type
Reading	40	untimed	multiple choice, short answers, extended answers
Math	42	untimed	multiple choice, short answers, extended answers
Writing	2	untimed	essay
Communication	8	untimed	multiple choice, short answers, extended answers

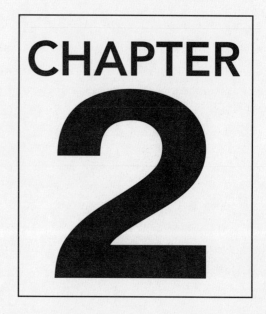

CHAPTER

2

TEST-TAKING TIPS AND STRATEGIES

The best way to prepare for your science exit-level exam is to set up a good study plan, and then stick to it. Ideally, you should start prepping a month or two before the test. We don't mean that you should devote every waking moment of the next four to eight weeks to studying, nor should you let studying interfere with your normal life. Don't sacrifice time you would normally spend on homework, at soccer practice, or hanging out with your friends. Instead, set aside just thirty minutes a day for your preparation.

Take a nice, deep breath, because everything that could possibly appear on your science exit-level exam is already tucked away in your brain. You won't be tested on anything that your teachers didn't already cover. And as long as you've managed to pass your science classes, you're in good shape for the test. All you need to do now is to wake up your brain with a review of the material. And that's where this book comes in.

This book will help you review everything you've already learned in your science classes quickly and easily. Each of the four review chapters focuses on a different subject—biology, chemistry, physics, and earth sciences. If you've already thumbed through the pages, you might be nervous about just how much science review we've included in this book. Not to fear, though! Rather than throw a lot of stuff at you at once, each chapter is broken down into shorter reviews of the major concepts in that subject. That way, you can prepare a little at a time, which will help you refresh and strengthen what you already know about science as well as put your mind at ease before you take your exam.

> Scientists have shown that students have an easier time remembering what they've studied when they don't cram. So don't wait until the night before your exam to hit the books. Spread your studying out over a couple of weeks or months.

Focus on one subject review in this book each week, and one topic each day. Don't push yourself to cover more than one topic a day because if you cram too much in at one time, you aren't likely to remember much of it later. Read the topic carefully, and then try the Pop Quiz that follows. Unlike the pop quizzes your teachers spring on you without warning, these quizzes won't make your stomach queasy or your forehead to break out with sweat. For one thing, you already know they're coming (because we just told you about them!), so you won't be surprised. More important, the pop quizzes are a great way to measure how much you know about each topic that will appear on your exit exam. When you get a question right, you can be confident that you understand the topic. But if you have trouble answering a Pop Quiz question, you can crack open your textbook and class notes for more in-depth review.

> Hopefully, you save your notebooks at the end of each school year. If, however, your ninth grade science notes are at the bottom of a landfill or are lost in the back of your bedroom closet, borrow the notes from someone who is taking the class now or ask your old teacher if you can borrow a copy of the textbook.

Once you've finished all of the review chapters and pop quizzes, jump to the last part of the book and try the final review questions. Afterward, you'll find the correct answers, but even more importantly, you'll find detailed explanations of the questions. Use these explanations to decide if you need to go back to your textbook for more review.

Your Test-Day Strategy

The night before your exit-level exam, don't bother studying. If you don't know it now, you won't by the time you sit down to take the test. Besides, cramming will just make you nervous. Instead, get everything ready for the next day. Set out your clothes, your pens and pencils, a calculator and ruler (if they're allowed in the test), a light snack to munch on if you get a break during the exam, and a watch to keep track of your time. Watch a little television, read a magazine, or take a long, relaxing bath before you go to bed—anything to get your mind off the test. Set your alarm clock and, to play it safe, ask your mom or dad to make sure you're up on time in the morning. And get to bed at a reasonable hour so you can get a solid night's sleep.

> This is not the day to wear your brand-new shoes that haven't been broken in yet. Instead, dress to be comfortable, not to impress your classmates.

Once you wake up, eat a nutritious breakfast. No, don't grab a candy bar or a can of soda! The sugar might make you feel good at first, but a bowl of cereal or a piece of fruit will help your brain function better as the day goes on. If you have time, try to squeeze in a little exercise, too. You don't have to run a marathon first thing in the morning, but a little stretching will relax your body.

Rushing will just make you feel nervous when you sit down to your exam, so try to get to the test site a little early. Pick a desk in a well-lit area, and try sitting in it for a few minutes. If it squeaks or the legs are uneven, try another. Sure, people might give you weird stares, but who cares? You don't want any annoying little details disturbing you while you're taking your exam. Also, avoid sitting near a window or the door. The fewer distractions, the better! As the proctor passes out the test, take a deep breath, roll your neck a few times, crack your knuckles—anything to relax—and when you're told to start, dive right on in to the test booklet. You'll be all set.

> Bring a watch (without an alarm) to your exam. Lay it on the desk, next to your test booklet, so you can keep an eye on the time.

A lot of test takers waste precious time by losing their places on the answer sheet. Place your test booklet on top of the sheet and use it as a placeholder. Keep the top of the booklet just below the next answer space. That way, you won't have to stop working to figure out where the next answer gets marked. Also, if you decide to skip a question, make sure you leave it blank on your answer sheet, or **lightly** circle it so you'll remember to come back to it later. Before you hand in your exam, however, make sure you completely erase anything you circle on the answer sheet. Most multiple-choice tests are graded by machines that might misread a stray or forgotten mark as a wrong answer!

What's on the Test?

Although science exit-level tests differ from one state to the next, most consist of multiple-choice questions, and some also ask you to write short answers or to fill in graphs or charts. Ask your teacher or guidance counselor for specific details about your state's exit-level exam. All tests, however, will test you on four things:

- **Content Knowledge:** Have you remembered all of the facts, formulas, and definitions you've learned in your science classes?

- **Thinking Skills:** Do you know how to analyze and draw conclusions from data?

- **Procedural Skills:** Can you understand scientific procedures, like which tools to use for an experiment or how to collect data?

- **Application Skills:** Do you know how to read and interpret charts and maps?

Like we said earlier, you've already got the content in your head, and this book will help you release all of that information. But what about the other three points?

It turns out that you've been learning your whole life how to do this stuff. And it's easy to avoid making mistakes when you come across questions that test those three skills:

1. **Read everything carefully.** Be sure you know exactly what the question is asking you, that you understand all of the data, and that you're clear about what the answer choices are.

2. **There aren't any trick questions on the test.** So don't look for hidden meanings. Everything you need to know to answer a question will be provided for you right there in the test booklet.

3. **Consider every answer choice.** Your job is to find the best, most complete answer to a question. So don't choose the first one that looks right. Another choice might answer the question better.

4. **Guess wisely.** If you don't know the answer to a multiple-choice question right away, eliminate those choices that you know are wrong. Your odds of correctly guessing will be higher if you have fewer choices to pick from.

5. **Use your time carefully.** Exit-level exams are timed tests. If you get stuck on a question, save it for later and move on to the next question.

6. **Check your work.** Don't mark the wrong bubble on your multiple-choice answer sheet. And if your test has short answers, address every part of the question—if you're asked to give three examples in your response, don't stop after one!

Taking a test that has as much riding on it as your high school diploma can be overwhelming. But you've already taken the first step toward success: you're reading this book. So get some paper and a pen or pencil, turn off the television, and let's get started.

PART

II

SCIENCE REVIEW

CHAPTER 3

BIOLOGY

Biology is the science of life. It is divided into four main topics: the molecule, the cell, the organism, and the population. Cellular biology studies the cell, which is the basic structural unit of living matter. Molecular biology explores the structure and action of nucleic acids and proteins as well as heredity and how organisms process the energy needed to sustain life. Organismal biology looks at individual forms of life, including humans. Population biology explores ecology and the study of organisms in their natural habitats.

The Cell Story

CELL THEORY

Back in the seventeenth century, the earliest microscopes were used to entertain the wealthy!

The concept of the cell has come a long way since Robert Hooke first came up with it back in 1665. Many people were shocked and fascinated to look through the lens of a microscope and see single-celled organisms floating around in their wine and crawling over their food. Thanks to the fields of Microscopy and Histology (study of tissue), we have learned quite a deal since then about cells.

Investigations of thin slices of specimens from living organisms led to the formulation of a **cell theory**:

1. The cell is the basic unit of structure and function for most living things.

2. Cells arise from pre-existing cells by independent, self-reproduction.

3. Living organisms are composed of one or more cells.

It is estimated that the human body is comprised of some 100 trillion cells.

Cells vary in size, shape, and function. A bacterial cell, for instance, is invisible to the naked eye. Bacteria only become visible when they appear as colonies of millions of cells. Yet a single muscle cell can reach 9 inches in length (a million times larger than a bacterial cell).

CELL STRUCTURE

Cells are the basis of life, heredity, structure, and function of every organism. Each cell is made up of different structures, called **organelles.** Cells have a **cell** or **plasma membrane** that surrounds the cell and is selectively permeable to what enters and exits the cell. Inside the membrane, the cell is filled with a gelatinous **cytoplasm**; organelles are embedded in this material. The **nucleus** is one of the most important organelles. Contained within the cell membrane, it contains all the genetic information for each cell.

> A great way to visualize cytoplasm and organelles is to think of those not-so-appetizing Jell-o desserts served at the cafeteria. The Jell-o is the cytoplasm and the chunks of fruit that float in it are the organelles.

Eu = true

Cells are classified as Eukaryotic (true-nucleus) or Prokaryotic (before-nucleus). **Prokaryotic** cells lack a nuclear membrane and membrane-bound organelles. They are unicellular, mainly microscopic organisms, such as bacteria and cyanobacteria. It is estimated that prokaryotes appeared some 3.5 billion years ago. Some scientists hypothesize that prokaryotic organisms began to live symbiotically with one another and evolved into eukaryotic cells. **Eukaryotes** include all the animal, plant, and protist cells. These cells are characterized by a true nucleus that is bound by a membrane and membrane-bounded subcellular organelles. Eukaryotes can be unicellular, as in the case of the *Amoeba*, or multicellular, as seen in humans.

Eukaryotic cells possess many organelles ("little organs") to carry out cellular processes such as energy production, waste disposal, cellular transport, and product production. The table below summarizes the functions of the major organelles found in animal and plant cells.

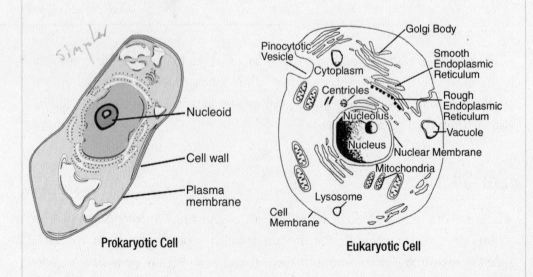

simpler

Prokaryotic Cell — Nucleoid, Cell wall, Plasma membrane

Eukaryotic Cell — Pinocytotic Vesicle, Cytoplasm, Centrioles, Nucleolus, Nucleus, Cell Membrane, Lysosome, Mitochondria, Nuclear Membrane, Vacuole, Rough Endoplasmic Reticulum, Smooth Endoplasmic Reticulum, Golgi Body

cwall maria

cell skin/armor

Summary of Organelle Function

Organelle		Structure Function	
Cell Membrane	A phospholipid bilayer embedded with complex proteins	Serves as a selectively permeable barrier to the external environment	
Endoplasmic Reticulum *Stomach?*	A membranous network of canals and vesicles. Some canals are covered by ribosomes (rough ER), and some don't have ribosomes (smooth ER)	Ribosomes perform protein synthesis in the rough ER. Internal transport occurs here. Smooth ER is the site for lipid and steroid hormone synthesis. It assists the breakdown of glycogen to glucose.	
Ribosome	Free and attached (to ER) bodies of mainly RNA with protein; composed of large and small subunits	Manufacture proteins from amino acids	
Golgi Apparatus	A network of flattened canals with associated vacuoles and vesicles	Center for modifying and packaging cellular products and carbohydrate synthesis	
Mitochondrion *lungs*	A double membrane structure. An outer smooth membrane and an inner membrane with folds called cristae	Site for cellular respiration; convert sugar molecules into ATP	
Nuclear Membrane	A double membrane with pores	A selective barrier between the nucleus and cytoplasm	*inner cwall* *cwall rose*
Nuclear Chromatin *Data center*	Thread-like DNA and protein; coiled threads form chromosomes for division	Stores genetic information; controls cell growth, reproduction, and overall metabolism	
Nucleolus *assistant*	Round body within nucleus; composed of RNA and protein	Participates in protein synthesis and may be involved in RNA transcription	
Lysosomes	Small membrane-enclosed bodies	Storage for many proteolytic enzymes	
Chloroplast *solar panels*	A structure of stacked membranes that contain chlorophyll	Site of photosynthesis in plants	

Summary of Organelle Function (continued)		
Organelle	**Structure**	**Function**
Cell Wall—plants only	A cellulose support structure around plant cells	Provides rigid frame for support
Cilium	Hair-like projections that have a 9+2 microtubule arrangement	Coordinates movement
Flagella	Whip-like extension from cell, similar to cilium	Involved in movement, such as in the sperm cell
Centriole	Rod-shaped structure with 9 sets of 3 fused tubules	Necessary for spindle formation during mitosis and meiosis

Cell Membrane and Transport

Cell membranes control the movement of materials into and out of the cell. They are composed of phosphates and lipids (fats). The Singer-Nicholson *fluid-mosaic* model suggests that membranes are fluid-like phospholipid bimolecular sheets with embedded proteins and carbohydrate chains. This phospholipid bilayer not only creates an effective lipid barrier, but the proteins and carbohydrates act as receptors or identifiers for the movement of molecules from external sources.

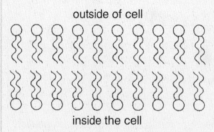

Phospholipid bilayer of cell membrane

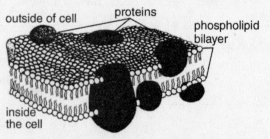

Cross-section of the cell membrane showing Fluid-mosaic nature

While many factors are necessary for cell survival, cellular transport is one of the most important. The movement of substances can be divided into two main categories, **passive** and **active transport**. Movement by passive transport includes *diffusion* and *osmosis*. These forms of movement transfer molecules along a concentration gradient (from high concentrations to low concentrations), but they require no energy. Imagine you're going to a movie theater. As you enter the lobby, what's the first thing you smell? Popcorn! The smell gets stronger as you walk toward the concession stand, but it fades once you find a seat. That's an act of simple diffusion. The highest concentration of the popcorn smell was at the concession stand, while the lowest concentration was in the movie theater, away from the concession stand.

Active transport is used when a cell needs to move a substance against a concentration gradient; to do this, a cell must use energy. A **carrier molecule** is used in movement across a semipermeable membrane. The molecule complexes with the substance that is being imported against the concentration gradient. ATP (adenosine triphosphate) is the form of energy used to complete the transport.

Some eukaryotic cells use different mechanisms to move large molecules and fluid components. **Endocytosis** is an active process whereby a cell encloses a particle in a membrane-bound sac that is pinched off from the cell membrane (*phagocytosis—cell eating*), or the cell will enclose small volumes of liquid (*pinocytosis—cell drinking*). **Exocytosis** is the reverse process of endocytosis. Instead of incorporating the particle into the cell, in exocytosis the particle is released from the cell.

Cellular Functions: Metabolism and Energy Pathways

All cells require a constant source of energy. Gathering, storing, and using this energy is referred to as a cell's **metabolism**. We consume nutrients to provide our bodies with the building blocks necessary to synthesize new materials needed by our cells. Unlike plants and some microscopic organisms, humans and other animals can't simply absorb energy by placing our hands on a slice of pizza and absorbing all of the pizza's nutrients through our skin. Instead, animal cells have to break food down in order to release the energy stored in the food.

> That old saying, "You are what you eat," isn't far from the truth. Think about that the next time you have a "Big Mac Attack."

This is done through a series of chemical reactions that occur in a *metabolic pathway*. Both plant and animal cells rely on metabolic pathways to convert substances into forms of energy that can be used by each cell. These conversions are mediated through enzymes. **Enzymes** are proteins that act as a biological catalyst.

They speed up the rate of a reaction by lowering the amount of activation energy needed and remain unchanged by the reaction they catalyze. Without enzymes it would take weeks, even months, for foods to break down completely. Imagine how you'd feel if your Thanksgiving turkey stayed in your stomach until New Year's Eve!

Enzymes are specific to the substrates they bind with. Think of your best friend. The two of you have a unique friendship that no one else has. You do stuff together and share secrets that you probably don't do and share with people who you aren't as close to. Well, each enzyme has a particular substrate as a best friend—except they probably don't swap CDs.

Each enzyme also has sets of optimal conditions under which they work best. These conditions include pH, temperature, concentrations, and inhibitors. The enzyme salivary amylase, which is produced in the mouth, works best at a pH of 7 (neutral). But the pH of the stomach's gastric juice has a pH of 2 or 3 (acidic). When salivary amylase is swallowed with chewed up food and enters the stomach, it is no longer active.

Enzymes can also be **denatured.** The enzyme's three-dimensional shape can change when its optimal conditions are altered. A denatured enzyme is an ineffective catalyst because its altered shape no longer fits with its substrate. Lastly, enzymes are necessary for the chemical reactions of photosynthesis and respiration to occur.

Photosynthesis—Photosynthesis is a food manufacturing process used by plants. CO_2 (carbon dioxide) from the air and H_2O from the soil are transformed into organic compounds, in particular carbohydrates like glucose ($C_6H_{12}O_6$). This is an anabolic process in which the sugars that the plant produces through photosynthesis can be used to make other compounds. Plants harness the sun's light energy to fuel this conversion. Oxygen is a by-product of this reaction and is released into the atmosphere or used in cellular respiration. Here's what the summary equation of photosynthesis looks like:

$$6CO_2 + 6H_2O \xrightarrow[\text{chlorophyll and enzymes}]{\text{light}} C_6H_{12}O_6 + 6O_2$$

Respiration—Respiration, or cellular respiration, is used to free chemical energy from molecules of glucose for biological work. Cellular respiration occurs in the mitochondria of the cell. Both plants and animals perform this. There are many types of respiration, but you're most familiar with **aerobic respiration**. It converts carbohydrates into carbon dioxide, water, and high energy molecules of ATP. Here's the overall summary equation for aerobic respiration:

$$C_6H_{12}O_6 + 6O_2 \xrightarrow{\text{enzymes}} 6CO_2 + 6H_2O + ATP$$

Respiration begins in the cytoplasm of the cell in a process known as **glycolysis** (sugar breaking). The products of glycolysis then move to the mitochondria, where they are converted into energy-rich ATP molecules. **Catabolic** reactions such as respiration produce energy by the breakdown of larger molecules. The oxygen produced by photosynthesis is necessary for cellular respiration, and the carbon dioxide produced by respiration is necessary for photosynthesis.

> Photosynthesis and cellular respiration are the Yin and Yang of energy. They are part of a cycle of energy that is necessary for life to exist.

MOLECULAR BASIS OF LIFE: DNA, RNA, AND PROTEIN SYNTHESIS

DNA

Every form of life exists because of **DNA (deoxyribonucleic acid)**. It controls the manufacture of proteins and passes genetic material from one cell to another. DNA is comprised of nucleic acids that are formed from smaller structures, called **nucleotides.** Each nucleotide is comprised of a phosphate molecule, a sugar molecule, and a nitrogenous base. The nitrogenous bases are divided into two main groups: **Purines,** which are A (adenine) and G (guanine), have a double ring structure. **Pyrimidines,** which are C (cytosine), T (thymine), and U (uracil, which is only found in RNA), have a single ring structure. These nucleotides are the four-letter language of DNA. They combine to make simple words. While these words may not make much sense in English, in the language of DNA, they direct the making of a protein.

HIGH STAKES

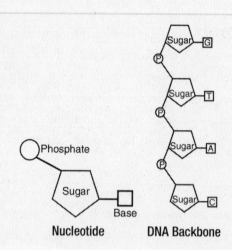

Nucleotide   DNA Backbone

In 1953, James Watson and Francis Crick produced the double helix model of DNA. Along this structure, nucleotides arrange themselves in a spiral. The nucleotides base pair with one another in a **complementary** fashion. Adenine base pairs with Thymine (A–T), and Cytosine base pairs with Guanine (C–G). Hydrogen bonds hold the complementary base pairs together. Theoretically, this is the only possible base pairing scheme allowable for DNA, but the order of the base pairs along a strand can vary greatly. The structure of a DNA strand is arranged like a twisted or coiled ladder. The sides of the ladder are created by bonds between alternating units of sugars and phosphate groups. The rungs of the ladder are created by the complementary base pairs of A to T and C to G, and each member of a base pair is attached to a sugar on its side of the ladder.

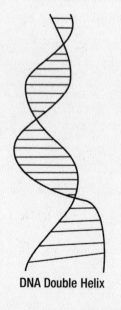

DNA Double Helix

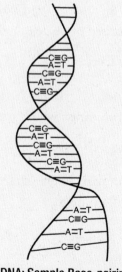

DNA: Sample Base-pairing

RNA and Protein Synthesis

DNA, like an encyclopedia or a dictionary, is our permanent genetic reference index. And just like those reference books in the library that you can't check out, DNA cannot leave the nucleus. However, the instructions encoded in DNA must be moved from the nucleus in order to direct activity within the cell. So copies of the instructions are made in the form of RNA. The RNA can then carry out the specifics of cellular activity. **RNA (ribonucleic acid)** exits the nucleus in three forms: **messenger RNA** (mRNA), **transfer RNA** (tRNA), and **ribosomal RNA** (rRNA). Each type is synthesized from DNA. RNA differs from DNA in several aspects:

1. It uses a different sugar molecule (ribose sugar).

2. It is single-stranded.

3. Instead of Thymine (T), it uses Uracil (U) as its nitrogenous base to pair with Adenine (A).

All three types of RNA play an important role in protein synthesis.

DNA is the basis for all protein synthesis that occurs in cells. Proteins are the foundations for structural and functional components of every cell in the body. They can exist in many forms, such as hair, feathers, and enzymes. However, all proteins share a key element in their make-up—amino acids. **Amino acids** are molecules containing an amino group (NH_2) and a carboxyl group (COOH). Like Legos or Lincoln Logs, they link to make proteins.

There are twenty amino acids that combine in different ways to form a language. Each word in this language can be translated into a protein. The DNA code holds the key to this language; the code translates into an amino acid. The amino acids are then grouped together to make a specific protein. The code of DNA is read in a sequence of three nucleotides at once, a "triplet." This triplet is referred to as a **codon**. A codon can code for a particular amino acid or it can act as a "promotor" region to initiate synthesis or as an "end" region to stop synthesis.

Protein synthesis can be divided into two main parts:

- *Transcription*—to write the code by converting DNA to RNA

- *Translation*—to decipher the code by matching codon with its correct amino acid

The following table highlights the main steps in each process.

Transcription for mRNA Production	Translation or Protein Synthesis
1. Enzymes open the helix of DNA and stabilize the open helix to expose bases.	1. mRNA leaves the nucleus and moves to the cytoplasm, where it associates with two subunits of ribosomes.
2. On the coding strand, RNA polymerase attaches to start codon as the promotor region.	2. At the ribosomes, the mRNA contains the nitrogenous bases, which are read as codons and translated into amino acids.
3. RNA polymerase adds nucleotides complementary to the DNA coding strand (except Adenine, which base pairs with Uracil in RNA).	3. tRNA molecules carry one amino acid at a time to complex with mRNA at ribosomes. tRNA molecules attach to complementary mRNA.
4. Other enzymes correct any mistakes in coding, and when the "stop" codon is reached, the RNA molecule detaches and the DNA helix recoils.	4. As additional tRNA molecules bring more amino acids and base pair with mRNA, the amino acids form peptide bonds until the designated protein is complete.
5. The newly synthesized mRNA molecule leaves the nucleus and enters the cytoplasm.	5. The protein is released and can have several fates inside the cell or be exported from the cell.

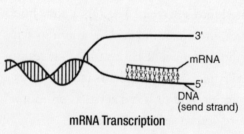

mRNA Transcription

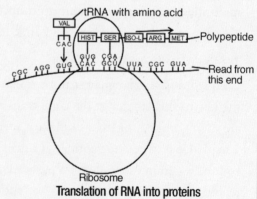

Translation of RNA into proteins

Cellular Reproduction: Mitosis and Meiosis

Mitosis

All cells must have a mechanism for perpetuation, growth, maintenance, and repair. If you ever had a bad haircut or a painful sunburn, in time your hair grew back and your skin peeled to reveal new skin. You can thank cellular division for this. Eukaryotic cells (both plant and animal) have a highly specialized nucleus that regulates these processes by encoding this information in molecules of DNA. The process of cell division begins first with the nuclear division, before **cytokinesis** (division of the remainder of the cell). Eukaryotic cells normally possess nuclei that carry two sets of genetic information and are said to be **diploid**. Those that carry only one set of genetic information are said to be **haploid**.

There are two kinds of nuclear division: **mitosis** (body cell nuclear division that results in diploid nuclei producing identical diploid cells) and **meiosis** (reduction division occurring in gonads—testes and ovaries—in which diploid nuclei produce non-identical haploid cells). The genetic information that needs to be divided is DNA. Unorganized DNA exits in the strand-like form called **chromatin**. Once a cell is ready to divide, this chromatin becomes coiled and condensed with proteins into darkly staining structures called chromosomes. **Chromosomes** carry **genes** that are units of inheritance (we'll talk about that later in the chapter). Chromosomes in a non-dividing cell exist in a duplicated state in which two copies of itself (or **sister chromatids**) are attached together at a central point, the **centromere**.

All eukaryotic cells undergo the same basic life cycle, but the amount of time spent in each stage varies.

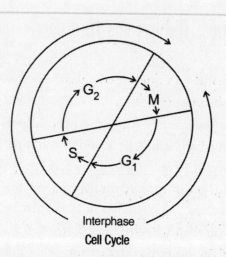

Interphase
Cell Cycle

There are five stages of the cell cycle. **Interphase** occurs between mitotic divisions and is divided into 3 main parts:

- **First Growth (or G1)**—The cell increases its volume and makes important components like mRNA, tRNA, and enzymes.

- **Synthesis (or S)**—DNA replication occurs in preparation of distribution to gametes.

- **Second Growth (or G2)**—Final preparations are made for mitosis to begin.

The four sequential stages of mitosis are as follows:

Prophase

- Nuclear envelope dissolves

- Chromatin organizes into chromosomes

- Centrioles migration and spindle formation

Metaphase

- Duplicated chromosomes align at the equatorial plane of cell

Anaphase

- Each chromatid of a duplicated chromosome separates and moves toward opposite ends of cell

Telophase

- A nuclear envelope develops around daughter

- Chromosomes uncoil and revert back to chromatin

- Division of the cytoplasm occurs (*cytokinesis*)

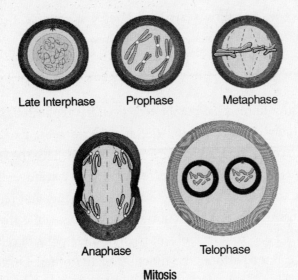

Late Interphase   Prophase   Metaphase

Anaphase   Telophase

Mitosis

Animal cell division is similar to plant cell division, but there are a few differences. In animal cells, cytokinesis results in a *cleavage furrow*, which divides the cytoplasm. In plant cells, a *cell plate* forms in the center and progresses to the cell membrane. This results in a cell wall separating the two cells.

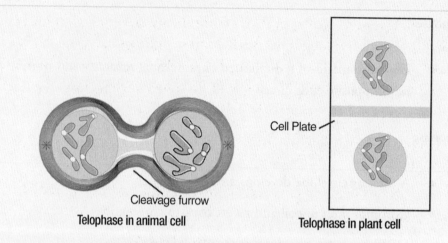

Cell Plate

Cleavage furrow

Telophase in animal cell

Telophase in plant cell

Stem cells have been the subject of much research in recent years. Some successful preliminary research suggests that they can reverse diseases by creating healthy cell division in previously diseased cells, which can slow down or stop the advance of a pathology.

In animal cells, after mitosis has completed, a cell has replicated the same genetic information initially donated by the egg and sperm cells. Except for random mutations, all the cells produced by mitosis in the body have the same genes. The earliest cells created by mitosis are referred to as **stem cells**. Cells then **differentiate** into specialized cells by activating some genes and repressing others. For example, muscle cells produce contractile proteins while thyroid cells produce hormones that control metabolism. Each of these types of cells has a specific function, but it cannot perform the function of the other. Differentiation also occurs in plant cells.

Meiosis

mvh osis hngh

Meiosis is a form of sexual reproduction that eukaryotic cells use so parents can donate genetic information to their offspring. This form of reproduction involves **gametes** (reproductive cells) produced from **gonads** (reproductive organs that produce these cells). In humans, the testes produce sperm and the ovaries produce ova (eggs). Non-reproductive cells contain 23 pairs of chromosomes (22 non-sex-related or autosomal chromosome pairs and 1 pair for sex determination—XX or XY). However, each sperm and each ova only contains 22 single chromosomes and one sex chromosome, or half of the genetic equivalent for a human cell. The genetic complement is restored once an ovum is fertilized by a sperm cell, creating a **zygote**. What would happen if the egg and sperm did not go through meiosis? Each pair of our 23 pairs of chromosomes would have four chromosomes instead of two, for a total of 92 chromosomes! This would be a mutation that probably would not be able to sustain life.

Like mitosis, there are similar stages of division. However, there are also three major differences:

1. Meiosis is a form of **reduction division**, which reduces the number of chromosomes in half.

2. It takes two divisional processes to accomplish this.

3. The resulting daughter nucleus is genetically different from the mother cell it divided from.

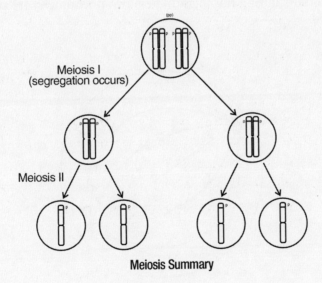

Meiosis Summary

Meiosis I

Interphase occurs, wherein DNA is replicated in preparation for division.

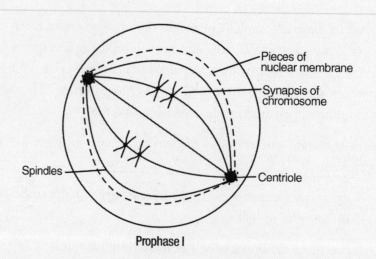

Prophase I

Prophase I: The nuclear envelope dissolves and chromatin organizes into chromosomes, a process called **synapsis**. Reshuffling of genetic information or **crossing over** also occurs during this phase. These two phenomena are absent in mitosis.

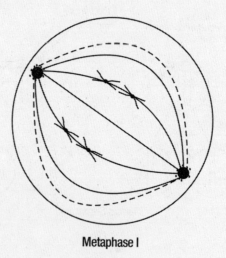

Metaphase I

Metaphase I: The synapsed chromosomes move as a unit to the equatorial plane.

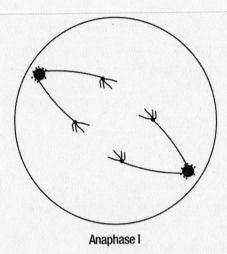

Anaphase I

Anaphase I: Chromosome pairs separate, and each duplicated chromosome moves to opposite poles of the cell. Thus, half of the chromosomes end up at one end of the cell, and half end up at the other end.

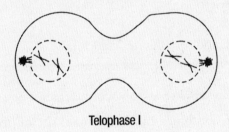

Telophase I

Telophase I: A nuclear envelope reforms around each new daughter nuclei.

Meiosis II begins immediately after meiosis I, with no time for cell growth or DNA synthesis.

Meiosis II

Prophase II: This stage begins again and is similar to Prophase I, except synapsis and crossing over do not occur. The cell is now haploid.

Metaphase II: Individual chromosomes move to the central equator of the cell in each daughter cell.

Anaphase II: Chromatids from each chromosome divide and move to opposite poles. They can now be called daughter chromosomes.

Telophase II: As cytokinesis occurs, four new daughter cells develop, each with a different genetic combination. Nuclear envelopes return around the daughter nuclei, chromosomes uncoil, and the daughter cells differentiate into gametes (either egg or sperm).

POP QUIZ

Congratulations! You made it through the first section in this chapter. It was a long one, so now it's time to see how much you've learned.

1. A muscle cell may have thousands of

    (A) chloroplasts.

    (B) mitochondria.

    (C) flagella.

    (D) cytoskeleton.

2. The smooth endoplasmic reticulum is
    (A) a pair of small cylinders composed of triplet tubules.
    (B) the assembly site of polypeptide chains.
    (C) free of ribosomes and is the main site of lipid synthesis in many cells.
    (D) the plastids found in plants.

3. Which of the following cellular structures is present in plant cells but not animal cells?
    (A) Cell wall
    (B) Lysosomes
    (C) Golgi bodies
    (D) Nucleus

4. Membranes consist of

   (A) a lipid bilayer.

   (B) nucleic acids.

   (C) phospholipids and proteins.

   (D) both (A) and (C).

5. An enzyme is best described as

   (A) a lipid.

   (B) protein.

   (C) a catalyst.

   (B) both (B) and (C).

6. Plants need ____ and ____ to carry out photosynthesis.

   (A) oxygen; water

   (B) oxygen; CO_2

   (C) CO_2; H_2O

   (D) sugar; water

7. If parent cell X has sixteen chromosomes and undergoes mitosis, the resulting cells will have how many chromosomes?

   (A) 16

   (B) 32

   (C) 8

   (D) 64

Answers

1. **The correct answer is (B).** Mitochondria convert glucose into ATP, so it makes sense that the high energy consuming muscle cells will have more mitochondria than the average cell.

2. **The correct answer is (C).** The smooth endoplasmic reticulum is free of ribosomes and is the main site of lipid synthesis in many cells.

3. **The correct answer is (A).** Choices (B), (C), and (D) are organelles that both plant and animal cells have in common.

4. **The correct answer is (D).** Cell membranes are classified as phospho-lipid bilayers interspersed with proteins.

5. **The correct answer is (D).** An enzyme is both a protein and a catalyst.

6. **The correct answer is (C).** Plants use carbon dioxide and water to fuel photosynthesis, as well as light. In the process, they give off oxygen.

7. **The correct answer is (A).** When a parent cell undergoes mitosis, the resulting daughter cells receive an identical number of chromosomes as the parent.

96% first try

Pass the Genes, Please: Genetics Review

Gregor Mendel was an Austrian monk who, in the nineteenth century, produced the first experimentally based theories on inheritance. He worked with pure breeding pea plants that had definite and distinct traits. From his work, Mendel established principles that are the basis for modern genetics. He stated that two factors govern each trait and that each parent donates one of each of these two factors to their offspring. He discovered that traits can exist in alternate forms, called **alleles**. An allele can be dominate or recessive. Mendel's **laws of independent assortment** and **segregation** explain how these traits are passed onto offspring.

> The objective of the *Human Genome Project* is to map out the complete human genome, meaning all the thousands of genes found on the 46 human chromosomes.

We now know that the traits Mendel discovered are controlled by **genes**. Genes exist as heritable units on a chromosome. A chromosome may possess thousands of genes. Since each human is a product of the combination of both maternal and paternal chromosomes (23 from the egg and 23 from the sperm), we carry genes from both parents. Genes determine our physical and mental development. However, they don't have to control these characteristics in the same way because a gene can be a **dominant** allele for a trait or a **recessive** allele for a trait. Dominant alleles are expressed and can mask the expression of recessive alleles. Recessive alleles can only be expressed when they are in the **homozygous state**, where both alleles are the same. The **heterozygous state** exists when the alleles are different.

> Examples of human traits include the ability to roll your tongue, if your ear lobes are attached to the side of your head, the color of your eyes and hair, and your blood type.

In human genetics, we often discuss characteristics as **phenotypes**. A person's phenotypes are any physical traits that are expressed by his or her genes. Hair color is an example of phenotype. The phenotype of a trait can be altered, such as when you dye your hair blue. But your genes will continue to produce your normal hair color, so you won't have to live with blue hair forever—especially if orange becomes the 'in' color. The **genotype** represents all the genes that dictate the expression of a person's phenotype. When certain genotypes of the parents are known for a specific trait, a **Punnet square** can be used to predict the probability of the expression of this trait in their offspring. Not all traits are inherited in the same manner, however, so we need to consider several patterns of inheritance.

PATTERNS OF INHERITANCE

Monohybrid Inheritance

Monohybrid (Single Factor) Inheritance represents a genetic cross involving only a single trait carried on autosomes (chromosome pairs 1–22). Let's consider tongue rolling. The ability to roll the sides of the tongue up to form a U shape is controlled by a dominant allele. We will designate **R** as the dominant gene for tongue rolling and **r** for the recessive gene for no tongue rolling. To construct a Punnet square for a cross such as this, the genes present in the gametes for one parent are placed along the side of the square and the genes in the gametes for the other parent are placed along the top. The proper configuration is seen below:

(Parents) **RR × rr**

The Punnett square for this cross:

	R	R
r	Rr	Rr
r	Rr	Rr

All the resulting offspring of this cross are genotypically heterozygous dominant (Rr), so phenotypically all will be tongue rollers. Now, members of this first generation can be crossed to assess the probability of inheritance.

(Parents) **Rr × Rr**

The Punnett square for this cross:

	R	r
R	RR	Rr
r	Rr	rr

In this cross, we can predict phenotypically that 3 out of 4 squares will be dominant, or that there is a 75 percent probability that the offspring will be tongue rollers. Genotypically, there is a 25 percent chance that a tongue roller will be homozygous dominant, a 50 percent chance that a tongue roller will be heterozygous dominant, and a 25 percent chance that the offspring will be recessive for tongue rolling and will lack this quirky ability. A genotypic and phenotypic ratio can be expressed from this cross:

Genotypic—1:2:1

Phenotypic—3:1

Dihybrid Inheritance

Dihybrid (Double Factor) Inheritance involves following two traits, independent of one another. For this type of cross, a Punnet square can also be used. It is now useful to use an example from nature, such as the texture and color of pea plants.

In this problem, a yellow wrinkled pea will be crossed with a green smooth pea. The yellow color (Y) is dominant to green (y) and the smooth texture (S) is dominant to wrinkled (s). A cross between a purebred green, smooth pea plant with a yellow, wrinkled pea plant yields the following results:

(Parents) **SSYY × ssyy**

The Punnett square for this cross:

	SY	**SY**	**SY**	**SY**
sy	SsYy	SsYy	SsYy	SsYy
sy	SsYy	SsYy	SsYy	SsYy
sy	SsYy	SsYy	SsYy	SsYy
sy	SsYy	SsYy	SsYy	SsYy

All the offspring from this cross will be phenotypically 100 percent green and smooth. Genotypically, they will all be heterozygous dominant for both traits. If we cross two heterozygous peas to one another, though, the offspring will not all look alike. In the cross on the following page, notice all the different genotypes produced:

SsYy × SsYy

	SY	Sy	sY	sy
SY	SSYY	SSYy	SsYY	SsYy
Sy	SSYy	SSyy	SsYy	Ssyy
sY	SsYY	SsYy	ssYY	ssYy
sy	SsYy	Ssyy	ssYy	ssyy

If you take a minute to count up all the different phenotypes, you should also notice that there are four specific types in a 9:3:3:1 ratio. There are 9 squares that show dominance for both traits, 3 squares that show dominance for one trait and recessive for the other, another 3 squares that show dominance for one trait and recessive for the other, and one square that shows recessive for both traits.

Incomplete Dominance

Some allele pairs that don't exhibit the dominance or recessive characteristics are exhibited in the previous examples. Genes may show incomplete dominance, allowing neither allele to be dominant to the other. This creates a unique situation in the heterozygous condition. The heterozygous organism will appear different from the homozygous dominant or the homozygous recessive state. Think back to grade school when you learned to combine different colors. What happened when you mixed yellow and blue? You created a shade of green. This illustrates incomplete dominance—neither yellow nor blue was the dominant color. An example from the world of biology can be seen in the plant kingdom, with the snapdragon flower. By crossing a pure breeding red snapdragon to a pure breeding white snapdragon, all of the resulting offspring will be pink, a uniquely different phenotype.

snapdragons show incomplete dominance!

W = White flower
W' = Red flower
WW' = Pink flower

WW × **W'W'**   (white × red)

	W	**W**
W'	**WW'**	**WW'**
W'	**WW'**	**WW'**

WW'   (all are pink)

All offspring produced from this cross are phenotypically pink in color. If two pink flowers are crossed, however, all three phenotypes occur:

WW' × **WW'**   (pink)

	W	**W'**
W	**WW**	**WW'**
W'	**WW'**	**W'W'**

25% white: 50% pink: 25% red

Sex-Linkage

> Traits that are carried on the 23rd pair of chromosomes are said to be "sex-linked."

In humans, sex is determined by one set of sex chromosomes at the 23rd pair. If the pair of chromosomes are homozygous for X (XX), this designates a female. Males are heterozygous (XY). Traits that are carried on the 23rd pair of chromosomes are said to be "sex-linked." Since more of these genes are found carried on the X than the Y chromosome, these traits were once referred to as "X-linked." Examples of traits whose genes are carried on the X chromosomes are genes for blood clotting and for controlling color vision. Defects in these genes can produce disorders such as hemophilia and color blindness.

Multiple Alleles

For a few traits, there are many alleles for a particular gene location on a chromosome. The ABO blood group system is a human example of this phenomenon. Both the A and B alleles are dominant. When they are together, they show **codominance** by both expressing themselves. The A and B allele are also dominant to the O allele. These alleles generate the four different blood types:

- AA or AO = Type A

- BB or BO = Type B

- AB = Type AB

- OO = Type O

Pop Quiz

Good job! You've reached the end of another section, so it's time for another Pop Quiz. If you feel a little shaky on a topic, pull out your biology book and review that section.

1. An allele is
   - (A) a gene pair.
   - (B) an observable trait.
   - (C) the offspring of first generation crosses.
   - (D) all the different molecular forms of a gene that exist.

2. Genes whose effect "masks" the effect of its partner are
   - (A) diploid.
   - (B) homozygous.
   - (C) dominant allele.
   - (D) true-breeding.

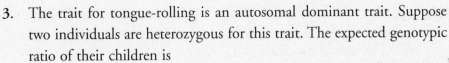

3. The trait for tongue-rolling is an autosomal dominant trait. Suppose two individuals are heterozygous for this trait. The expected genotypic ratio of their children is

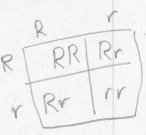

(A) 1:1.

(B) 1:2:1.

(C) 3:1.

(D) 100 percent non-tongue rollers.

4. Male humans transmit their Y chromosome to

(A) sons only.

(B) daughters only.

(C) both sons and daughters.

(D) Human males do not transmit Y chromosomes.

5. Red-green color blindness is a sex-linked recessive trait in humans. A colorblind woman and a man with normal vision have a son. What are the chances that the son is color blind? What are the chances that a daughter born to this couple will be color blind?

(A) 100 percent; 100 percent

(B) 50 percent; 0 percent

(C) 100 percent; 0 percent

(D) 50 percent; 100 percent

4/6

6. A man who is heterozygous for type A blood (AO) has a child with a woman heterozygous for type B (BO) blood. What is the possible blood type of the child?

(A) Type B blood

(B) Type O blood

(C) Type AB blood

(D) Type A blood

(E) All of the above could be possible blood types.

ANSWERS

1. The correct answer is (D).

2. The correct answer is (C).

3. The correct answer is (B). Since both individuals are heterozygous, the cross is Tt × Tt (assuming you use the gene assignment T = dominant, t = recessive). The Punnet square will yield 1:4 TT; 2:4 Tt; and 1:4 tt, or 1:2:1. Choice (C) is the phenotypic ratio.

4. The correct answer is (A). In order for a fertilized egg to become masculinized, a Y chromosome must be present to confer maleness. Therefore, the Y chromosome dictates that a male develops from the fertilized egg.

5. The correct answer is (C). Sex-linked traits, although mainly seen in men, are not restricted to men. It is best to write out the cross and do the Punnet square where C = normal and c = color blind. Remember, only XX gives information for females and XY gives information for males.

$$
X^C \ Y \quad
\begin{array}{c|c|c}
 & X^c & X^c \\
\hline
X^c & X^C X^c & X^c Y \\
\hline
X^c & X^C X^c & X^c Y \\
\end{array}
$$

female $X^c\, X^c$ × male $X^C Y$

6. The correct answer is (E). A cross of AO × BO shows the appearance of all possible blood types at 25 percent probability for each.

Forces Unseen: Bacteria and Viruses

BACTERIA

Bacteria, also known as **microbes** or **germs**, are microscopic organisms that reproduce primarily asexually. This may come as a surprise, but most organisms (including humans) are covered inside and out with what's referred to as a normal **flora** of bacterial populations. Metabolically speaking, an organism would be at a severe disadvantage and quite unusual if it didn't have bacteria.

> There are more than 2,000 known species of bacteria, and some scientists speculate that this represents less than 1 percent of all the bacteria on Earth!

Bacteria are classified as either **autotrophs** (they synthesize food by converting light to chemical energy) or as **heterotrophs** (they require other organisms to serve as a food source). Bacteria are grouped under Kingdom Prokaryotae, also known *Monera,* and are subdivided into three main groups based on staining reactions, shape, motility, metabolism, reproduction, and endospore formation:

- **Eubacteria** (true bacteria) come in three shapes: **coccus** (spherical), **bacillus** (rod-shaped), and **spirillum** (spiral-shaped). An example would be *Escherichia coli,* or *E. coli,* a bacterium that grows in small numbers as a part of the natural flora of the skin, the intestinal tract, and the genital tract. However, under a compromised immunity and overgrowth of this bacterium, a person can become extremely ill and even die.

- **Cyanobacteria** perform photosynthesis to convert light energy into chemical energy for food. The green gooey stuff you sometimes see in standing pools of water (also known as pond scum) is an example of cyanobacteria. It is theorized that Earth's early atmosphere was converted to one containing oxygen when photosynthetic bacteria released oxygen into the atmosphere.

- **Archaeobacteria** is a recently discovered group of bacteria. These microcrobes are typically found in extreme environments, such as on glaciers and in underwater volcanic vents.

Bacteria have simple structures. Since they are prokaryotes, they lack a membrane-bound nucleus and membrane-bound organelles. The picture below shows the basic body plan for a typical bacterium. Bacteria contain strands of DNA known as a **nucleoid**, a **plasma membrane**, a **cell wall**, and a **capsule**. This simple body allows for the rapid division of a bacterium, usually by way of *binary fission*. This is a form of asexual reproduction that does not involve division of complex structures, as seen in mitosis and meiosis.

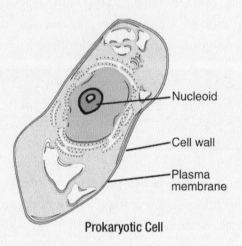

Prokaryotic Cell

Humans, Bacteria, and the Environment

When most people think of bacteria, they think of disease-causing organisms. Many bacteria actually serve beneficial and necessary functions to humans and the environment. Bacteria function as **decomposers**, **nitrogen fixers**, and **symbionts,** and a small percentage are **pathogenic**. Some microbes, such as **saprophytes,** recycle dead materials and sewage into smaller molecules that can be returned to the environment. The pharmaceutical industry uses bacteria in the manufacture of antibiotics and vitamins. Many of the foods we eat, such as yogurt and cheese, are the product of bacterial metabolism. Alcohol, acids, and many other chemicals are products of bacterial cultures. Plants also benefit from relationships with bacteria. The roots of bean plants form a symbiotic relationship with bacteria that are capable of converting atmospheric nitrogen into a useable form, which not only benefits the plant but also the soil surrounding the plants. This process is known as **nitrogen fixation**. The cycling of nitrogen is achieved exclusively by bacteria.

The relationships formed by symbiotic bacteria can be **mutualistic, commensalistic,** or **parasitic**.

- Mutualistic relationships occur when both organisms rely on each other to live.

- Commensal relationships develop when the microbe benefits and the host does not, but there are no ill affects to the host.

- Parasitism is a one-way relationship where the bacteria benefit and the host suffers negative side affects, such as illness. These bacteria are **pathogens,** or disease-causing agents.

Humans and other organisms share a mutualistic relationship with some bacteria. The digestive system in humans relies on intestinal bacteria to produce antibiotics that prevent the growth of pathogenic bacteria. Bacteria also aid in digestion. Herbivores, such as cows, lack the enzyme needed to digest cellulose, so they depend on methanogens to convert their food into simple sugars. The methane gas (CH_4) produced as a by-product of these microbes is used as a fuel source by humans in some parts of the world.

But then there are the **pathogens** that cause disease and death. Pathogenic bacteria invade healthy tissues. Their metabolic processes release enzymes that destroy the normal physiology of this tissue. Some diseases caused by pathogenic bacterium are leprosy, syphilis, gonorrhea, tuberculosis, strep throat, and Lyme disease. Other pathogens produce toxins as a product of their bacterial metabolism that are poisonous to humans. Botulism, for example, is caused by a toxin that infects food and liquids. When it is ingested, it can cause illness and death.

> Several generations of bacteria can develop in a matter of hours, or even minutes!

To combat pathogens, antibiotics have been developed to disrupt bacterial metabolism. Researchers find this a daunting task because the growth rate of bacteria is extremely rapid and some bacteria can develop immunity to an antibiotic, especially when we overuse antibiotics. They divide rapidly and create a new and more virulent strain. For example, antibiotics such as penicillin are now ineffective against more resistant strains of bacteria, so stronger antibiotics must constantly be developed. Antibiotics weaken and rupture the cell wall of bacteria and cause the death of the cell. Scientists attack this problem from new angles, such as enzyme therapies and vaccines that react to specific proteins of some strains in bacteria and interrupt their growth.

Viruses

Viruses have confounded scientists since their discovery at the end of the nineteenth century. Some scientists theorize that viruses are the simplest forms of life, others say they are nonliving, and still other scientists say that they are parasites that have evolved to a highly specific state. One thing is clear, however. Viruses, unlike most other organisms, do not neatly fit into one of the five major kingdoms because they are incapable of sustaining life and of reproducing by themselves. Therefore, they are usually considered as separate entities.

Viruses are infectious particles that act as **obligate intracellular parasites** in all types of organisms. They can only reproduce inside a living cell. Once inside the host cell, viruses take over the genetic machinery of the host cell and produce more viruses. Viruses consist of a core of nucleic acid that can be either DNA or RNA in origin, which is surrounded by a protein coat. They are the smallest infectious agents known to man. Viruses have decimated plants and animals and are the cause of many devastating human diseases, such as AIDS/HIV, hepatitis B, and herpes.

Viral Action

Most of the organisms occupying the five kingdoms are not immune from viral invasions.

Viruses differ from bacteria in their simplified body structure and composition and their mode of replication. Viruses absolutely depend on a living host cell for replication. These living cells can be of plant, bacterial, or animal origin. Viruses are host-specific, in that they invade only one type of cell, which provides necessary receptor sites for the virus to attach itself. For example, the virus that causes polio attaches to neurons, the virus responsible for mumps attaches to salivary glands, and the virus that causes chicken pox attaches to skin cells. A viral infection follows five phases:

1. **Attachment:** The virus attaches to receptor sites on a host cell. Glyco-proteins (proteins with carbohydrates attached) on a cell's membrane usually serve as receptor sites for viral attachment.

2. **Penetration:** The virus injects its nucleic acid into the host cell. The head and tail remain outside the cell.

3. **Biosynthesis:** The viral nucleic acid now directs the synthesis. Initially, the virus uses the host cell's nucleotides and enzymes to make copies of its DNA. In a later phase, any RNA transcribed as mRNA is from viral origin for the synthesis of its nucleic acids, proteins, enzymes, and other components.

4. **Maturation:** Viral genes direct assembly of complete virions (a complete and fully developed viral particle). For simpler viruses, this assembly of head and tail units occurs spontaneously.

5. **Release or Lysis:** The plasma membrane of the host cell eventually breaks open (lyses). These released viral particles are prepared to infect the nearest vulnerable host cell.

Some bacteria, as previously mentioned, contain RNA instead of DNA. RNA viral replication is essentially the same except for several different modes of mRNA production among different types of RNA viruses. **Retroviruses** use a unique enzyme called **reverse transcriptase,** which allows the RNA of a virus to synthesize a complementary strand of DNA. This enzyme is called reverse because it directs transcriptions from RNA to DNA, which is the opposite of the standard mode of transcription from DNA to RNA. Scientists involved in molecular genetics and biotechnology have exploited the capabilities of this reverse transcriptase to manufacture copies of specific DNA molecules.

This form of replication also requires that the viral DNA be integrated into the host cell's DNA, meaning the host cell's chromosome. At this point, the virus remains a permanent mosaic of the chromosome. The HIV-1 and HIV-2 viruses that cause AIDS belong to this group and are difficult to treat. They often remain in a latent state and only replicate when the cell replicates or they become active and replicate, producing new viruses that then spread to nearby cells. The HIV virus also has a staggering mutation rate. A single individual may develop many different strains over the course of the infection, which decreases the effectiveness of most drug therapies.

> The Chinese were the first to experiment with vaccines as early as the eleventh century.

To treat viral infections, prevention is the key. Early investigations into the spread of disease, in particular smallpox, prompted the development of vaccines. In 1796, Dr. Edward Jenner discovered that milkmaids who contracted cowpox from cows showed a natural immunity against the more virulent smallpox. From this discovery, a new form of disease prevention was born. Vaccines are developed by using nonpathogenic strains of viruses or killed viral strains. The vaccine is introduced into an organism. Immunity occurs when the organism's immune system produces antibodies to fight the inactive virus. If the organism ever encounters these particles again, it has already developed a defense.

Genetic engineering has even created the ability to allow some other organism to produce inactive components of a virus. For example, in recent years, "edible vaccines" have been developed. Plants such as bananas can be engineered by splicing genes from a bacterium or virus with a bacterium that naturally occurs in the soil that the plant is grown in. The bacterium in the soil then infects the growing plant, transferring the foreign gene along with it. Scientists hope that in this way, mass quantities of vaccines can be produced inexpensively and distributed to areas of the world that lack conventional health care. Another new take on vaccines uses "naked" DNA from a virus that is injected into muscle or skin cells. The host cell produces minute amounts of viral antigens as directed by the viral DNA and initiates an immune response. These new approaches represent the constant struggle of man against these unseen and potentially deadly invaders.

Pop Quiz

You're on a roll! Answer the questions or go back and do some more review.

1. Cyanobacteria require _____ as their source of energy.
   - (A) protein
   - (B) sulfur
   - (C) sunlight
   - (D) roots

2. A substance that interferes with gene expression or other normal functions of bacteria is a(n)

   (A) antibiotic.

   (B) prion.

   (C) viroid.

   (D) bacteriophage.

3. Which of the following diseases is not caused by a virus?

   (A) Smallpox

   (B) Polio

   (C) Influenza

   (D) Syphilis

4. Saprophytes are

   (A) viruses that infect bacteria.

   (B) recyclers that convert dead materials and sewage into reusable molecules.

   (C) bacteria that make cheese and yogurt.

   (D) plasmids.

5. Methanogens produce _____ as a result of cellulose digestion in the guts of cows.

   (A) nitrogen gas

   (B) carbon dioxide

   (C) methane gas

   (D) heterocysts

6. Why is the enzyme reverse transcriptase called "reverse"?

   (A) It directs transcriptions from RNA to DNA.

   (B) It directs transcriptions from DNA to RNA.

   (C) Transcription is directed from DNA to plasmid.

   (D) Transcription is directed from RNA to bacteriophage.

Answers

1. The correct answer is (C). Cyanobacteria are the photosynthetic bacteria.

2. The correct answer is (A).

3. The correct answer is (D). Choices (A), (B), and (C) are all caused by viruses.

4. The correct answer is (B). Choice (A) refers to a bacteriophage, choice (B) refers to commercial strains of friendly bacteria, and choice (D) refers to loops of DNA within bacteria.

5. The correct answer is (C).

6. The correct answer is (A). Reverse transcriptase allows the retrovirus to manufacture its viral DNA by using an RNA strand as the template.

The Keys to the Kingdoms

All organisms are not alike. Many centuries ago, **Aristotle** created a classification system that organized organisms according to movement. If something moved, it was of animal origin, and if it did not move, it was of plant/vegetable origin. Unfortunately for Aristotle, though, later scientific investigations proved this system to be faulty.

> You've probably classified organisms, too. Do words like preppy, goth, geek, and jock sound familiar?

Carl von Linne (**Carolus Linnaeus**) made the next major step in bringing order to the natural world. He laid the foundation for **taxonomy**, the system of classification and nomenclature (naming). Linneaus used Latin to name organisms, so that everyone involved in the field of science could use a universal language for the names of organisms. He then created a system called **binomial nomenclature**, which uses a two-part name that illustrates the special characteristics of an organism. The binomial was more precise than common names and later evolved into the genus and species of modern taxonomic classification.

> The genus is capitalized and the species is not, and if not italicized, the name should be underlined.

Genus	species		Genus	species
<u>Homo</u>	<u>sapien</u>	or	*Homo*	*sapien*

Modern classification schemes incorporate five major groups, called kingdoms. This is the largest grouping category. As classification continues, it becomes increasingly specific. The major groups for taxanomic classification are:

Modern Taxonomy

Kingdom
Phylum
Class
Order
Family
Genus
Species

In plants, the term **division** is used instead of phylum. A great way to remember the order is with a mnemonic (memory tool) such as *King Pat Can Order Fresh Green Salad.* The first letter of each word corresponds to the first letter of each major category. If this mnemonic is too corny, feel free to make your own.

Kingdom Prokaryotae (Monerans)

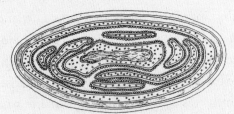

Typical Prokaryotic Cell

> To review the body plan of bacteria, see pages 51-52.

Members of this kingdom are bacteria and cyanobacteria. These are simple, single-celled, microscopic organisms. The cell wall of bacteria enables microbiologists to Gram stain bacteria for identification. These organisms play different roles in our environments. Some are pathogenic, others are nitrogen fixers, and still others act as decomposers.

Bacterial Shapes

Bacteria exist in three basic shapes:

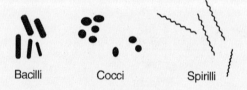

Bacilli   Cocci   Spirilli

Bacteria Types

There are 4800 different kinds of bacteria, and most need oxygen to live. These are **aerobic** (oxygen dependent) bacteria. Other bacteria do not need oxygen to live and are **anaerobic** (non-oxygen dependent). Within the group of anaerobes, some find oxygen poisonous and will die if subjected to large amounts; these are **obligate** bacteria. Other anaerobic bacteria, the **facultative** type, can withstand small amounts of oxygen.

Cyanobacteria

These autotrophic bacteria are photosynthetic, and because of the pigment color they produce, cyanobacteria are also known as blue-green algae. If a polluted body of water contains appropriate and abundant nutrients, a growth explosion of algae can occur, creating a "floating carpet" or algal bloom. Cyanobacteria can also form symbiotic relationships; lichens are the product of fungi and cyanobacteria living together. These bacteria contributed to the increase of free oxygen in Earth's early atmosphere, which was critical for eukaryotic life based on aerobic respiration.

KINGDOM PROTISTA

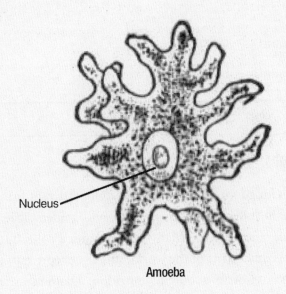

Nucleus

Amoeba

Protozoans

> Can you believe that there are more than 60,000 known species of protists? Thank goodness you'll only need to know a few for your exam!

Many members of this kingdom are single-celled, motile organisms. However, some form colonial relationships. These are eukaryotic cells with a true nucleus and other structures found in more advanced cells. Protozoa are classified on locomotion and how they obtain food. Two common protozoans are *Amoeba* and *Paramecium*. The amoeba are heterotrophic, formless cells that use pseudopods to move and engulf food by phagocytosis. Paramecium, which are also heterotrophic, move by using cilia. The cilia are also used to direct a current of water containing food into the organism's gullet (like a mouth and stomach all in one).

Some protists are pathogenic. The sporozoans in phylum apicomplexa contain a species called P*lasmodium vivax,* which causes malaria, a disease that is responsible for millions of deaths worldwide. Another protistan that is pathogenic to humans belongs to the species Trypanosoma. *Trypanosma brucei* causes *African sleeping sickness* and *Trypanosoma cruzi* causes *Chagas*. Both are debilitating, wasting diseases.

Examples of Animal-like Protistans

- Amoeba

- Paramecium

- Trypanosoma

Recall the process of phagocytosis from page 27.

Plantlike Autotrophs: Algae

Algae is classified in kingdom protista, but it is quite different from amoebas and paramecium. Algae includes green, brown, red, and golden algae as well as diatoms, dinoflagellates, and euglena. Many seaweeds are a collection of algal cells, and in Asia as well as other parts of the world, this algae represents a major part of the human diet because of its abundant nutrition. Diatoms are used commercially for the reflective and abrasive nature of their shells. Paints used for marking the lanes on highways often contain diatomaceous earth. Some toothpastes also contain these shells for abrasive action. Probably the most curious of these organisms is Euglena. The euglena are normally autotrophic—they contain chloroplasts with pigment for photosynthesis. However, under low light or the absence of light, they can switch to a heterotrophic mode. They move by flagella, which is more characteristic of protozoans. (These guys are all mixed up!)

Plant-like protistans can also be pathogenic. Some species of dinoflagellates undergo explosive population growth, creating seas of red or brown. This is called "red tide," and it is responsible for the death of fish and occasionally people due to its high production of neurotoxins.

Examples of Plant-like Protistans

- Red, brown, and green algae
- Dinoflagellates
- Diatoms
- Phytoplankton
- Euglenoids

Funguslike Heterotrophs: Slime Molds

This is another type of Protist—and a rather gross one at that. You've probably seen this stuff if you've ever gone camping or hiking. It hangs out in dark, warm, moist areas, like on the soil or rotting leaves or logs, and looks grayish-white, yellow, or bright red. It resembles a fungus because a portion of its lifecycle creates a multicellular entity that forms spores.

KINGDOM MYCETAE

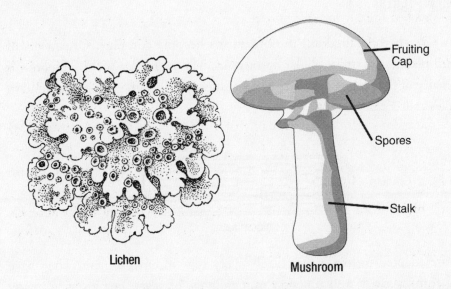

Lichen

Mushroom

Fruiting Cap

Spores

Stalk

> Fungus is a major commercial food product. Mushrooms, blue cheese, beer, soy sauce, and the citric acid that makes your soda tart are just a few fungus products.

Fungus is the common name for members of the Kingdom Mycetae. They are mainly nonmotile, nonphotosynthetic heterotrophic organisms. The majority are multicellular, like molds and mushrooms, but there are a few unicellular types, like yeast. Fungi survive and disperse by forming spores, which are made sexually or asexually. When released, the spores are carried by wind or water and can travel thousands of kilometers from their point of origin. **Saprophytes** absorb nutrients from dead organisms. **Symbiotic fungus**, on the other hand, can be either **parasitic** (causing athlete's foot and ringworm) or **mutualistic** (lichens).

Members of Kingdom Fungi

- Molds

- Mushrooms

- Yeast

- Lichens (symbiosis between fungi and algae or fungi and cyanobacteria)

Kingdom Plantae

Once we reach this kingdom, the organisms become complex. Organisms of kingdom plantae are multicellular autotrophs. The highlight of this kingdom is the presence of the photosynthetic pigment **chlorophyll**. This pigment is found in organelles called chloroplasts.

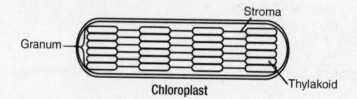

Plants are adapted to live in practically every type of environment. They have evolved form, activity, and function over millions of years. For instance, many developed vascular tissues to live on land. Others have hard, woody tissues for support. And some possess ovaries. The multitude of plants within this kingdom is staggering! To keep it simple, let's review the two major groups of plants.

Division Bryophyta (Bryophytes)—Nonvascular Plants

The simplest form of plants, Bryophytes are nonvascular and have no true roots, stems, or leaves. Lacking these structures, bryophytes are limited in two ways:

(1) They cannot grow very high, on average only a few inches in height.

(2) They must live near moisture.

During reproduction, the motile sperm swim to the eggs. Bryophytes exhibit an **alternation of generations,** which explains their reproduction. The dominant generation in most plants is diploid. However, adult bryophytes are haploid. The plant enters a diploid form when the sperm unites with the egg. Spores are produced and undergo meiosis, creating another haploid plant. These plants alternate between the haploid and diploid form, with the haploid form dominating the cycle.

- Mosses

- Liverworts

- Hornworts

Vascular Plants

Vascular plants represent the vast majority of plants. These plants are mainly diploid throughout their lifecycle and represent a successful adaptation for land living, as seen in their complex vascular tissues. They produce haploid sperm and eggs. Eggs are manufactured in the **ovary** and sperm in **pollen** granules.

Types of Vascular Tissue

- Dermal—the outer portion, including stomates and hair cells, with aerial portions covered with a waxy cuticle to prevent water loss

- Vascular—Found in roots, stems, and leaves, they move water throughout the plant.

    Xylem—hollow cells that form a tube; tubes carry water from soil into roots and transport to aboveground portions of plant

    Phloem—thickened sieve-like cells that transport organic molecules produced in one part of the plant to storage regions in another part; for example, the sugars produced by photosynthesis in the leaf move to the root for storage

Types of Basic Vegetative Organs

- Roots—anchor plant into soil; take up water and nutrients from soil; we eat a variety of roots, like carrots and radishes

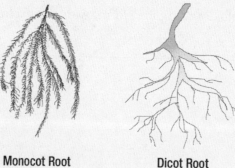

Monocot Root   Dicot Root

- Stems—support leaves and transport raw materials from roots to leaves and synthesized food from leaves to roots; some edible examples of stems are potatoes, yams, celery, and sugar cane

- Leaves—the major photosynthetic portion of a plant; transpiration occurs in leaves in which water is lost to assist the flow of water and nutrients from roots to leaves

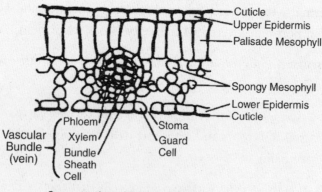

Cross section of a typical leaf

Major Parts of a Typical Leaf

- *Epidermis*—outer layer of cells that prevents water loss; may contain a cuticle

- *Palisades Layer*—vertically arranged chloroplasts for maximum photosynthesis

- *Spongy Layer*—loosely arranged chloroplasts that allow for water, oxygen, and carbon dioxide circulation

- *Guard Cells*—epidermal cells that change shape according to water amounts in leaf; they create tiny openings called stomates, which close or open to control the rate of water loss and gas exchange

- *Vascular Bundles*—xylem and phloem tissues in bundles

Seedless Vascular Plants

- Lycophytes—epiphytic (commensal) plants that live off of other plants; produce spores

    Club mosses

- Sphenophytes—spore producers that resemble a horse's tail; one member of this   group, *scouring rushes*, was used by early Americans for "scouring" pots and pans; also spore-producing

    Horsetails

    Scouring rushes

- Pterophytes—contain spore-bearing capsules on underside of leaf called *sori*

    Ferns

Seed-Producing Vascular Plants

Basic Reproductive Organs

- Seed—a specialized structure that contains an *embryo* enclosed in an outer, protective covering, the seed coat; both gymnosperms and angiosperms produce seeds. Under the right conditions and with water, the seed can germinate and grow into the adult plant.

- Pollen—small dust-like granules produced by both gymnosperms and angiosperms

Gymnosperms

Literally translated as "naked seed," this first group of vascular plants produces seeds on the surfaces of woody, leaf-like structures called **cones**. Gymnosperm cones are reproductive structures: male cones produce pollen, and female cones produce ovules on the same tree. During *pollination*, wind, insects, and rain carry the pollen to the eggs of the female cone.

- Pine

- Cedar

- Ginkgo

Angiosperms

Fruits taste so good to encourage animals to eat them. This helps with seed dispersal.

This group of plants is considered the highest order of evolution in the plant kingdom. Unlike the gymnosperms, angiosperms produce coated seeds that are enclosed by tissues of the ovary on the flower. The ovary and other tissues develop into the mature structure known as the fruit. Many fruit are edible and are used as food sources for humans like apples, oranges, and tomatoes. In fact, when you eat a piece of fruit, you are actually consuming a plant's mature ovary.

There are 300,000 varieties of plants that produce flowers, fruits, and seeds. In fact, all flowering plants are considered angiosperms, so this is an extremely large group of plants. There are two major categories:

Monocots

The seeds of monocots contain structures called cotyledons. Cotyledons contain the embryo and store nutrients for germination of the embryo. Monocots contain only one cotyledon. Monocot plants also show different arrangements in vascular bundles, leaf venation, and the number and arrangement of petals on flowers.

- grasses such as rye, corn, wheat, and rice

- orchids

Dicots

Dicot plants have two cotyledons and encompass the majority of angiosperms—about 180,000 varieties. These plants include most herbaceous (nonwoody) plants, flowering shrubs, and trees. They also show specific arrangements of vascular bundles, leaf venation, and petal arrangement of flowers.

- legumes (beans)

- apples

- oak trees

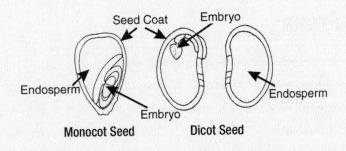

Angiosperm Reproductive Organs

Flowers are the specialized reproductive organs for flowering plants. They contain both the male and female portions of the plant. You should already be familiar with the parts of the flower, so we'll just do a quick review of the main parts:

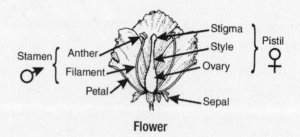

Flower

- **Petals**—the floral portions of the plant, usually ornate to attract pollinators

- **Pistil**—the female reproductive parts
    Stigma—the portion on which pollen lands
    Style—the slender tube-like portion between the stigma and ovary
    Ovary—contains the egg and site of fertilization; the ovary matures into the fruit with seeds
- **Stamen**—the male reproductive parts

    Anther—produces pollen

    Filament—the stalk on which the anther sits

- **Sepals**—the protective portion of the unopened flower

Kingdom Animalia

There are at least four million known species of animals.

This final kingdom contains animals that have adapted to live in practically every environment on Earth. The diversity in this kingdom is incredible. From habitat to size and from form to color, animals show amazing variety. They are multicellular, **heterotrophic** organisms, meaning they must obtain food by consuming other organisms. Humans are classified under this kingdom. So what does it take to be an animal anyway?

- Animals can move from place to place during all stages of their life and can move one part of their body in respect to the other parts.

- Animals are not photosynthetic.

- Animals reproduce sexually, although some may reproduce asexually as well.

- Animals are multicellular, with many cells organizing into tissues and then into complex organ systems.

Ok, let's review the major groups of animals, beginning with the more basic forms and advancing to the more complex forms.

> Hang in there, we're almost done with this section!

Phylum Porifera (sponges)

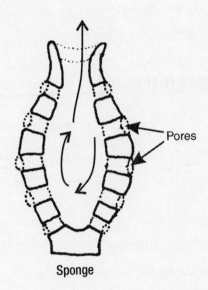

Pores

Sponge

- Members: Marine and Freshwater Sponges

- Features: Stationary (sessile) organisms as adult, contain pores for circulation of water and food

Phylum Cnidaria (cnidarians)

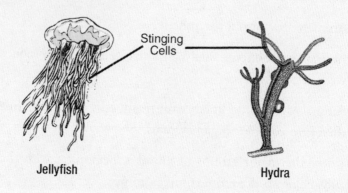

Jellyfish   Stinging Cells   Hydra

- Members: Jellyfish, Corals, Sea Anemone
- Features: Secrete hard protective covering around themselves; have a two-form lifecycle, a **polyp** and **medusa** stage, with the medusa being free-floating and the sessile polyp producing the medusae; possess tentacles and stinging cells

Phylum Platyhelminthes (flatworms)

Planaria

- Members: Planarians, Tapeworms, and Flukes
- Features: *Planarians* are free-living, nonsegmented carnivores with a sac-type digestive system. *Tapeworms* are segmented parasites that live in the digestive tract of vertebrates and have no digestive system. *Flukes* are both external and internal parasites with flattened bodies that live off of fluids from their host

Phylum Aschelminthes (roundworms)

Roundworm

- Members: Nematodes, Pinworms

- Features: Cylindrical bodies and a complete digestive tract, not segmented, can be free-living and parasitic, especially useful in recycling in soil habitats

Phylum Annelida (segmented worms)

- Members: Earthworm, Leech, Polychaete

- Features: Occupy marine environments (except earthworms); have segmented bodies; can be parasitic, as seen in the blood-sucking leech; have developed organ systems such as circulatory, muscular, digestive, and nervous

Phylum Arthropoda (arthropods)

Insect

Chilopod

Diplopod

Arachnid

Crustacean

- Members: **Class Insecta** (insects), **Class Arachnida** (spiders), **Class Diploda** (millipedes), **Class Chilopoda** (centipedes), **Class Crustacea** (crustaceans)

- Features: Some possess a head thorax and abdomen (Insects, Spiders); have appendages such as jointed legs, antennae, mouthparts, wings; external exoskeleton armor; metamorphose from egg, larva, pupa, to adult; most are terrestrial, with some marine dwellers (class crustacea)

Phylum Mollusca (mollusks)

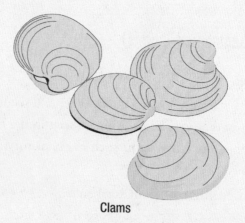

Clams

- Members: Bivalves (Clam, Mussels), Squid, Snail, Octopus

- Features: Soft bodies (some are protected by shells); some have ventral, muscular foot (bivalves); internal organs in visceral region

Phylum Echinodermata (echinoderms)

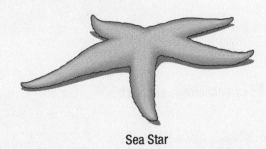

Sea Star

- Members: Starfish, Sand dollar, Sea cucumber

- Features: Marine dwelling; possess tube feet and water circulating system; spines on surface

Phylum Chordata Vertebrata

Chordate and Mammal

This is the most advanced group of animals when considering evolutionary development, so we're going to go into a bit more detail here. Three evolutionary developments make the chordata phylum so advanced:

(1) Notochord development, which is generally the precursor to a vertebral column

(2) A dorsal nerve chord, which in some animals differentiates into a brain and spinal cord

(3) Pharyngeal gill slits for carbon dioxide/oxygen exchange (these appear as pharyngeal folds in higher animals)

Class Chondrichthyes (cartilagenous fish)

- Members: Sharks and Rays
- Features: Cartilage skeleton, fins

Class Osteichthyes (bony fish)

- Members: Trout, Bass, Carp
- Features: Bony skeleton, fins, and scales; use gills to process oxygen from water; mainly external fertilization

Class Amphibia (amphibians)

- Members: Frog, Salamander, Toad
- Features: No scales, moist skin, external fertilization, metamorphosis occurs, three-chambered heart

Class Reptilia (reptiles)

- Members: Snake, Turtle
- Features: Scales on body, internal fertilization, membrane covers egg

Class Aves (birds)

- Members: Chicken, Crow, Eagle
- Features: Feathers cover body, internal fertilization, eggs enclosed in calcium-enriched shell, four-chambered heart

Class Mammalia (mammals)

- Members: (This class is pretty big, so only a few main orders will be listed)

    Monotremes (primitive egg-laying mammal)—duck-bill platypus

    Marsupials (carry young in pouch on mother's body)—kangaroo

    Rodents (incisor teeth have continual growth)—rat, squirrel, mouse

    Cetaceans (marine, forelimbs modified to flippers)—dolphin, porpoise, whale

    Carnivore (meat-eaters)—dogs, wolves, cats

    Primates (large brain, stand erect, ability to grasp and hold objects)—human, ape, monkey, lemur

- Features: Hair covers body, feed young with mammary glands, internal fertilization, four-chambered heart

Pop Quiz

Another whopper of a section completed! Take the quiz or go study any problematic areas in your textbook or class notes.

1. Spherical bacteria are

    (A) bacilli.

    (B) spirillus.

    (C) spirochetes.

    (D) cocci.

2. Obligate anaerobic bacteria may be killed by high doses of

    (A) oxygen.

    (B) carbon dioxide.

    (C) carbon monoxide.

    (D) nitrogen.

3. Ameoba move by _____; paramecium move by _____.

   (A) cilia; pseudopods

   (B) pseudopods; cilia

   (C) flagella; cilia

   (D) pseudopods; flagella

4. Population "blooms" of _____ cause "red tides" and the death of many fish.

   (A) *Plasmodium*

   (B) diatoms

   (C) dinoflagellates

   (D) *Euglena*

5. The organism that causes *Athlete's foot* is

   (A) bacterial.

   (B) fungal.

   (C) protist.

   (D) viral.

6. A group of plants producing seeds by means of flowers is

   (A) angiosperms.

   (B) gymnosperms.

   (C) bryophytes.

   (D) liverworts.

7. _____ have internal conducting tissues to move water and solutes throughout the plant.

   (A) Lycophyte plants

   (B) Avascular plants

   (C) Bryophyte plants

   (D) Vascular plants

8. Monocots and dicots are groups of

   (A) gymnosperms.

   (B) club mosses.

   (C) angiosperms.

   (D) ferns.

For questions 9–13, use the following key to select which phylum each group of animals belongs:

   (A) Phylum Chordata

   (B) Phylum Cnidaria

   (C) Phylum Annelida

   (D) Phylum Mollusca

   (E) Phylum Echinodermata

   (F) None of these

9. Snakes, bony fish, lampreys, and cows

10. Spiders, crabs, millipedes, and insects

11. Hydra, corals, jellyfish, and sea anemones

12. Clams, mussels, squid, and octopus

13. Sea stars, sand dollars, and sea cucumbers

14. The first three levels of taxonomic classification are

   (A) kingdom, class, family.

   (B) kingdom, phylum, order.

   (C) kingdom, genus, species.

   (D) kingdom, phylum, class

Answers

1. The correct answer is (D).

2. The correct answer is (A). Oxygen can be lethal to anaerobic organisms that do not use oxygen to fuel their metabolic pathways.

3. The correct answer is (B).

4. The correct answer is (C). Choice (A), Plasmodium, causes malaria, and choices (B) and (D) do not cause pathogens to occur.

5. The correct answer is (B).

6. The correct answer is (A).

7. The correct answer is (D). Choices (A), (B), and (C) refer to plants that lack vascular tissues.

8. The correct answer is (C).

9. The correct answer is (A).

10. The correct answer is (F).

11. The correct answer is (B).

12. The correct answer is (D).

13. The correct answer is (E).

14. The correct answer is (D).

The Body Factory

The human body is a remarkable and precise balance of many organ systems working in unison. Each of these systems is coordinated and affects one another in various ways. **Homeostasis** is the process in which the organ systems work together to keep the body in balance. The easiest way to examine how this works is to look at each system separately.

The Integumentary System

The integumentary system includes skin, sweat glands, oil glands, hair, and nails. Think of it as a protective coating: It's waterproof, self-repairing, stretchable, washable, and durable, and it is the largest organ in the body. Our skin is a barrier between our bodies and the external environment. Skin prevents water loss, mechanical and chemical damage, and microbial invasion. It also accounts for about 7 percent of the total body weight of an average adult and covers a surface area of 1.5–2 meters.

> Tactile regions of the body, such as the palms of the hand and soles of the feet, have thicker skin than elsewhere.

Skin is composed of two distinct regions: the **epidermis** and the **dermis**. These two regions are further divided into several functional layers.

> The third region just beneath the skin is the hypodermis. It is not considered a part of the skin, but it serves a protective function similar to skin.

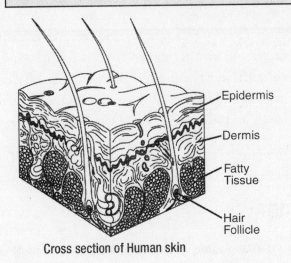

Cross section of Human skin

- **Epidermis**—highly keratinized structure consisting of 4–5 separate layers

  - *Stratum Corneum*—The outermost layer of cells, 20–30 cell layers thick. This layer consists of cells that are filled with keratin and hardened plasma membranes that protect the skin from physical and chemical abrasion and penetration.

- *Stratum Lucidum* —This layer is only present in thick skin. It represents an intermediate layer of flattened, dead keratinocytes (epidermal cells that produce keratin).

- *Stratum Granulosum* —The depth of this layer is about 3–5 layers deep. This strata represents the initiation of keratin precursors like keratohyalin and lamellated granules, which contribute to the waterproofing and toughening of the upper layers of skin.

- *Stratum Spinosum*—A layer of irregular-shaped cells that are filled with *prekeratin*.

- *Stratum Basale* —The deepest layer of cells that represent the stem cells of the epidermis. Rapid mitotic division in this region has been associated with an alternate name, *stratum germanitivum* ("germinating layer").

- **Dermis**—This is the second major skin division and lies beneath the epidermis. This connective tissue layer is divided into 2 layers, the papillary layer and the reticular layer.

  - *Papillary Layer*—This thin layer of connective tissues contains blood vessels, and its upper layer is folded into ridges called *dermal papillae*. These papillae lie on top of elevations called dermal ridges. The dermal ridges then form epidermal ridges on the hands and feet, which are better known as "fingerprints."

  - *Reticular Layer*—The second layer of dense connective tissue of the dermis

THE SKELETAL SYSTEM

The human skeletal system is a feat of nature that rivals and surpasses any man-made machine. It supports the body and acts as a lever system for the muscles, creating movement at joints. Some important functions of bone include:

- Movement
- Support
- Protection
- Mineral repository
- Blood cell formation

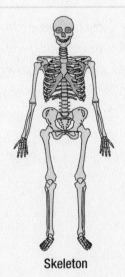

Skeleton

There are 206 bones in the vertebrate skeletal scheme. They are divided into two major groups, the **axial skeleton** (80 bones that run the axis of the skeleton) and the **appendicular skeleton** (126 bones that include the limbs and the pectoral and pelvic girdles).

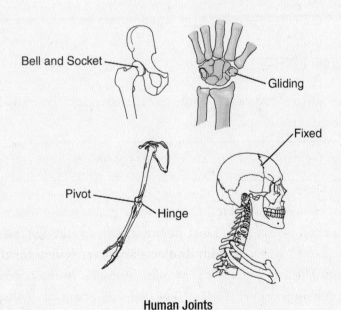

Human Joints

Bones articulate, or meet, with one another at **joints**. To prevent the bones from rubbing against each other, cartilage lines the joints. Depending on the type of movement seen at a joint, the cartilage can provide either a smooth articulating surface or a strong adhesion between bones. Several types of joints connect bones to one another. **Synovial joints** allow for a variety of movements, such as running. They contain a cavity lined with elastic connective tissue and are lubricated by *synovial fluid*. **Sutures** are another form of joint. They connect cranial bones in an interlocking fashion and are immovable. Many joints utilize a band-like type of connective tissue known as a **ligament** to stabilize movable joints. **Tendons** attach muscles to bone at joints.

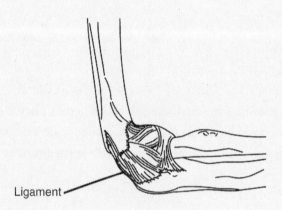

Ligament

THE MUSCULAR SYSTEM

There are more than 600 muscles in the human body, and there are three types of muscle: skeletal, cardiac, and smooth.

> The myofilaments give skeletal muscle its striated appearance.

Skeletal muscles are responsible for the body's movement and are attached to bone at either end by tendons. On a microscopic level, the fibers that make up skeletal muscles are elongated, cylindrical, multinucleate cells that are encased by a **sarcolemma**. The sarcolemma is a membrane similar to the cell membrane of other cells containing a single nucleus. The diameter of one of these muscle fibers can range from 10 to 100 mm and can be as long as 30 cm. Within each muscle fiber, there are smaller units, called **myofibrils**. Each myofibril contains still smaller **myofilaments** that are comprised of specific proteins, such as *actin* and *myosin*. These proteins comprise the main components of the **sarcomere**. When the actin and myosin slide back and forth, the sarcomere shortens. And when the sarcomeres within a muscle fiber shorten, the entire fiber shortens, too. A muscle is comprised of many bundles of these fibers working together. When all the sarcomeres contract, the entire muscle shortens.

Each time a muscle contracts and shortens itself, it moves the body part it is attached to. But a skeletal muscle does not work on its own. It works with another muscle. For example, let's say you wanted to raise your forearm. Your biceps brachii muscle will contract and raise the forearm (this muscle is known as the prime mover or **agonist**). Your triceps brachii, however, acts as an **antagonist** to the biceps and will relax.

Other forms of muscle in the human body are cardiac and smooth muscle. **Cardiac muscle** is found in the walls of the heart. This muscle allows for the strong pumping action of the heart's ventricles. **Smooth muscle** is found in the walls of hollow organs, like the stomach and intestines. Cardiac and smooth muscles differ from skeletal muscles in several ways:

- They have different structures.

- They have different nervous system coordination.

- The movement of skeletal muscle is voluntary—you have conscious control over it. Cardiac and smooth muscles, however, move involuntary—you can't control them consciously. Instead, they work without you realizing it.

THE NERVOUS SYSTEM

The nervous and endocrine systems are responsible for coordinating all of the physiological processes in the body. The nervous system serves as a rapid response system, so it is the major regulator of these processes. Actions such as the blink of an eye, the beating of the heart, breathing, and digestion are controlled by this system. The endocrine system, which we'll talk about later, responds more slowly and is actually controlled by the nervous system.

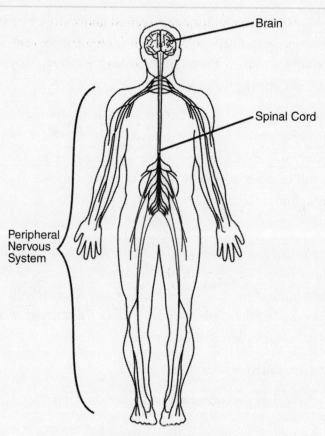

Peripheral Nervous System

The major organs of the nervous system are divided into two groups:

- **Peripheral nervous system,** which contains the cranial and spinal nerves and the ganglia, carries impulses from the sensory neurons to the central nervous system.

- **Central nervous system,** which contains the brain and spinal cord, processes the incoming sensory information and translates it into instructions. It then sends those instructions to the appropriate organs of the body, so the body can respond to the initial sensory information.

The **neuron** is the functional unit of nervous tissue that is used by the central and peripheral nervous systems. Neurons maintain an electrical charge on their outer surface by pumping ions such as Na and K across the cell membrane. These cells vary in shape and function, but generally the cell body is the central region of the neuron. Long nerve fibers extend from it. One type of nerve fiber, the **dendrites,** is the receptive region where impulses are received and moved to the cell body. The **axons** are another type of nerve fiber in which impulses are generated. Axons take impulses away from the cell body and transport them to another neuron or organ. Bundles of axons from many neurons comprise a **nerve**.

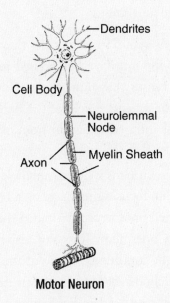

Motor Neuron

In between adjacent neurons, there is a space called a **synapse**. Neurons send messages to one another across this space via **neurotransmitters**—chemical messengers. Neurotransmitters, like acetylcholine, move from the cell body to the axonal terminals, where they are stored until an impulse travels down the axon. The neurotransmitters move from the neuron's axonal terminal, across the synapse, and to the neighboring neuron or organ, where it delivers the message that initiates a response in the neighboring neuron or organ.

Special Senses

Taste, vision, hearing, balance, and smell are integral parts of the nervous system. They allow us to interact with and interpret external stimuli as well as monitor internal changes of a chemical or physical nature. There are several classifications of sensory perception receptors:

- **Proprioceptors** (found in higher animals) are in the skin and muscles and detect pressure, temperature, pain, and touch.

- **Photoreceptors** perceive visible light stimuli.

- **Chemoreceptors** function in chemical perception.

- **Mechanoreceptors** detect mechanical energy stimuli.

- **Thermoreceptors** detect thermal stimuli.

- **Hair cells** (found in vertebrates) are in the inner ear and detect changes in gravitational pull and sound.

Many animals utilize these senses, and in some cases they have a "super" sensitive capacity. (Dogs like the bloodhound have heightened senses of smell and hearing.) Other animals possess senses that humans lack altogether. For instance, some species of birds detect the magnetic field of the Earth. Honeybees see ultraviolet light. Rattlesnakes sense infrared radiation from objects at a distance.

The Eye—Visual perception in humans is like a camera lens. Light enters through an adjustable lens that, like film, focuses the image on a receptor called the **retina**. Within the retina are specialized photoreceptors called **rods** and **cones** that detect different properties of light. Cones allow for color vision and visual acuity, and rods are responsive in low light conditions. Some of the simpler organisms, like *euglena,* use eyespots that merely detect light intensity. Arthropods such as grasshoppers possess a compound eye that lets light enter at different angles—this enhances their sight in dim light. Other animals, such as deer and mice, are color blind—they only see shades of gray.

> Cones allow for color vision and visual acuity and rods are responsive in low light conditions.

The Ear—In higher animals, the ear is subdivided into three regions: the outer, the middle, and the inner ear. The outer ear consists of the **pinna** (a cartilagenous, funnel-like structure), the **external auditory meatus** (the ear canal), and the **tympanic membrane** (the eardrum). The middle ear contains the three ear ossicles: the **malleus** (hammer), the **incus** (anvil), and the **stapes** (stirrup). An **eustachian tube** in the middle ear opens into the throat and allows for pressure stabilization. The inner ear contains the receptors for hearing, balance, and equilibrium and uses three structures to carry out these processes:

- The three **semicircular canals** lie in three distinct planes and can detect dynamic equilibrium or acceleration of the head.

- The **saccule** and **utricle** contain **otoliths**, which are calcium carbonate crystals embedded in a gelatinous substance that stimulates hair cells. The saccule and utricle detect the body's position in relation to gravity.

- The **cochlea** is a complex of canals filled with fluid that is displaced by sound energy. Within this complex is the **spiral organ of corti**. It has hair cells that detect sound energy.

Hearing is both a mechanical and neural event. Sound waves are funneled into the ear via the external auditory meatus and arrive at the tympanic membrane. The tympanic membrane sends the vibratory motion at the same frequency it was received to the ear ossicles. The motion is transferred to the middle ear, from the malleus to the incus to the stapes. The stapes sends this energy through the **oval window** and into the inner ear. The fluids in the inner ear are displaced by this motion, which in turn stimulates hair cells that synapse with sensory neurons. These neurons then send messages to the auditory centers of the brain.

The Endocrine System

> Growth hormone is responsible for the growth spurt you experienced at puberty—and for all of the clothes you outgrew, practically overnight!

The human endocrine system is comprised of specialized organs called **glands** that secrete chemical messengers called **hormones**. These hormones are carried throughout the body by the circulatory system, but they have only site-specific responses and can only attach to recognized receptor molecules of certain cells. The response time of hormones varies according to the outcome that is needed. For instance, epinephrine and norepinephrine (released from the adrenal medulla gland) can cause a rapid behavioral response known as the "flight or fight" response. This causes the heart rate, blood pressure, and breathing rate to increase as well as to direct blood to skeletal muscle. (Maybe you've felt some of these symptoms right before a big test!) Human growth hormone has a much slower response time. It stimulates the growth of cells over a period of several years. The table below lists each major gland, the major hormones it releases, and its function.

Major Endocrine Glands and Functions

Endocrine Gland	Hormones Released	Functions
*Pituitary (both anterior and posterior)	1. Growth hormone 2. Anti-diuretic hormone	1. Regulator of muscle, bone, and connective tissue growth 2. Increases re-uptake of water into blood from renal tubules; increases blood pressure
Thyroid	1. Thyroxin 2. Calcitonin	1. Regulates cellular metabolism 2. Decreases calcium ions in blood
Parathyroid	1. Parathyroid hormone	1. Increases calcium ions in blood
Pancreas	1. Insulin 2. Glucagon	1. Lowers blood-sugar levels; increases rate of metabolism of stored sugar 2. Increases blood sugar levels by converting glycogen to glucose; synthesizes glucose; and releases glucose to blood from liver cells
Adrenal glands	1. Corticosteroid 2. Epinephrine	1. Decreases sodium ion excretion; influences cellular metabolism and provides resistance stressors; contributes to secondary sexual characteristics during puberty 2. Increases blood sugar levels, heart rate, blood pressure, and respiratory rate; shunts blood to skeletal muscle. Mobilizes the sympathetic nervous system for short-term stressors or emergencies
Testes	1. Testosterone	1. Starts the maturation of male reproductive organs, secondary sexual characteristics at puberty, and sex drive
Ovaries	1. Estrogen 2. Progesterone	1. Initiates maturation of female reproductive organs and secondary sexual characteristics at puberty 2. Promotes breast development and menstrual cycle

*The pituitary gland has an effect on all of the major glands. The few listed in this table do not represent the total number of hormones released from the pituitary.

The Cardiovascular System

Multicellular organisms like humans consist of trillions of cells that need a rapid and efficient way to meet their physiological needs. During cellular metabolism, cells take in nutrients, create waste, and store, make, and use molecules—all of which need to be transported to other parts of the body. The cardiovascular system addresses transportation by using several integrated parts.

> The **tricuspid** valve is on the right side of the heart, and the **bicuspid** or **mitral** valve is on the left side.

Blood carries material and dissipates heat (we'll talk more about it in a little while). The **heart** is a cone-shaped organ that pumps blood from one part of the body to another. It has four chambers: The right and left upper elastic chambers are the **atria**. The right and left lower pumping chambers are the **ventricles**. Atrio-ventricular valves separate the atria from the ventricles. The valves ensure that blood circulates through the heart in one direction, from the atria to the ventricles, preventing a regurgitation of blood as the ventricles contract. The heart pumps blood into **arteries,** which distribute the blood to the organs. Blood is pumped into successively smaller arteries until it enters thin-walled vessels called **capillaries.** Blood is diffused through capillary beds so material can be exchanged between the blood and organ tissues. Blood then percolates through the capillary beds and into **veins,** which gradually merge with larger veins until the blood returns to the heart.

Cardiac Physiology

Because their tasks are different, the right and left sides of the heart differ. The right side of the heart pumps blood to the lungs, which are near the heart. Therefore, the right ventricle does not have to work hard. The larger left ventricle, however, pumps blood to the aorta, which delivers blood to the rest of the body. The left ventricle must contract with greater force, and this force creates a higher pressure in the arteries. Each contraction of the heart is reflected in the heartbeat.

Heart and Associated Vessels

The average adult's heart beats 72 times per minute. When you take your pulse after you've exercised, you are actually measuring your heartbeat rate; the pulse rate and heartbeat rates are the same.

Blood pressure is measured through the heartbeat. There are two phases to a heartbeat. The systolic pressure is the first phase. It represents the strong contraction of the ventricles as blood is pumped into the aorta. The diastolic pressure is the second phase. It represents ventricular relaxation.

Blood

Blood is a fluid connective tissue consisting of **formed elements.** Approximately 55 percent of these elements are blood suspended in a fluid matrix called **plasma.** Blood plasma is made of proteins, ions, and metabolites. Blood transports molecules, cells, and heat from one body region to another. The formed elements—*erythrocytes* (red blood cells), *leukocytes* (white blood cells), and *thrombocytes* (platelets)—perform very different functions and circulate at different percentages. The following table outlines some of the basic functions of blood plasma and the formed elements.

Functions of Blood Plasma and Formed Elements

Component	Description	Functions
Blood plasma	Composed about 90 percent of water; 7-8 percent plasma proteins; about 3 percent other variables	Transports wastes, nutrients, hormones, electrolytes, proteins, etc.
Erythrocytes (Red blood cells)	Biconcave disk-shaped cells; anucleate; contain hemoglobin to bind oxygen molecules; life span of 100-120 days; average number in adults is about 4.5-5.5 million cells per cubic millimeter	Carry oxygen and carbon dioxide gases
Leukocytes •Neutrophil •Basophil •Eosinophil •Lymphocyte •Monocyte (White blood cells)	Leukocytes number between 4,000-11,000 per cubic millimeter; each cell is nucleated	Defense mechanisms against disease, tumors, parasites, toxins, and bacteria; can move from blood to tissues (diapedesis); produce antibodies for long-term protection
Thrombocytes	Cytoplasmic fragments numbering 250,000 to 500,000 per cubic millimeter	Seal small ruptures in blood vessels; assist in blood clotting

THE RESPIRATORY SYSTEM

The cyclic exchange of respiratory gases within an organism is known as **respiration. Cellular respiration** involves the production of ATP molecules within the mitochondria; oxygen is used, and carbon dioxide is produced. The process of exchanging gases between blood and tissues is called **internal respiration,** whereas **external respiration** exchanges gases between blood and air. The process of breathing incorporates specific structures for the cycling of gases in and out of the body, illustrating external respiration. Breathing varies greatly within the animal kingdom. Most vertebrates use lungs for gas exchange. Animals such as frogs use both

a lung and moist skin to exchange gases. Mammals have the most complex respiratory systems, with successively smaller branching tubes that open into vascularized sacs. The main components of the human respiratory system are as follows:

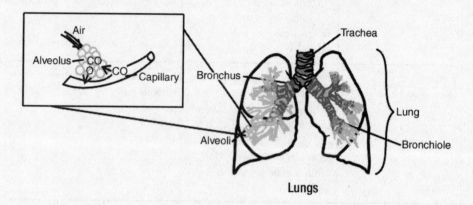

Lungs

- **Nose and Nasal Passages**—Within the nose, narrow chambers and elevations open to the nares externally and the throat internally. The passages are lined with hairs and mucus that filter, warm, and moisten inhaled air.

- **Pharynx** (throat)—A passage that doubles as an access way for both air and food

- **Larynx** (voice box)—A box of cartilage and muscle that houses the *glottis*, an opening that allows air to move from the pharynx to the larynx and ultimately to the trachea. The vocal chords are also found here.

- **Trachea** (windpipe)—Inferior to the trachea, this tube-like structure consists of cartilagenous rings ("**c-rings**") that keep the trachea open during the pressure changes that occur during breathing. It is lined with ciliated cells, which are interspersed with mucus-secreting cells. These components trap debris and move it out of the pharynx.

- **Bronchi**—Two large tubes that branch off the trachea as it enters the lungs. Each tube gets successively smaller and phases into *bronchioles*.

The human lung contains 300 million alveoli. In surface area, they cover a space of 70 square meters, which is about 100 times the surface area of skin.

- **Alveoli of Lungs**—Respiratory bronchioles terminate in sacs called alveolar sacs, which contain alveoli. The sacs are covered with capillaries to facilitate gas exchange across the thin walls of the alveoli.

- **Diaphragm**—The diaphragm and chest muscles create pressure and volume changes in the lungs. These changes create pressure differences between the outside air and the interior lung cavity. Air is forced in and out due to the differences in these pressure and volume changes.

THE DIGESTIVE SYSTEM

Cells need a constant supply of nutrients to use for energy and as building blocks for the assembly of macromolecules. The digestive system allocates and processes these nutrients. The human digestive system, in all its complex functions, is nothing more than a long muscular tube extending from the mouth to the anus. Along this pathway are several modified pouches and segments to perform specific tasks, including the following:

- Nutrient intake

- Mechanical and chemical processes of digestion

- Nutrient uptake

- Elimination of undigested material

To illustrate the functions of the parts of the digestive system, let's see what happens when you ingest a potato chip:

1. **Mouth**—Mechanical digestion begins here. The teeth and tongue masticate, or chew, the potato chip. Salivary amylase enzyme, produced by salivary glands, starts the hydrolysis of starch and dextrines. Saliva also assists in moistening the potato chip and forming the chewed-up pieces into a ball, or *bolus*, that can be easily swallowed.

2. **Pharynx**—During the swallowing process, the bolus of potato chip is pushed into the pharynx, where it slides over the epiglottis and into the esophagus. The epiglottis is the guardian of the airway—it momentarily seals the glottis during the swallowing process.

3. **Esophagus**—The muscular tube extending from the pharynx to the stomach. The potato chip moves down the esophagus by *peristalsis*, a rhythmic contraction that also occurs in the intestines.

4. **Stomach**—Both mechanical and chemical functions occur here. The stomach temporarily stores the potato chip, releasing small quantities of it at a time. The muscles in the walls of the stomach churn, mixing the chip with gastric juice and pepsin (called chyme). The pepsin digests proteins.

5. **Small Intestines**—The majority of chemical digestion and nutrient absorption occurs in the three segments of the small intestine. The **pancreas** delivers several pancreatic enzymes: trypsin, which breaks large polypeptides into amino acids; amylase, which changes polysaccharides to simpler forms; and lipase, which breaks fat down into glycerol and fatty acids. The **liver** produces bile, which physically emulsifies fats to improve digestion by lipase enzyme. All nutrient absorption, except of fatty acids and glycerol, occurs in the **small intestine**. The blood then moves into capillaries, and the nutrient-laden blood is taken to the liver and then to the body tissue. Fatty acids and glycerol are absorbed through a specialized system and are dispersed throughout the body by the lymphatic system. Because the small intestine has a great amount of surface area, chemical digestion and absorption are enhanced.

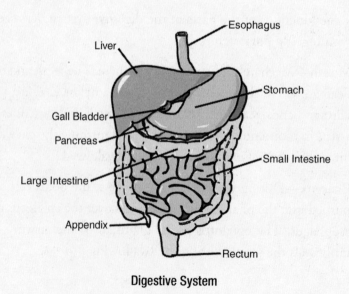

Digestive System

> The liver processes absorbed sugars, vitamins, amino acids, and minerals. Aside from its bile-producing functions, glycogen is stored here. The liver can also mobilize excess sugars and convert them into fats, destroy old red blood cells as well as produce blood proteins, and alter amino acids.

6. **Large Intestines**—Not all of the potato chip will be digested; some of it will move into the large intestine to be processed. Any water and available minerals from the chip are absorbed into the blood vessels of the walls of the large intestine and are returned to circulation. Bacterial action produces vitamin K, which is also absorbed into blood vessels and returned to circulation. The remainder of bacteria and undigested potato chip form the main component of *feces*.

7. **Rectum**—This is the storage site for accumulated feces until *defecation*, the excretion of feces.

8. **Anus**—The anal sphincter relaxes and the walls of the rectum contract until the feces is released from the body.

The mammalian digestive system works on a time-released food distribution plan, so it isn't necessary to constantly eat. This allows for activities besides feeding—like sleeping, doing homework, playing baseball, watching tv . . .

THE URINARY SYSTEM

Cellular metabolism of every organism produces waste products, like urea and nitrogenous wastes, that need to be separated from useful products, like water, and then disposed of. Simple organisms perform this by diffusing waste directly into their surrounding environment. For example, the flame cells of platyhelminthes collect and release waste along the sides of their bodies. More complex organisms, on the other hand, use a tube system to excrete wastes. The earthworm employs nephridia to collect accumulated fluids in tubule-like structures, which are then excreted.

The vertebrates have one of the most complex excretory systems of all organisms. It centers around the **kidney**, which is responsible for several functions:

- Blood filtration (the kidneys separate the filtrate from cellular components within blood)

- Monitoring of waste concentrations in blood

- Reabsorption from filtrate

- Return of reusable components back to blood

- Secretion for eventual removal of filtrate

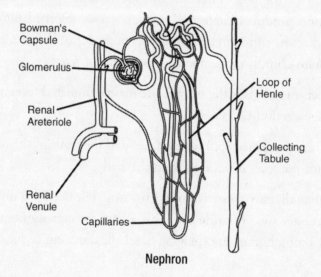

Nephron

Each kidney is composed of more than two million specialized units called **nephrons**. Each nephron consists of a tuft of capillaries called the **glomerulus**, which is surrounded by a cup-shaped structure, the **Bowman's (glomerular) capsule**. In addition, each nephron is divided into three distinct parts: the proximal convoluted tubule, the loop of henle (nephron), and the distal convoluted tubule.

Homeostasis means balance.

Nephrons play a huge role in maintaining homeostasis by retaining useful substances and getting rid of waste products. At this very moment, your trillions cells are going about their business, making things, storing things, and creating waste

products. For example, most cells utilize proteins in their day-to-day operations. In metabolizing these proteins, cells create nitrogenous waste that they have to get rid of. The liver will assist by converting nitrogenous waste into urea. This urea then must be transferred, via the circulatory system, to the kidneys. The waste then gets filtered through the glomerulus and the Bowman's capsule. At this point, the filtrate must pass through a series of tubules. Any useable molecules, including water, are reabsorbed and returned to circulation. Whatever is still left after this reabsorption process is waste, which is moved through the ureter to the bladder, where it waits to be excreted. Once that "urgent" moment arrives, urine passes through the urethra and out of the body.

The Reproductive System

Mention of the reproductive system probably conjures up embarrassing memories from health class. But at least we can review this system without using one of those corny health films from the 1970s! As you know, the primary goal of the reproductive system is the continuation of a species. There are many forms of reproduction, yet the degree of an organism's complexity is a good indicator of how it reproduces.

Asexual reproduction does not require any of the complex structures used by eukaryotic cells. Binary fission is a type of asexual reproduction that is used by prokaryotic cells like bacteria. These cells merely replicate a simple loop of DNA and then undergo cytokinesis. Fragmentation, as seen in phylum Porifera (Sponges), is another asexual form of reproduction in which a piece of the body breaks away and matures into a larger form. Vertebrates, on the other hand, produce gametes from reproductive organs, the gonads.

HIGH STAKES

Remember, gametes are sperm and egg cells that undergo meiotic division.

Female Basics

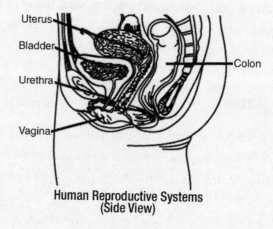

Uterus
Bladder
Urethra
Vagina
Colon

**Human Reproductive Systems
(Side View)**

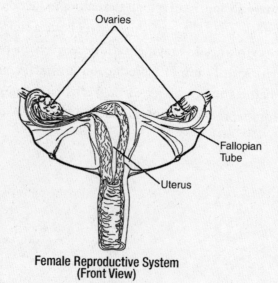

Ovaries

Fallopian
Tube

Uterus

**Female Reproductive System
(Front View)**

Females produce ova, or eggs, within their main reproductive structures, the **ovaries**. The process of **menstruation**, or **menses**, allows for one egg to be released each cycle. The pituitary gland releases the hormone FSH, which stimulates egg production and begins the menstrual cycle. Once an egg is released from an ovary (known as *ovulation*), it travels to the **Fallopian (uterine) tubes.** Another hormone, **estrogen,** is now produced in the follicle that just released the egg. Estrogen sends a signal to the pituitary gland to produce LH, which then converts the follicle into **corpus luteum**, a tissue that continues to make estrogen and an additional hormone, progesterone. Together, these two hormones support pregnancy. Progesterone in particular creates a growing population of blood vessels in the lining of the **uterus.**

> An embryo develops from the initial zygote, a fertilized egg.

Egg fertilization occurs in the fallopian tubes. The embryo that develops after fertilization implants itself to the lining of the uterus. The embryo releases hormones to support levels of LH and to inhibit any FSH until some time after birth. As the zygote undergoes cell division, distinct developmental stages occur: the blastula and the gastrula. The blastula is a fluid-filled cavity surrounded by a single layer of cells. The gastrula forms next and gives rise to important germ layers:

- The **ectoderm** for epidermis and neural organs

- The **endoderm** for the inner lining of respiratory and digestive organs

- The **mesoderm,** which is the precursor to all other major tissues of systems, such as the skeletal, muscular, and reproductive systems

At the end of the eighth week of human development, the embryonic period ends and the fetal period begins. From this point until birth, the forming baby is referred to as a **fetus** because distinct features can be seen.

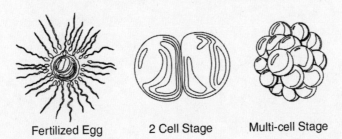

Fertilized Egg   2 Cell Stage   Multi-cell Stage

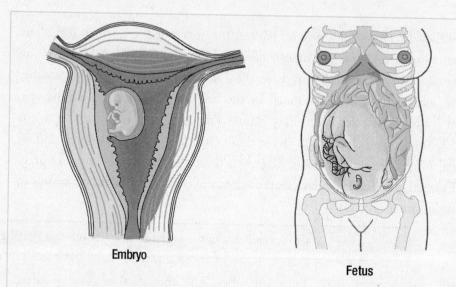

Embryo

Fetus

If fertilization does not occur, however, the unfertilized egg signals the break-down for corpus luteum. The egg and its newly created uterine lining are sloughed off the walls of the uterus and moved out of the body. This begins menstruation, a cyclic process that repeats approximately every twenty-eight days, alternating ovaries for egg release.

Male Basics

> Remember, meiosis results in the production of sperm cells.

Males manufacture sperm within their major reproductive organ, the **testes**. Men can reproduce sperm cells on a continuous basis throughout their lives, unlike women. The hormone testosterone signals and maintains sperm production. As with the female reproductive system, the pituitary hormone FSH stimulates the production of sperm cells, a process known as spermatogenesis.

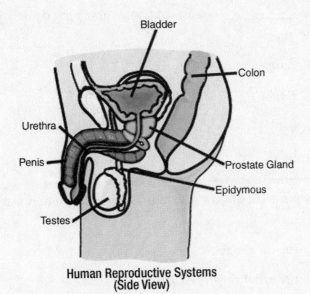

Human Reproductive Systems
(Side View)

POP QUIZ

Try the Pop Quiz to see if you need to review anything in more detail.

1. _____ conduct messages toward the cell body of a neuron.

    (A) Dendrites

    (B) Axons

    (C) Schwann cells

    (D) ATP

2. The _____ consists of tissue containing densely packed photoreceptors.

    (A) pinna

    (B) retina

    (C) iris

    (D) lens

3. The principal place in the human ear where sound waves are amplified is

    (A) the ear canal.

    (B) the spiral organ of Corti.

    (C) the middle ear.

    (D) the sclera.

    (E) None of the above

4. Thyroxine and triiodothyronine are two main hormones secreted by the

    (A) pancreas.

    (B) thyroid gland.

    (C) adrenal gland.

    (D) parathyroid.

5. The _____ gland controls the release of hormones from other endocrine glands; it is controlled by the _____.

   (A) hypothalamus; pancreas

   (B) pituitary; parathyroid

   (C) thyroid; thalamus

   (D) pituitary; hypothalamus

6. The sun's ultraviolet rays induce _____ production in melano-cytes.

   (A) collagen

   (B) melanin

   (C) keratin

   (D) elastin

7. A suture is

   (A) a bone cell.

   (B) a lever system.

   (C) an interlocking joint between cranial bones.

   (D) connective tissue sheets between muscle groups.

8. When the _____ contract(s), the elbow joint bends (flexes).

   (A) biceps brachii

   (B) triceps brachii

   (C) tricep and bicep brachii

   (D) None of the above

9. The sarcomere of a muscle fiber

   (A) is the site of blood-cell formation.

   (B) attaches muscle to bone.

   (C) secretes bone-dissolving enzymes.

   (D) is the function unit of muscular contraction.

10. Most of the oxygen in human blood is transported by

   (A) plasma.

   (B) hemoglobin.

   (C) serum.

   (D) leukocytes.

11. Gas exchange through skin is a characteristic common with

   (A) birds.

   (B) amphibians.

   (C) reptiles.

   (D) mammals.

12. The greatest amount of absorption of digested materials occurs in the

   (A) liver.

   (B) colon.

   (C) small intestines.

   (D) pharynx.

13. An entire subunit of a kidney that purifies blood and restores solute and water balance is called the

   (A) nephron.

   (B) glomerulus.

   (C) ureter.

   (D) loop of Henle.

   (E) None of the above

14. The structure that conveys the egg from the ovary to the uterus is the

   (A) seminal vesicle.

   (B) vagina.

   (C) ureter.

   (D) fallopian tube.

CHAPTER
3

SPT/HSPA, FCAT, MEAP HST, GEE21, Regents Exams, SOL, NCCT
T, AHSGE, GHSGT, BST, BSAP, WASL, CAHSEE, TAAS, OGT, HSPT/H   CAT, MEAP HST, N
SPT/HSPA, FCAT, MEAP HST, GEE21, Regents Exams, SOL, NCCT, A   GHSGT, BST, BSAI

Answers

1. **The correct answer is (A).**

2. **The correct answer is (B).** Choice (A) is the outer portion of the ear. Choices (C) and (D) refer to parts of the eye, but neither has photoreceptive functions.

3. **The correct answer is (C).** The middle ear contains the ear ossicles and the typanic membrane, which are involved with conduction and amplification of sound waves.

4. **The correct answer is (B).**

5. **The correct answer is (D).** The pituitary gland is considered the master gland and is controlled by the hypothalamus region of the brain.

6. **The correct answer is (B).** Choices (A), (C), and (D) are proteins produced by specialized cells called fibroblasts.

7. **The correct answer is (C).**

8. **The correct answer is (A).**

9. **The correct answer is (D).**

10. **The correct answer is (B).**

11. **The correct answer is (B).** Amphibians such as frogs have moist skin membranes through which respiratory gases can diffuse.

12. **The correct answer is (C).** Choice (A), the liver, is involved in detoxification and bile production. Choice (B), the colon, reabsorbs water, compacts and moves feces for removal, and converts some vitamins. Choice (D), the pharynx, is a pathway to the esophagus.

13. **The correct answer is (A).**

14. **The correct answer is (D).**

Ecology

It is fitting that the biology section ends with ecology because it is defined as the interactions between communities of organisms and the environment. In this section, we will briefly explore the environment and how animals and humans interact with and affect it. We commonly associate ecology with environmental or ecological issues. In a way, these loose terms bring ecology to us in a form that's easier to understand because we see it in action. Often, however, they encompass many different aspects of ecology, so let's first review some basic concepts of ecology starting with our Earth.

THE BIOSPHERE

Earth is comprised of four main components. The **biosphere** represents the realm of life consisting of plants and animals that are either living or in the process of decay. The other three components, the **lithosphere**, **atmosphere**, and **hydrosphere**, interact with the biosphere.

We will cover the lithosphere, atmosphere, and hydrosphere in the Earth Sciences chapter.

THE ENVIRONMENT AND ECOSYSTEM

Ecologists define an environment as any component that can influence an organism during its lifetime. These environmental influences can be divided into two categories:

- *Biotic Factors*—living things that affect an organism

- *Abiotic Factors*—nonliving things, such as water, air, geology, and the sun, that can affect an organism. Interactions between these produce temperature, wind, erosion, and humidity

Both of these factors are interrelated. For example, plants rely on many abiotic factors for proper growth, including rainfall and temperature. If these factors should rise or fall dramatically in a particular region, plant growth will fall, which in turn will reduce food sources and habitats for animals.

Ecosystems represent both the biotic and abiotic conditions under which the biotic communities live. In other words, an ecosystem is the interaction of different populations of organisms and their environment. Think of your high school as an ecosystem. Students represent the human population. Any insects, plants, or even mold that may be growing on the bologna sandwich you left in your locker over the weekend are all separate populations. All these populations interact with each other as well as the nonliving components of the school environment. Your high school ecosystem does not exist in a vacuum, however. The populations of your school will also interact and blend with other ecosystems, such as the parking lot outside your school.

Biomes

Similar ecosystems are often grouped together to form larger ecosystems called **biomes**. While more extensive in size and complexity than an ecosystem, biomes are still biotic communities subjected to abiotic environmental factors. Biomes also support different organisms—both plant and animal—due to their differences in geography, climate, and resource. As we review some of the major biomes of the world, let's begin with the coldest in the north and progress toward the equator. We will not consider aquatic biomes here, but it's important to understand that biomes include swamps and marshes, lakes and rivers, estuaries, the inter-tidal zone, and the ocean.

- Tundra

  Region: Northernmost biome, to the north of coniferous forest

  Climate: Bitter cold with thin soil covering a permanent layer of frost

  Vegetation: Consists of lichens, mosses, grasses, and small shrubs

  Animals: Vary according to the season: lemmings, arctic fox, arctic hare, lynx, grizzly bear, caribou, reindeer, musk ox

- Coniferous Forest

  Region: Northern portions of North America, Europe, and Asia

  Climate: Cold, but not as cold as the tundra, the winters are long

  Vegetation: Consists of coniferous trees (pine, fir, spruce) and small amounts of deciduous trees

Animals: Large and small herbivores such as moose, elk, mice, and hares and some predators like the lynx, foxes, bears, and wolverines

- Temperate Forests

    Region: West and central Europe, eastern Asia, and eastern North America

    Climate: Seasonal, temperatures are below freezing in the winter and summers are warm and humid

    Vegetation: Deciduous (leaf-shedding) and coniferous trees, ferns, lichens, moss

    Animals: Many mammals like squirrels, porcupines, raccoons, black bears, coyotes

- Tropical Rain Forests

    Region: Central America, northern South America, some parts of Africa and Asia

    Climate: No seasonal variation, high temperatures around 28°C, acidic soil, heavy and frequent rainfall

    Vegetation: Dense canopy created by tall trees, many symbiotic plant-tree relationships

    Animals: Extreme diversity in animals, many exotic types of insects, large numbers of birds, amphibians, and reptiles; a few large predators like tigers

- Grasslands

    Region: Central Russia, Siberia, southern India, northern Australia, some portions of Africa and South America

    Climate: Seasonal, hot and dry in summers, heavy rainfall in wet season; frequent brush fires, thick, rich soils

    Vegetation: Variety of grass species and bushes, few woodlands

    Animals: Mainly large grazing species such as bison, rhinos, zebras, giraffes; predators—wolves, hyenas, lions, leopards; some birds and burrowing animals like prairie dogs

- Deserts

  Region: Northern and southwestern Africa, southwestern United States, northern Mexico, Australia, and parts of Asia and Middle East

  Climate: Hot, dry climate by day and cold nights, very little rainfall, thin soil

  Vegetation: Drought-adapted plants such as cacti, shrubs, and bushes with shallow roots or long tap roots

  Animals: Mainly reptiles and some rodents, owls, vultures, hawks, and many insects

CATEGORIES OF ORGANISMS

> Remember that biotic = living and abiotic = nonliving.

Within each ecosystem, there is a definite structure to the biotic communities and abiotic environmental factors; within the biotic communities are many species of organisms that coexist together. These organisms are divided into separate categories that interact with one another based on their main source of food. All ecosystems have the same three basic categories of organisms, which interrelate in predictable ways:

Producers

- Autotrophic
- Mainly green plants, some microorganisms
- Use the solar energy to convert nutrients
- Main portion of biomass

Consumers

- Heterotrophic
- Do not use sunlight for food source

  Herbivore (Primary Consumers)—feed directly on producers
  Carnivore (Secondary Consumers)—feed only on other consumers

Omnivore—feed on both producers and consumers

Decomposers

- Heterotrophic

- Feed on dead material: plants of all kinds, fecal waste, dead animals

- Recycle raw materials to the ecosystem

Feed Me! Food Chains and Food Webs

Food Chains

Let's imagine that on a lazy summer day some fish are swimming in a lake. The fish are eating plankton and other small organisms. You decide to go fishing at this lake, and you get a pretty decent catch. You fry some of the fish for dinner. This is an example of a simple food chain. In an ecosystem, food chains illustrate simple feeding pathways between organisms. In the previous example, a pathway exits from one organism to another in a chain:

Plankton → Fish → Man

Food chains represent a transfer of energy from one organism to another. All organisms need a source of food to survive, so all organisms engage in food chains.

Food Webs

Humans don't only eat fish, herbivore populations don't only eat one kind of plant, and carnivore populations don't consume only one type of herbivore. So food webs link many food chains together to represent complex feeding relationships. Communities of animals within a particular ecosystem participate in the creation of a food web, which is the same as a food chain, only on a much larger scale. Energy (food) moves through a series of levels—producer to herbivore to carnivore. These levels are called trophic levels (trophic means feeding). The diagram below shows the hierarchy of the feeding levels:

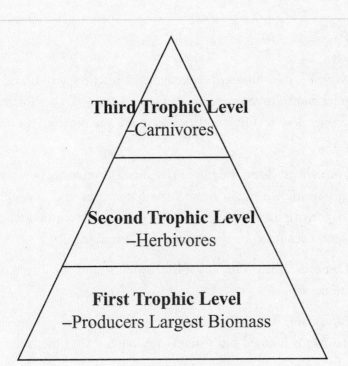

Third Trophic Level
–Carnivores

Second Trophic Level
–Herbivores

First Trophic Level
–Producers Largest Biomass

Living Arrangements

> Examples of habitats are pineland communities, a forest community, or an arid, grassy plain.

Feeding relationships dominate the structure of an ecosystem. However, an ecosystem isn't just one giant free-for-all with severe interspecies competition. Communities within an ecosystem support many different animals, and animals of the same species or **populations** within a community are specially adapted to their surroundings. Each population of animals occupies a **habitat**, a certain place a species is best suited to live according to its biological adaptations. Different species can even become "specialists" within their habitats by occupying a **niche**. A niche refers to all specific biotic and abiotic elements an organism incorporates for its survival, such as feeding location, food source, feeding schedule, source of shelter, and nesting location. For example, many birds may occupy a forest community, but some eat seeds and others eat worms and insects; some birds eat high up in a tree and others closer to the ground.

SYMBIOSIS

Just as you have relationships with your parents, teachers, and friends, other species develop relationships. **Symbiosis** refers to relationships organisms develop as a result of living close to one another. There are three basic types of symbiotic relationships:

- **Mutualism:** Both organisms rely on each other to live; an example of this relationship can be seen with termites and *trichonympha*. The trichonympha protist lives in the gut of the termite and converts the wood consumed by the termite into a usable form.

- **Commensalism:** One organism benefits, and the effects to the other are neutral.

- **Parasitism:** A one-way relationship in which the parasite benefits and the *host* is harmed but usually not killed; over time, the negative side effects can overcome an organism.

NATURAL RESOURCES

A **resource** is anything we obtain from the environment to meet our needs. **Renewable** resources, such as air and water, are replenished in the environment through natural cycles. Many natural resources are finite, however: when the supply is depleted, it is gone forever. These are called **nonrenewable** resources, and they include copper, iron, oil, coal, and natural gas. We will look at the differences between renewable and nonrenewable resources by exploring energy.

Renewable Energy

Renewable energy sources can be replenished in a short period of time. The five renewable sources used most often include hydropower (water), solar, wind, geothermal, and biomass.

Biomass—Biomass is organic material that has stored sunlight in the form of chemical energy. It includes wood, straw, and manure.

Solar—Solar energy is the sun's solar radiation that reaches the Earth. It can be converted directly or indirectly into other forms of energy, such as heat and electricity.

Hydropower—Hydropower is created when moving water, such as a river or a waterfall, is directed, harnessed, or channeled. Water flows through a pipe and then turns the blades in a turbine to spin a generator that produces electricity.

Wind—Humans have used the wind as an energy source for thousands of years. For example, sails capture wind to propel boats, and windmills use wind to generate electricity.

Geothermal—When steam and hot water have been naturally trapped in the Earth's crust, engineers drill into the crust and allow the heat to escape, either as steam or very hot water. The steam then turns a turbine that generates electricity. This is known as geothermal energy.

Nonrenewable Energy

Nonrenewable energy sources are extracted from the earth as liquids, gases, and solids. Oil, coal, and natural gas are considered fossil fuels because they formed from the buried remains of plants and animals that lived millions of years ago. Uranium ore, a solid, is mined and converted to a fuel. Uranium is not a fossil fuel.

Oil—Oil is formed from the remains of marine animals and plants that have been covered by layers of mud. Heat and pressure from these layers turn the remains into crude oil. After the oil is removed from the ground, it is sent to a refinery, where the different parts of the crude oil are separated into useable products, including motor gasoline, propane, ink, bubble gum, and dishwashing liquid.

Coal—Coal beds are found near the ground's surface. Power plants burn coal to make steam, which turns turbines to generate electricity. Separated ingredients of coal (such as methanol and ethylene) are used to make plastics, tar, and fertilizers. It is also an integral part of the steel-making process.

Natural Gas—Like oil and coal, natural gas is formed when plants and animals remains decay and are covered by mud and soil. Pressure and heat change this organic material natural gas. The main ingredient in natural gas is methane. It is used to heat homes and is an essential material for products such as paints, fertilizer, and antifreeze.

Nuclear power—A nuclear power plant produces energy through the fissioning or splitting of uranium atoms, which creates heat. That heat boils water to make the steam that turns a turbine-generator. The part of the plant where the heat is produced is called the reactor core.

Pop Quiz

This was a long chapter, but don't you feel better knowing that you've just finished reading the last biology section? You're that much closer to being prepared to ace your exit-level exam! If there were any areas in which you felt a little shaky, go back to your textbook and review in more detail. But if you feel confident and want to move forward, you have three options:

Option A: Take the last biology Pop Quiz.

Option B: Take the biology review in Chapter 7.

Option C: Continue to Chapter 4 to start reviewing chemistry.

1. Animals that eat animals that eat plants are called

    (A) producers.

    (B) decomposers.

    (C) secondary consumers.

    (D) primary consumers.

2. A grassland region characterized by bitter cold, thin soil, and a layer of permanent frost is a

   (A) tropical forest.

   (B) temperate forest.

   (C) tundra.

   (D) coniferous forest.

3. A pattern of interaction between two species in which one benefits while the other does not benefit but is not harmed in the process is

   (A) commensalism.

   (B) mutualism.

   (C) parasitism.

   (D) neutralism.

4. Integrated groups of food chains are called a

   (A) habitat.

   (B) food web.

   (C) community.

   (D) competitive consumers.

5. The way an organism lives in relation to other members of its biotic community and abiotic factors is called a

   (A) habitat.

   (B) biome.

   (C) niche.

   (D) food chain.

ANSWERS

1. **The correct answer is (C).** Producers, choice (A), are plants; decomposers, choice (B), live on dead or decaying material; and primary consumers, choice (D), are animals that eat plants.

2. **The correct answer is (C).** A tropical rainforest, choice (A), is characterized by no seasonal variations, high temperatures, and heavy rainfall. A temperate forest, choice (B), is seasonal with temperatures below freezing during winter months. A coniferous forest, choice (D), has long, cold winters, but it is not as cold as the tundra.

3. **The correct answer is (A).** Choice (B) refers to a relationship where both organisms benefit. Choice (C) is a relationship in which one organism benefits and the other is harmed. Choice (D) is not an ecological term.

4. **The correct answer is (B).**

5. **The correct answer is (C).** Choice (A) refers to where an organism lives, choice (B) refers to a very large community in a region with a particular type of climate, and choice (D) describes a simple feeding relationship that shows the transfer of energy from one organism to the next.

CHEMISTRY

Chemistry is the study of the composition, interactions, properties, and structure of matter and the changes that matter undergoes. It involves looking at ways to take substances apart and put the parts together again in new ways. For example, scientists are able to create substances as varied as metal alloys, paint, plastics, medicine, and perfumes by manipulating elements and compounds.

Know Your Measurements

The ability to convert measurements in chemistry is very important. Let's say you need 1 liter of solution for an experiment, but you've got a graduated cylinder that only holds 50 milliliters of solution. What should you do? If you know how to convert milliliters to liters, you can figure out pretty quickly that you need to fill that cylinder 20 times to equal 1 liter of solution.

In order to measure and report an object's mass, temperature, volume, or any other physical property it may have, you need to have some standard units of reference. In chemistry, the units of measurement are expressed using the metric system. The metric system is based on the number 10. Each subunit is a fraction of 10.

> In the United States, we use non-metric units in everyday life—measurements like feet and pounds. But the metric system is used in science and is much easier to work with.

Measurements for Length (based on multiples of the meter)

m = meter, cm = centimeter, mm = millimeter, km = kilometers

1m = 100cm	or	1cm = 0.01 m
1m = 1000mm	or	1mm = 0.001m
1cm = 10mm	or	1mm = 0.1 cm
1km = 1000m	or	1m = 0.001km

U.S. Customary Measurements in Relation to Metric Measurements

1 mile (mi) = 5280 feet (ft.)

1 yard (yd) = 3 ft.

1ft. = 12 inches/30.48 cm./0.3048 m

1 inch = 2.54 cm

1 meter = 39.37 inches/3.280 ft.

Measurements for Mass (based on multiples of the gram)

g = gram, mg = milligram, mcg = microgram

1 gram = 1000 milligrams	or	1 mg = 0.001g
1 kilogram = 1000 grams	or	1g = 0.001kg
1milligram = 1000 micrograms	or	1mcg = 0.001mg

U.S. Customary Measurements in Relation to Metric Measurements

1 pound (lb) = 16 ounces (oz)

1kg = 2.205 lb

1oz = 28.35 grams

1 lb = 453.6 grams

> One of the easiest ways to get a question wrong is to answer with the wrong unit of measurement. To avoid this mistake, convert as much as you can into the required units. For example, if the numbers in a question use grams, but the answer choices are in milligrams, convert everything before you start making your calculations.

Measurements for Liquid Volumes (based on multiples of the milliliter)

mL = milliliter, L = liter, gal = gallon, qt = quart, pt = pint

1mL = 0.001 L	or	1L = 1000mL
1mL = 1000 mL(microliter)	or	1mL = 0.001mL

U.S. Customary Measurements in Relation to Metric Measurements

1 gallon = 4 quarts

1 quart = 2 pints

1 pint = 16 liquid ounces

1 liter = 1.057 quarts/2.113 pints/33.81 oz./3.785 gal

Measurements for Temperature Readings in Celsius, Fahrenheit, and Kelvin

The **Celsius** (°C) or centigrade scale is the most commonly used measurement for temperature in science. The **Fahrenheit** (°F) scale is five-ninths the size of the degree Celsius. The **Kelvin** scale is used to illustrate temperatures of gases. To convert Celsius to Fahrenheit, use one of the following equations:

Fahrenheit to Celsius: $C = \dfrac{5°C}{9°F} \times (F - 32°F)$

Celsius to Fahrenheit: $F = \dfrac{9°F}{5°C} \times (C + 32°F)$

Common Temperatures in Celsius and Fahrenheit		
__Common Temperatures__	__°F__	__°C__
Normal Body Temperature	98.6	37
Boiling Water	212	100
Average Room Temperature	68	20
Frozen Water	32	0

BASIC LABORATORY EQUIPMENT AND SAFETY

Your exit-level exam may ask you questions about some of the instruments used to take these measurements as well as general laboratory equipment. Let's divide them into groups based on similar properties.

Glassware

- Beaker

- Erlenmeyer Flask

- Test Tube

- Funnel

Measurements

- Graduated Cylinder—measures liquids

- Triple Beam Balance—weighs solids

- pH Meter—measures acid/base ratio of liquids

- Spectrophotometer—reads the wavelength of light absorbed by a substance

- Pipette—glass tube with units along the length for accurate measurements of liquid

- Volumetric Flask—calibrated to a specific volume for solution preparation

- Thermometer—takes temperature readings

General Lab Equipment

- Microscope—used to view microscopic objects by passing light through a series of lenses and magnifying the image

- Burners—range from hot plates to gas burners

- Tongs—used to hold items that may be hot

Laboratory Safety

Laboratories contain chemicals and equipment that can be hazardous if not handled properly. The following safety protocols may sound like common sense, but hey, it can't hurt to list them anyway:

- Never consume foods or liquids in the lab.

- When handling chemicals or burners, **always** wear safety goggles and gloves.

- Do not handle hot glassware without appropriate safety gloves.

- Keep burners and glassware away from edges of tables/benches; they can easily fall and break.

- Follow all of your teacher's safety rules for all tools used in lab.

- Never smell a chemical directly from the bottle.

- Follow all safety protocols for cleaning up spilled chemicals.

Pop Quiz

1. How many centimeters are in 6.54 inches?

   (A) 65.4 cm

   (B) 14.4 cm

   (C) .654 cm

   (D) 16.6 cm

2. A patient is rushed to the emergency room with a temperature of 105 °F. What is his temperature in degrees Celsius?

   (A) 10.5 °C

   (B) 40.55 °C

   (C) 37 °C

   (D) 22 °C

3. Your mass is 64 kilograms. What is this measurement in pounds?

   (A) 141.12 lbs.

   (B) 160 lbs.

   (C) 60.5 lbs.

   (D) 120 lbs.

4. If a gas tank holds 18 gallons, how many liters does it hold?

   (A) 36 L

   (B) 6.8 13L

   (C) 68.13 L

   (D) 9 L

ANSWERS

1. The correct answer is **(D)**. The conversion for this problem is as follows:

$$6.54 \text{ in} \times \frac{2.54 \text{ cm}}{1 \text{ in}} = 16.61 \text{ cm}$$

2. The correct answer is **(B)**. The conversion for this problem is as follows:

$$C = \frac{5°C}{9°F}(F - 32°F)$$

$$C = \frac{5°C}{9°F}(105°F - 32°F)$$

$$C = \frac{5°C(73°F)}{9°F}$$

$$C = \frac{365°C}{9} = 40.55°C$$

3. The correct answer is **(A)**. Knowing the conversion factor of 1kg = 2.205 lb. makes this a simple multiplication problem.

$$64 \text{ kg} \times \frac{2.205 \text{ lb}}{1 \text{ kg}} = 141.12 \text{ lb}$$

4. The correct answer is **(C)**. Choice (A) is incorrect because it only doubles the amount for liters. 3.785 liters equals 1 gallon, so the conversion is as follows:

$$18 \text{ gal} = \frac{3.785L}{1 \text{ gal}} = 68.13L$$

CHAPTER
4

Let's Get Physical About Matter

Matter describes anything that occupies space and has mass. It is found in everything, but not all matter is the same. Just compare the matter found in concrete to the matter in a cheese steak. Not exactly the same thing, huh? Both are considered matter, yet each has properties that makes it uniquely different. In fact, there are only four basic properties that are shared by all matter:

- **Mass** describes the relative inertia of an object, which means that it is hard to get an object into motion and difficult to slow down once it starts moving. Imagine a huge boulder rolling down a hill, or your Aunt Bertha running toward you to give you a big wet kiss on the forehead, and you get the picture. **Inertia** is the resistance to any kind of change in motion, so in a way mass describes inertia in terms of numbers and units. Mass is not affected by gravity, so when Aunt Bertha starts chasing after you for that kiss, she will have the same mass whether she's running toward you on the ground or leaping off the top step on the staircase!

- **Weight,** unlike mass, fluctuates according to where you are in the universe. It is a measure of gravitational force of attraction that Earth exerts on an object. On the moon, the gravitational pull is one-sixth that of Earth, so an object will weigh less on the moon. This explains why it looks like astronauts float when they walk on the moon.

- **Volume** is the measure of space something can occupy. An empty glass can potentially hold a specific amount of fluid, and when empty it can hold air. When the space of the glass is occupied by either the fluid or air, it represents the volume.

> Don't confuse density with heaviness. A pound of M&Ms is just as heavy as a pound of spinach, but the volume of M&Ms will not be the same as the volume of spinach.

- **Density** is a ratio of mass per unit volume. It represents the relationship between how much mass per unit volume an object has. This relationship can be expressed or calculated with the formula $D = \dfrac{mass}{volume}$. Density is expressed as g/mL (mass in grams and volume in milliliters). **Note:** 1mL is the same as 1 cubic centimeter or $1cm^3$ or 1cc, so if you see this, don't panic! These units are often used in medicine.

PHYSICAL STATES OF MATTER

There are four kinds of matter:

- **Gas:** Matter in the gaseous state relies on its container for both the shape and the volume. Example: Steam

- **Liquid:** Matter in the liquid state takes on the shape of whatever container it is put in. However, a liquid has a definite volume that does not depend on the container it is put in. Example: Water

- **Solid:** Matter in the solid state has a definite shape and volume regardless of the container. Example: Ice

- **Plasma:** A unique state of matter that only appears to be solid. In reality, it is an ionized gas. Questions about plasma won't appear on your exam, so don't worry about it.

Matter can change both physically and chemically. A **physical change** is a change in a substance's shape, size, or state. There is no chemical reaction involved with a physical change. The particles that make up the substance are essentially the same. So a diamond that is pulverized into diamond powder or a potato that gets mashed are both examples of a physical change. In each instance, the diamond and potato take on a different appearance, but they are still made of the same particles.

A chemical change is a bit different. When matter experiences a **chemical change**, it actually changes into a new substance with different properties from its former self. Okay, example time: let's use an egg. By now, you've probably learned how to scramble an egg, or you've at least watched someone else do it. When you crack the shell, the egg comes out translucent and fluid. However, when you scramble the egg in a pan and start cooking it, the egg turns yellow and becomes solid. It has changed chemically and cannot go back to its former composition.

Don't worry—cooking skills will not be tested on your exam!

POP QUIZ

1. The weight of an object

   (A) describes the relative inertia of an object.

   (B) is a reflection of gravitational force.

   (C) is equal to the mass of an object.

   (D) is not influenced by gravity.

2. Choose all the examples you think represent a *physical* change.

   (A) The shattering of a glass onto the floor

   (B) The decay of animal remains in a forest community

   (C) Cookie dough converted into cookies

   (D) Processing sirloin steak into ground beef

   (E) Evaporation

   (F) Rusting of iron

   (G) Freezing water

3. You are given a fruit drink with two distinct layers, a green layer of juice on the bottom and a yellow layer of juice on the top. No matter how much you stir the drink, the green settles back to the bottom and the yellow juice floats to the top. What conclusions can be drawn about the density of the liquids?

   (A) No conclusions can be drawn because it takes a vigorous shaking to get the layers to mix.

   (B) The green layer is less dense or lighter and sank faster than the yellow layer.

   (C) The green layer is more dense and sank to the bottom; the yellow layer is less dense and floats on the top.

   (D) The yellow layer is more dense and slower moving, so it remains on the top layer.

4. Which example represents a chemical change?

   (A) Mixing sugar into a cup of coffee

   (B) Condensation

   (C) Melting butter

   (D) Burning gasoline

Answers

1. **The correct answer is (B).** Choice (A) would not be the correct answer since it describes mass. Choice (C) is incorrect because mass and weight are two separate properties. Choice (D) is also incorrect since weight is influenced by gravity. Thus, choice (B) is the only answer that correctly describes weight and its relation to gravity.

2. **The correct answers are (A), (D), (E), and (G).** Each of these choices correctly describes a physical change.

   (A): The glass will break into smaller pieces of glass.

   (D): The sirloin steak is ground into smaller pieces.

   (E): Evaporation is a process in which liquid absorbs heat and changes into a gas. This phase change is still a physical change since the chemical properties of the water did not change.

   (G): Again, this is a phase change of water, which is physical.

3. **The correct answer is (C).** Liquids have density, just like solids or gases. In this example, the green juice was denser than the yellow juice, so the green juice sank to the bottom while the yellow juice floated to the top. Aside from a chemical reaction between the two juices, their respective densities keep them from mixing.

4. **The correct answer is (D).** Choices (A), (B), and (C) all represent physical changes. Choice (A), mixing sugar in coffee, is a physical change since it would be possible to separate them. Choices (B) and (C) are phase changes because they remain chemically unchanged. Choice (D) is correct because as gasoline burns, it turns into the substances water and carbon dioxide (exhaust fumes).

The Universe of the Atom

We are now entering the realm of the atom. You must grasp the basics of this section because everything else that you will be tested on in chemistry is based on this section. The pressure is on, but we know you can handle it. So far, we've been looking at matter as a whole. Now it's time to shift gears and focus on the smallest particles of matter.

ATOMIC THEORY: A BRIEF HISTORY

> Even now, physicists continue to investigate the nature of the atom.

All matter is made up of atoms. The word **atom** is derived from the Greek *atomos,* "not cuttable." Way back in 300 B.C.E., Greek philosophers began to ponder the divisibility of matter. They came up with the theory of the atom, but for many centuries, it was just that: a theory. Two thousand years would pass before scientific investigations were able to prove the theory and develop a modern atomic theory.

Timeline of Atomic Theory

Theories Constructing Laws of Chemical Combinations

(1754–1826) Joseph Proust

Law of Definite Proportions

(1743–1794) Antoine Lavoisier

Law of Conservation of Mass

(1766–1844) John Dalton

An English schoolteacher and chemist who was stimulated by theories of Proust, Dalton proposed that the essential difference between atoms is their mass. Dalton constructed the first table of relative atomic weights. He also postulated the **Law of Multiple Proportions**.

Theories Constructing Periodic Law

(1834–1907) Dmitri Mendeleev

In 1869, this Russian scientist published a chemistry book for his students in which he correctly ordered atoms by mass, allowed for longer periods in the transition elements, and predicted missing elements.

Theories Explaining Components of an Atomic Structure

(1856–1940) J.J. Thomson

An English physicist, Thomson was the first to conduct experiments exploring atomic composition. In 1904, he created the "Plum Pudding" model of the atom where the electrons are like raisins dispersed in a positive charge cloud, the pudding.

(1871–1937) Ernest Rutherford

In 1911, Rutherford discovered the "empty" nature of atoms with the mass of an atom concentrated at its central core, which he named the *nucleus*. By using alpha particles (positively formed helium nuclei), Rutherford observed that some of the particles were deflected by positively charged nuclei. Rutherford coined the term "half-life" and won the Nobel Prize in chemistry in 1908.

Theories on Electron Configuration

(1885–1962) Niels Bohr

In 1913, this Danish scientist proposed *energy levels* of an atom in which electrons remain their most stable as long as they reside in their lowest energy states. He likened energy levels to the orbits of planets; this led to his "solar system" model of an atom. Electrons occupy energy levels, and the probability of locating these electrons is difficult. Bohr won the Nobel Prize of 1922 in physics.

While each of these scientists helped advance modern atomic theory, not all of their research still holds true. In fact, many parts of these early theories have been proven wrong. However, they provided the fundamentals, which allowed other scientists to further investigate the atom.

Modern Atomic Theory: Modern Atomic Structure

It's about time we get into the meat of this atom business and look at the structure of the atom.

All matter is made up of atoms, and all atoms are made up of subatomic particles: **electrons**, **protons**, and **neutrons**. While all three particles have mass, there are three major differences:

- Electrons have a negative charge (-).

- Protons have a positive charge (+).

- Neutrons have no charge.

Electrons and protons can repulse and attract each other with their charges without physically touching. Here's an easy way to remember this:

> *Opposite charges attract* (electron to proton). *Like charges repel* (proton to proton or electron to electron).

Each atom has a specific arrangement for its subatomic particles. The **nucleus** of an atom, or central core, contains protons and neutrons. The electrons occupy several energy levels around the nucleus. In the past, scientists thought these energy levels orbited the nucleus like the planets orbit the sun. More recently, however, electron placement has been described like an "electron cloud" because the electrons move so rapidly. Think of the movement of the blades of a fan. The blades move so fast that it looks as though they are one continuous blur. Today, scientists know that an electron occupies a certain region of space. Each region contains electrons that move at relatively the same speed, which enables us to determine where an electron is at a certain time. The path an electron takes, however, to go from point to point is unpredictable. This is the Heisenberg uncertainty principle.

Max Planck observed that light is composed of bundles of energy called quanta. Quanta are photons of light and are determined by the frequency of a wave. Atoms absorb and give off light energy and other types of electromagnetic radiation. The electromagnetic spectrum includes the high frequency cosmic rays and the lower frequency power waves.

Planck's formula for calculating the energy of a wave is determined by its frequency. For example, ultraviolet radiation causes human skin cancer because of the high frequency and energy of its photons:

E = hf

E = energy

h = 6.6×10^{-34} Joules/Hertz (Planck's Constant)

f = frequency

To calculate the frequency of quantum of light with a wavelength of 6.6×10^{-7},

Velocity = frequency × wavelength

3×10^{8} m/sec = (frequency)(6×10^{-7}m)

frequency = 5×10^{14} Hz

Energy = (6.6×10^{-34} Joule/Hz)(5×10^{14} Hz)

= 3.3×10^{-19} Joules

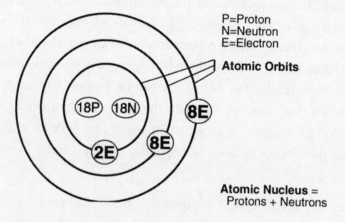

P=Proton
N=Neutron
E=Electron

Atomic Orbits

Atomic Nucleus =
Protons + Neutrons

ELECTRON CONFIGURATION

The number and location of electrons in any atom determine the type of chemical reactions the atom may participate in. **Electron configuration** is the distribution of electrons among available levels of an atom. Many models have been proposed to explain this concept, including the Bohr model of orbitals, which has been used to explain biologically important atoms, and its basic tenants are still in use. However, there is one major difference between the Bohr model and the modern model of atoms: We now know that electrons do not move in discrete orbitals. (Their movement is too complicated and too fast to know this with any precision, though.)

> Helium has 2 electrons. They occupy level 1, sublevel s, or 1s. So these electrons would be found in a spherical cloud around a Helium nucleus.

Electrons reside in regions called **atomic orbitals**. More specifically, there are certain energy states for electrons. The first energy level, *level 1,* is closest to the nucleus and holds 2 electrons. The second energy level, *level 2,* can have 8 electrons. The third energy level, *level 3,* can have 18 electrons. Within each energy level, there are sublevels, each of which contains one or more atomic orbitals. Level 1 has only one sublevel, named 1*s*. The '1' designates the level and the '*s*' denotes the shape of the orbital, spherical. Level 2 has two sublevels *s* and *p*, or 2*s* and 2*p*. The '*p*' level has three orbitals, each of which looks like a "figure 8." The axes of these orbitals are perpendicular and are designated *x, y,* and *z* (see below). The third energy level has three sublevels and three kinds of orbitals, one *s*, three *p*, and five of yet another type, the *d* orbital. There is also a fourth level, the *f* orbital. We're going to leave the *d* and *f* orbitals for your classroom textbook to explain. We'll just focus on orbitals *s* and *p*.

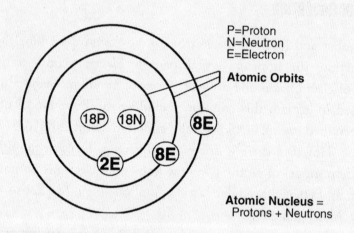

P=Proton
N=Neutron
E=Electron

Atomic Orbits

Atomic Nucleus =
Protons + Neutrons

Okay, one last point: The maximum number of electrons each orbital can hold is two, and they must spin in opposite directions. This stuff gets pretty confusing, so how about we try a practice problem to see the rules for electron configuration in action?

The Problem:

Given the atomic number of the first ten elements, figure out their electron configurations.

The Rules:

1. Use the atomic number for the number of electrons.

2. Put each electron in the energy levels, filling the lowest level first, and then proceed to the next level.

3. Only allow 8 electrons for level three. It can contain more, but extra electrons aren't placed in this level until atomic numbers above 20 are reached.

4. Level four is for the 19th and 20th electrons

The Answer:

Below are the first ten elements showing their electron configurations by *orbitals*.

	1s	2s	2p		
Hydrogen	↑				
Helium	↑↓				
Lithium	↑↓	↑			
Beryllium	↑↓	↑↓			
Baron	↑↓	↑↓	↑		
Carbon	↑↓	↑↓	↑	↑	
Nitrogen	↑↓	↑↓	↑	↑	↑
Oxygen	↑↓	↑↓	↑↓	↑	↑
Fluorine	↑↓	↑↓	↑↓	↑↓	↑
Neon	↑↓	↑↓	↑↓	↑↓	↑↓

Another way electron configuration can be shown is with dots, called the **electron dot configuration**. Let's use Beryllium (Be) from the above chart as an example to illustrate the dot formation.

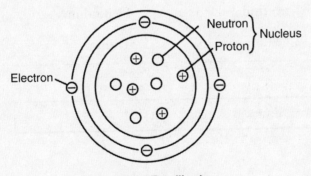

Typical Atom (Beryllium)

All right, enough about electrons! What about those other particles, neutrons and protons? Both protons and neutrons are found in the nucleus of an atom. Neutrons are neutral; they have no charge, but they have the same mass as positively charged protons. An atom is considered neutral in charge when the number of positive protons equals the number of negative electrons. For instance, carbon has six protons, so it also has six electrons.

The atoms of each element also have a specific number of protons. Protons determine the identity of an element. If we use carbon again, there are six protons in the nucleus. This number of protons is exclusive and unique to Carbon. No other element will have six protons in the nucleus. Therefore the number of protons can be used as a marker for an element. This marker is the **atomic number**. It represents the number of protons in an atom of an element. Since the number of protons equals the number of electrons, the atomic number also tells you how many electrons are present in the atom of a neutral element.

We haven't talked much about the neutron yet, and we're sure you can't wait! While all neutral atoms of an element have the same number of protons and electrons, they don't necessarily have the same number of neutrons. An **isotope** occurs when atoms of the same element differ in the number of neutrons in the nuclei. The following table shows an example of isotopes:

Hydrogen	
Hydrogen Form	Name of Isotope
Most common form 1 proton, no neutrons	Commonly called Hydrogen
1 proton, 1 neutron	Deuterium
1 proton, 2 neutrons	Tritium

Atomic Weight = # Protons + # Neutrons

Neutrons also determine the mass of atoms of an element. The **atomic weight** or **mass number** of an atom is the number of protons plus the number of neutrons. Knowing the atomic weight of an element is helpful when working with isotopes. Isotopes will vary in atomic weights (mass number) due to variations in the number of neutrons.

SHAPES OF MOLECULES

The valence shell electron pair repulsion model (VSEPR) is used in determining the shape of a molecule. The shape is very significant in determining the ability of a molecule to absorb energy. The VSEPR model states that each pair of electrons surrounding the central atom is considered to repel all the other electron pairs around the atom.

NUCLEAR ENERGY

Nuclear energy includes fission and fusion energy. Fission is the splitting of a uranium atom while fusion is the combining of hydrogen isotopes to form helium. The equation $E = mc^2$ is applied to these energy concepts.

Fission energy involves the release of alpha, beta, and gamma particles until a stable isotope is formed. Alpha, beta, and gamma particles are classified as ionizing radiation and can be mutagenic, teragenic, and carcinogenic in nature.

1) Alpha : helium nuclei

$$_{92}^{238}U \rightarrow {}_{90}^{234}Th + {}_{2}^{4}He \text{ (alph decay, positively charged)}$$

2) Beta : negatively charged electron

$$_{6}^{14}C \rightarrow {}_{7}^{14}N + {}_{1}^{0}e \text{ (beta)}$$

Pop Quiz

Whew! This was a heavyweight section! If you're still a little fuzzy, crack open your chemistry textbook. If not, march on to the Pop Quiz.

1. Protons = 6, neutrons = 9, electron = 6. The mass number or atomic weight is

    (A) 12.

    (B) 9.

    (C) 15.

    (D) 6.

2. Knowing that atom X has an atomic weight of 19, the possible combination of its particles could be

    (A) 19 electrons, 19 protons, 19 neutrons.

    (B) 19 electrons, 19 protons, 8 neutrons.

    (C) 9 electrons, 9 protons, 18 neutrons.

    (D) 9 clectrons, 9 protons, 10 neutrons.

3. One atom of oxygen has an atomic weight of 16 units, and another atom of oxygen has an atomic weight of 17 units. These atoms are

    (A) unstable.

    (B) isotopes.

    (C) ions.

    (D) reactants.

4. An atom has an atomic number of 12. Choose the following example of orbitals that best describes the electron placement.

    (A) 1*s*, 2*s*, 2*px*, 2*py*, 2*pz*, 3*s*

    (B) 1*s*, 2*s*, 3*s*, 3*px*, 3*py*, 3*pz*

    (C) 1*s*, 2*s*, 2*p*, 3*s*

    (D) 1*s*, 2*sx*, 2*sy*, 2*sz*

Answers

1. **The correct answer is (C).** The atomic weight is equal to the number of protons plus the number of neutrons. There are 6 protons and 9 neutrons in this example; together they total 15.

2. **The correct answer is (D).** Choices (A), (B), and (C) are not correct because the atomic weights calculated from the number of protons and neutrons given in these examples do not equal 19. Choice (D) is the only one in which all criteria are met.

3. **The correct answer is (B).** Atoms of the same element that differ in the number of neutrons are called isotopes.

4. **The correct answer is (A).** The atomic number is also the number of protons. This in turn gives you the number of electrons. By following the rules of electron placement, choice (A) should stand out like a pink elephant. Choices (B), (C), and (D) do not follow the rules.

It's Elementary: Elements, Compounds, and Mixtures

Elements

All right, so now we know that atoms are the smallest representatives of an element. But what's an element? Elements are substances composed of atoms that have the same nuclear charges and electron configurations. As these elements were being discovered, there became a need for classification. Dmitry Medeleev was the first scientist to notice that elements can be ordered into families based on similar chemical and physical properties. He observed that properties of elements appear to go through cycles, from elements with the lowest atomic weights to elements with the highest atomic weights. These cycles of properties were described as being **periodic,** meaning that they created patterns that affected how an element was grouped in the table.

Improvements were later made to Mendeleev's theory, in particular the discovery of the atomic number. The modern **periodic table of elements** now ranks elements according to the atomic number instead of the atomic weight. After further research, substantial evidence suggested that other properties of elements also vary periodically with the atomic number. Thus the **periodic law** was established:

Periodic Law: The properties of the elements are a periodic function of their atomic numbers.

Periodic Table of the Elements

A larger version of this table appears at the back of this book.

How to Read the Periodic Table

- **Horizontal Rows:** Each horizontal row is called a **period**. Elements within a period are dissimilar. Moving from left to right, the elements in a period change from metals to nonmetals, and atomic numbers and mass increase from left to right.

- **Vertical Columns:** Each vertical column is called a **group**. Groups contain elements that have similar properties due to the same number of electrons in the outer shell. Find Group IA on the periodic table. These are the **alkali metals,** which react with water to create an alkaline solution that is caustic. This means these solutions can burn your skin. Also check out Group 0. Members of this group are called **noble gases**. With a few exceptions, this group is the most stable. They have eight electrons in the outer energy level.

- **Groups:** The group number designates the number of electrons in the outside energy level. Groups have both numbers and letters. Below is the breakdown of the groups. Both atomic number and mass increase from top to bottom within a given group:

- The A series (IA–VIIA) is called the **representative elements.** It includes the noble gases of Group 0.

- The B series (IB–VIIB) is called the **transition elements.**

- The Lanthanide series elements (58–71) and the Actinide elements (90–103) are collectively called the **inner transition elements.**

Each element has its own calling card on the periodic table. Here's an example:

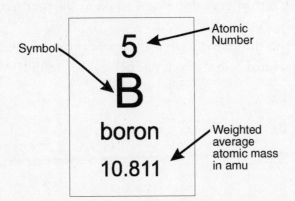

Did you know that most elements are metals? Only about twenty elements are nonmetals.

Elements fall into three categories, metals, nonmetals, and metalloids. **Metals** conduct electricity, are malleable, and can be drawn into wires or flattened into sheets. Metals can also be polished for shine and have high melting points (although mercury turns liquid at room temperature). Elements such as copper, silver, and gold are excellent examples of metals. **Nonmetals** are unsuitable for conducting electricity, and they are non-shiny. Also, some solid nonmetals are not very malleable and can shatter on impact. Finally, nonmetals have lower melting points than metals and are used in all electronic devices today.

The periodic table can be divided between metals and nonmetals (nonmetals occupy the upper right hand corner of the table). But there are a few elements that exist somewhere on the border between metals and nonmetals—they haven't actually picked a team to play on. **Metalloids** (no, not metalheads—metalloids) are elements such as silicon and boron that have properties that are similar to both metals and nonmetals.

Pop Quiz

Hey, guess what? It's that time again. Another section finished! Now that you've looked over the material on the elements, decide if a more in-depth textbook review is in order. If not, try the Pop Quiz below. Review the answers, and if you feel comfortable with your performance, go on to the next section.

1. Refer to the periodic table at the back page of the book. Of the elements listed below, which one belongs to group II A?

    (A) Ba

    (B) Bo

    (C) Zn

    (D) B

2. Refer to the periodic table at the back page of the book. How many electrons are in the outside level of an atom of chlorine?

    (A) 5

    (B) 8

    (C) 7

    (D) 2

3. A period refers to

    (A) the diagonal group of metalloids found between metals and non metals.

    (B) the horizontal rows of elements from left to right.

(C) the vertical columns of elements from top to bottom.

(D) the lanthanide series.

4. Refer to the periodic table at the back page of the book. What are the symbols for the following elements?

(A) Copper

(B) Lithium

(C) Iron

(D) Lead

(E) Sodium

(F) Silver

(G) Chlorine

(H) Manganese

Answers

1. **The correct answer is (A).** The only element from the choices given that exists in group IIA is Ba, Barium.

2. **The correct answer is (C).** Chlorine is in Group VIIA. Type A elements are representative, so the group number is also the same number of outer level electrons, 7.

3. **The correct answer is (B).** A period is a horizontal row of elements moving from left to right. Choice (C) would not be correct since this describes a group of elements.

4. **The correct answers are (A) Cu, (B) Li, (C) Fe, (D) Pb, (E) Na, (F) Ag, (H) Mn.** These are some common elements you should be familiar with. If any of these gave you a hard time, study a table of atomic weights and atomic numbers—this will give you the chemical symbols, too.

Opposites Attract: Compounds and Bonds

You like the WWF and your best friend is into ice-skating, but somehow the two of you coexist in a mutually satisfying relationship. Let's apply this to atoms to see how different atoms create friendships or bonds that are also mutually satisfying. There are two major types of "friendships" that atoms like to form: **ionic relationships** and **covalent relationships**. In this section, we're going to discuss important terms and laws that are related to these relationships.

Ions: Formation and Compounds

> Go back to the section "The Universe of the Atom" if you need to review.

Electrical forces of attraction hold matter together. However, as we learned earlier, an element's atoms are electrically neutral. So how can they attract each other if they are neutral? Well, atoms can't attract, but combinations of atoms can transfer electrons or share electrons to form compounds. Electronegativity is the ability of an element to attract electrons. Look at the periodic table on the inside back cover of this book. As you move from the left to the right and from the bottom to the top, electronegativity *increases*.

When atoms reorganize their electrons so metals can react with nonmetals, they are no longer called atoms. They become **ions.** An ion is an atom with a charge, either positive or negative. The neutral state is altered because the atom has either gained or lost electrons. When showing an ion, the charge is represented as a superscript to the right of the atom's symbol. When the ion has a positive charge, it is called a **cation** and it keeps the same name as the atoms from which it was made. However, when an ion is negative, it is called an **anion** and its name adds –*ide*. Here are some examples:

Examples of Ions

Group	Element	Symbol and name for its ion	
IA	Sodium	Na^{+1}	Sodium ion
	Lithium	Li^{+1}	Lithium ion
IIA	Magnesium	Mg^{+2}	Magnesium ion
	Calcium	Ca^{+2}	Calcium ion
IIIA	Aluminum	Al^{+3}	Aluminum ion
VIA	Oxygen	O^{-2}	Oxide ion
	Sulfur	S^{-2}	Sulfide ion
VIIA	Chlorine	Cl^{-1}	Chloride ion
	Fluorine	F^{-1}	Fluoride ion
	Iodine	I^{-1}	Iodide ion
*Transition elements	Copper	Cu^{+1}	Copper I
		Cu^{+2}	Copper II
Groups IIA–IIB	Iron	Fe^{+2}	Iron II
		Fe^{+3}	Iron III

*Note: Groups IIA–IIB have metals that can form more than one positive ion. These ions are named using Roman numerals to designate the charge on the atom.

Ions of opposite charges attract one another strongly. When they get together, they form compounds called—yeah, you guessed it—**ionic compounds.** Let's look at table salt. Normally, the parent elements, sodium and chlorine, can't be brought together. They react like mortal enemies. However, some changes in their electron configurations take place, which creates the ionic compound NaCl.

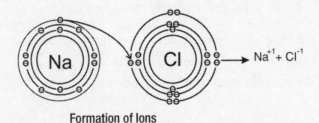

Formation of Ions

The one electron in the outermost energy level in the sodium ion was transferred to the seven outer elements in the chlorine ion, hence +1. The outermost energy level of the chloride ion gained an electron from the sodium. Now the net charge is −1, due to one extra electron. This forms a stable ionic bond with an octet formation.

Because like charges repel, all the new sodium ions move away from one another. The same is true for all the chloride ions. They attract each other to become stable. Thus, we have made sodium chloride—table salt. The net force of attraction between the oppositely charged ions is called the **ionic bond**.

Redox Reactions and Ionic Compounds

The simple reaction that drives the formation of ionic compounds is a **redox reaction**. This reaction draws its name from two important chemical events that occur during electron transfer:

- *red*uction: the gaining of electrons

- *ox*idation: the losing of electrons

In a redox reaction, one substance is the **oxidizer**—it causes the oxidation of the other substance by accepting electrons from it. The other substance is the **reducer**—it reduces a substance by giving it electrons. In table salt, sodium is the reducer because it gives electrons to the chlorine atom, which makes the chloride ion. Chlorine is the oxidizer; by accepting electrons from sodium, it oxidizes sodium atoms to ions. A key point to remember is that the oxidizing agent is always reduced; the reducing agent is always oxidized. Confusing? Then let's look at another example:

$$Mg \quad + \quad O_2 \quad \rightarrow \quad MgO$$

electron configuration	electron configuration	Magnesium Oxide
2 8 ②	2 ⑥	

Magnesium is the reducing agent. It reduces oxygen and loses 2 electrons, becoming Mg^{2+}, magnesium ion. **Oxygen** is the oxidizing agent. It oxidizes magnesium and gains 2 electrons, becoming O^{2-}, oxide ion.

Ionic Compounds: Names and Formulas

The formation of ionic compounds is a lot like Switzerland: they need to be neutral. So the ratios in which they assemble themselves must support electrical neutrality. The written expression of these ratios is a **chemical formula.** Chemical formulas represent the elements of the compound and the ratios of atoms present in the compound. For example, the formula for sodium chloride shows Na^+ and Cl^- in a ratio that is 1:1. The positive ion is always placed first in the formula. Another example, MgO (where Mg^{+2} is balanced by O^{-2}) shows an electrically neutral formula.

When atoms in formulas of ionic compounds are not in a 1:1 ratio, a subscript is used. For example, a compound made of calcium ions and chloride ions must have two Cl^- ions to one Ca^{+2} ion because it will take two Cl^- ions to balance every Ca ion with a +2 charge. So the formula would look like this:

$$Ca^{+2} + Cl_2 \rightarrow CaCl_2$$

Ionic compounds take on the names of their ions, so $CaCl_2$ is calcium chloride. Some metals, such as copper and iron, are given two names. Copper has two ions, each with two names. The copper (I) ion, for example, is also called cuprous ion, the older nomenclature. In common names of these ions, the *–ous* ending joins the ion with a lower charge, and the *–ic* ending follows the ions with the higher charge. These endings are still widely used, so it's a good idea to be familiar with both the modern and older names.

The number of atoms of element in a compound can be indicated by prefixes:

mono	(one atom)	carbon **mono**xide	CO
di	(two atoms)	nitrogen **di**oxide	NO_2
tri	(three atoms)		
tetra	(four atoms)		
penta	(five atoms)		

The smallest representation of an ionic compound formula is called a **formula unit.** This is the smallest sample of an ionic compound that still has the characteristics of the compound. As previously seen, the formula unit for sodium chloride is NaCl, and for magnesium oxide it is MgO. In NaCl, there are equal amounts of sodium and chlorine atoms in this compound. With MgO, there are equal amounts of magnesium and oxygen atoms.

Examples of Ionic Compounds

Sodium Fluoride—NaF   prevents cavities

Silver Chloride—AgCl   photographic film

Magnesium Sulfate—$MgSO_4$ laxative

Calcium Carbonate—$CaCO_3$ antacid

Writing Formulas for Ionic Compounds

Before we move on, let's practice writing an ionic compound (its formula). How would you write the formula for aluminum oxide?

1. Use the name to express the ions.

2. Al is a Group III element with an electrical charge +3. O, a Group VI element, has an electrical charge of –2. Since +3 isn't cancelled by –2, we must find the lowest common multiple of 2 and 3, which is 6 (2×3).

3. Now to balance the charges, multiply the smallest number of aluminum ions that give a product of +6 and smallest amount of oxide ions that give a total charge of –6. For Al, 2 Al^{+3} ions are needed, $[2 \times (3+) = +6]$. For O, 3 O^{-2} ions are needed $[3 \times (-2) = -6]$.

4. Once we establish the ratio as $2Al^{+3}$ to $3O^{-2}$, writing the formula is a piece of cake. Write Al first with a subscript 2, and O next with a subscript of 3. *Voila!* Al_2O_3.

The Octet Rule

What's so noble about noble gases? Go back to page 142, "How to Read the Periodic Table," if you don't remember.

All of the ions generated when sodium combines with chlorine or magnesium with oxygen have eight electrons in their outermost energy level (shells). Atoms and ions whose outermost energy shell contains eight electrons enjoy more stability than those that lack eight electrons at this level. This outer octet is similar to the electron configuration of noble gases. For example, sodium (in group IA) loses one electron from its outermost energy level 3 to become Na^+ ion. The energy level just before the outermost level, level 2, now becomes the outside level. This new outer octet resembles the noble gas neon. Let's try another example. Magnesium (in group IIA) loses two electrons from level 3 to become Mg^{+2} ion. Magnesium's level 2 becomes a stable octet, and it, too, resembles neon.

> Don't ask why noble gases are so stable. No one really knows—
> they just are!

At this point, both the sodium and magnesium ions are chemically stable. But keep in mind that this stability is due to balanced charges. When sodium atoms and chlorine atoms come together, they forget about neutrality and become stable. So any ions formed must express noble gas electron configurations. In fact, this reaction occurs so regularly between representative metals and nonmetals that it is now a law called the **octet rule:**

> Atoms that achieve eight electrons in their outermost energy levels by the transfer or sharing of electrons will acquire unusual stability, such as that of the nearest noble gas.

The charge that is seen on an ion is the **oxidation number.** Knowing the octet rule lets us accurately predict the oxidation numbers of ions most likely generated by representative elements. Here are some Groups and their respective oxidation numbers:

Group	Oxidation Number
IA	+1
IIA	+2
IIIA	+3
VIA	-2
VIIA	-1
0	no oxidation number

MOLECULES: FORMATION AND COMPOUNDS

Previously, we explored how metals and nonmetals can coexist in harmony by "completing" each other. However, there are also some nonmetals whose atoms cannot become ions by the transfer of electrons. In particular, the nonmetals of Groups IVA and VA infrequently become ions. So some other form of bonding occurs, especially because one of these elements, carbon, occurs in more compounds than any other element because of its valence of four.

Compounds that are composed only of nonmetals consist of **molecules** instead of ions. Molecules are small particles of neutral charge, consist of at least two atoms, and have enough electrons to make the system neutral. A compound consisting of molecules is called a **molecular compound**. Let's do some hierarchy to keep everything clear:

- Atoms are the basic units of elements.

- Ions are the basic units of ionic compounds.

- Molecules are the basic units of molecular compounds—in fact, molecules are the **formula units** of molecular compounds as well.

There are exceptions. Some elements exist with two atoms to each molecule—they react with themselves. These are diatomic molecules. They contain atoms of only one element. Some examples of these are:

$$Cl_2 \qquad Cl—Cl$$
$$O_2 \qquad O—O$$
$$N_2 \qquad N—N$$
$$I_2 \qquad I—I$$
$$Br_2 \qquad Br—Br$$
$$F_2 \qquad F—F$$
$$H_2 \qquad H—H$$

Some of these diatomic atoms were used in previous ionic formulas. They just weren't written as a chemist would write them. We'll look at this later, when we get to the chemical math section.

Covalent bonds are formed by the sharing pairs of electrons between atoms. G.N. Lewis, the scientist who brought us Lewis dot diagrams, discovered that one outer level electron from each atom could be shared between their atomic nuclei. Below are two ways covalent bonds can be depicted in the PCl_3 molecule:

a)   a condensed electron-dot configuration where only outer electrons are shown

b)   the bond-line structure

$$:\ddot{Cl}:\ddot{P}:\ddot{Cl}: \qquad :\ddot{Cl}-\ddot{P}-\ddot{Cl}:$$
$$:\ddot{Cl}: \qquad\qquad :\ddot{Cl}:$$

A few pages back, we discussed the octet rule. Well, this rule also applies to covalent bonds. If we count the shared pair for each atom in the PCl_3 molecule, each has eight electrons in the outermost energy level.

So far, we've just looked at one pair of electrons shared between atoms. However, two or three pairs of electrons can be shared in forming covalent bonds. The three main covalent bonding patterns are:

- **Single Bond:** the sharing of one pair of electrons

- **Double Bond:** the sharing of two pairs of electrons

- **Triple Bond:** the sharing of three pairs of electrons

$$H-\underset{\underset{H}{|}}{\overset{\overset{H}{|}}{C}}-H \qquad O=C=O \qquad H-C\equiv C-H$$

Methane   Carbon Dioxide   Ethyne

Covalence

An easy way to remember covalence is to subtract the group number from eight, (8(octet) – group number).

Some atoms of nonmetal elements differ in their ability to share electrons. Oxygen can form two bonds, nitrogen can form three bonds, and carbon can form four bonds. **Covalence** is the covalent combining ability of an element. It equals the number of electrons needed by atoms of an element to obtain stability, like the noble gases. (The Octet Rule applies here.) For example, a hydrogen atom only needs one more electron to satisfy the octet rule, so its covalence is 1. An easy way to remember covalence is to subtract the group number from eight, (8(octet) – group number). Check out the table below. It shows several groups and their covalence. Covalence indicates the number of lines (bonds) that must come off an atom in a structure, and it also dictates the correct structure.

Groups and Their Covalence Numbers

Group	Covalence Numbers
IVA—Carbon Family	8–4 = 4 covalence
VA—Nitrogen Family	8–5 = 3 covalence
VI—Oxygen Family	8–6 = 2 covalence
VII—Halogen Family	8–7 = 1 covalence

CHEMICALS AND THE BODY

Many elements and compounds that are used in every-day life can have negative effects on the human body. Here are a few:

Benzene (C_6H_6) is a chemical found in gasoline, paint removers, pesticides, and cigarette smoke. It is carcinogenic and causes aplastic anemia and depression of bone marrow as well as inhibits antibody production.

Arsenic (As) is found in food preservatives, the computer and electronics industry, insecticides, and tobacco. It causes sudden or disruptive memory loss, a lack of concentration, and numbness and loss of sensation in the limbs.

Toluene (C_7H_8) is a widely used organic solvent in gasoline and paint. It can cause fetal solvent syndrome, craniofacial and limb deformities, central nervous system defects, and intellectual impairment.

Lead (Pb) is found in old paints, imported pottery and lead pipes. It also used to be used in gasoline. Lead interferes with the early development of the brain network, can cause impaired intelligence, and can concentrate in the bones, where it can be mobilized into the bloodstream.

Pop Quiz

Yes! Another section finished. If there's anything that you really didn't get, just review it in your chemistry textbook. Try the Pop Quiz to check on how well you understand it.

1. The difference between an atom and an ion is

    (A) an ion is charged; an atom is electrically neutral.

    (B) an atom is charged; an ion is electrically neutral.

    (C) they differ by the number of neutrons.

    (D) they do not differ.

2. Write the formula for aluminum and sulfur; what is the compound's name?

    (A) Al_3S_2; aluminum sulfate

    (B) Al_2S_2; aluminum sulfur

    (C) Al_2S_3; aluminum sulfide

    (D) Al_2S; aluminum sulfite

3. Cl_2 is an example of

    (A) covalence.

    (B) atomic weight.

    (C) a radical.

    (D) a diatomic molecule.

4. Write the name of Na_2S.

   (A) Sodium sulfide

   (B) Sodium sulfate

   (C) Sodium sulfur

   (D) Sodium sulfic

5. Which of the following structural formulas represents the molecular formula for CCl_4?

   (A) 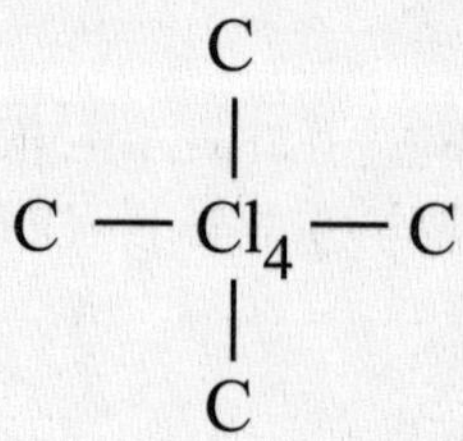
   $$\begin{array}{c} C \\ | \\ C - Cl_4 - C \\ | \\ C \end{array}$$

   (B)
   $$\begin{array}{c} Cl \\ | \\ Cl - C - Cl \\ | \\ Cl \end{array}$$

   (C)
   $$\begin{array}{c} Cl_4 \\ | \\ Cl_4 - C - Cl_4 \\ | \\ Cl_4 \end{array}$$

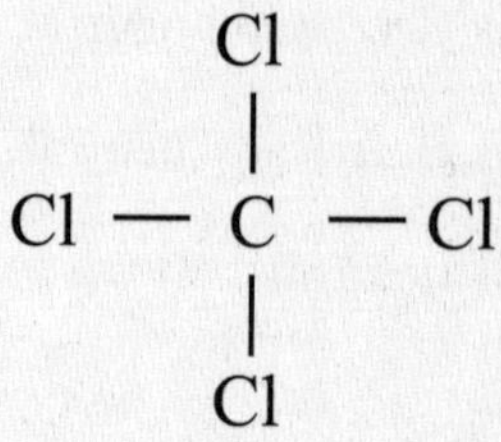

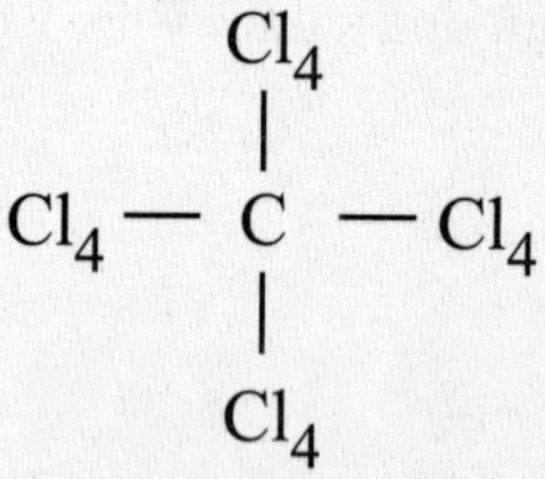

   (D) $Cl - C - Cl - C - Cl - C - Cl$

6. Calcium has an atomic number of 20. Using this info, give the charge of the calcium ion.

   (A) +3

   (B) −2

   (C) +2

   (D) −3

Answers

1. **The correct answer is (A).** Choices (B) and (D) are incorrect because atoms are electrically neutral. When atoms of metals and nonmetals want to react, they have to rearrange their electron configurations to form ionic bonds. To do this, they adopt an electrical charge to interact and become ions. Choice (C) refers to an isotope.

2. **The correct answer is (C).** Al ion has a charge of +3, and S ion has a charge of –2. The lowest common multiple of 2 and 3 is 6. So we need 2 Al [2 × (+3)]= +6 and 3 S [3 × (-2)]= -6. For balanced charges, the ratio must be Al_2S_3, or aluminum sulfide. Remember the suffix –*ide* is used with the root of the name of the negative element of the compound.

3. **The correct answer is (D).** Atoms of the same element sometimes react with themselves and form covalent bonds.

4. **The correct answer is (A).** The name is assembled in the order in which the ions appear in the formula. The symbol Na stands for sodium, the symbol S stands for sulfur. However, as stated earlier, the suffix –*ide* is added to the negative, nonmetal elements of a compound.

5. **The correct answer is (B).** The Group IVA, of which carbon is a member, have four outer electrons. They need four more electrons to satisfy their octet, so they have a covalence of 4. So carbon forms four bonds with the Cl ion for carbon tetrachloride.

6. **The correct answer is (C).** By writing the electron configuration of calcium, we can figure out the charge.

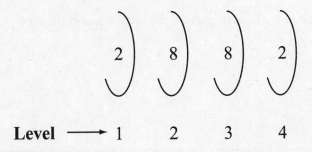

Calcium needs to lose two electrons to form a stable ion. By giving up the two electrons in energy level 4, the net charge on the particle becomes +2, or Ca^{+2}. Another way to do this is by using the periodic table. Find calcium in Group IIA. All of Group IIA elements have two outside electrons, and all of these can satisfy the octet rule by losing those two electrons. So all Group IIA ions have a charge of +2.

Chemical Reactions: Chemical Math

Before you conjure up any nightmarish memories of algebra, geometry, or calculus, relax! Chemical math is essential to understanding chemical reactions—but it is also very simple. In previous sections, we have learned the following:

- Atoms combine in whole number ratios to form compounds.

- Formula units react in the same way, forming whole number units.

Let's use this information to learn how to write chemical equations. Then we'll have a quick refresher on weight relationships in chemical equations, what scientists call stoichiometry.

CHEMICAL EQUATIONS

A **chemical equation** is shorthand for a chemical reaction. Chemical reactions have two basic parts:

- The formulas of the **reactants** (reacting substances) are on the left of the equation, separated by a plus sign.

- The formulas of the **products** are written on the right, with an arrow separating the reactants from the products.

Let's look at some examples of chemical equations:

A) $C + O_2 \rightarrow CO$

   and

B) $Fe + O_2 \rightarrow FeO$

One important thing to remember: in chemical reactions, atoms are conserved.

In the first example, the reactants C and O_2 produce CO. In the second example, Fe and O_2 produce FeO. However these equation are incomplete because they are not **balanced**. To balance an equation, the same number of each kind of atom must appear on both sides of the equation. In the first example, there are two oxygen atoms, but there is only one on the left side. **The Law of Conservation of Mass** states that in chemical reactions, the total mass of the reacting substance equals the total mass of the products formed. So in conserving O atoms, a **coefficient** is used. (A coefficient is just a number used when reactants are not in a 1:1 ratio. They help to balance the equation. Place the coefficient 2 before the CO:

$$C + O_2 \rightarrow 2CO$$

Ok, now we have two molecules of CO. The O is balanced, but the C atoms are now unbalanced. There are 2C atoms on the right, but only 1 on the left. By placing another 2 coefficient on the left in front of the C, the equation is properly balanced:

$$2C + O_2 \rightarrow 2CO$$

Balancing equations shouldn't be difficult if you follow these basic guidelines:

1. Identify the reactants from the products.

2. Write the correct formulas for all reactants and products.

3. Add coefficients as needed to conserve atoms.

4. Choose the reactant that has the highest number of different atoms and start by balancing an atom that is in only one reactant and one product.

Now let's balance $Fe + O_2 \rightarrow FeO$. First we need to write the correct formulas in the format of an equation:

$$Fe + O_2 \rightarrow Fe_2O_3 \text{ (unbalanced equation)}$$

There is a subscript of 2 in O_2 and a subscript of 3 in Fe_2O_3. To balance, use a coefficient of 3 for O_2, so there will be 6 O atoms on the left side of the equation. Then use the coefficient 2 for Fe_2O_3, so there will be 6 O atoms on the right.

$$Fe + 3O_2 \rightarrow 2Fe_2 O_3 \text{ (unbalanced equation)}$$

With the coefficient 2 in front of the formula Fe_2O_3, we now have four Fe atoms on the right. To correct this, we add a coefficient of 4 on the left for Fe.

$$4Fe + 3O_2 \rightarrow 2Fe_2O_3 \text{ (balanced equation)}$$

Did you notice that the subscripts never changed in these equations? Once the formulas are established, coefficients are used to balance an equation. By changing subscripts, the actual formula is changed, which can result in a totally different substance!

FORMULA AND MOLECULAR WEIGHTS

A compound's **formula weights** are the sum of the atomic weights. For instance, let's imagine that your family is a compound. You, your parents, and your brothers and sisters make up the formula for this compound. Each of you has a separate weight (maybe Dad weighs 220 pounds, Mom 145 pounds, you're 128 pounds, and your little brother is 59 pounds). Each of your separate weights can combine for a formula weight (552 pounds).

For a chemistry example, let's figure out the formula weight for NaCl.

> 1 atom of Na has an atomic weight of 23.0
>
> 1 atom of Cl has an atomic weight of 35.5
>
> Therefore, 23.0 + 35.5 = 58.5 total amu

*Note, atomic weights have been rounded to the first decimal point. amu is frequently used to refer to the weights of atoms and molecules as "atomic mass units."

Formula weight is the same thing as molecular weight, so if you see molecular weight on your test, think formula. Let's try another example:

Calculate the formula weight for **Mg(OH)$_2$**.

> You should try memorizing the most common elements' atomic weights. It'll save you time on your exam!

1. Use the periodic table to write down all of the atomic weights of elements present:

    Mg, 24.3   O, 16.0   H, 1.0

2. Next, use subscripts and coefficients to see how many times an element occurs in the formula. Multiply this by the atomic weight of the element:

$$1Mg = 1 \times 24.3 \qquad 2O = 2 \times 16.0 \qquad 2H = 2 \times 1.0$$

3. Add the product of each:

$$24.3 + 32 + 2 = \textbf{58.3 g}$$

We've just found the formula weight for Milk of Magnesia, $Mg(OH)_2$. Now that you know how to do this, you won't need to take a tablespoon before your exam!

AVOGADRO'S NUMBER AND THE MOLE

According to Italian chemist Amadeo Avogadro, the number $\textbf{6.02} \times \textbf{10}^{23}$ is the number of formula units in a pure sample of a substance with a mass that is numerically equal to the formula weight in grams. Okay, so in layman's terms **Avogadro's number** allows chemists to signify particles too small to be seen and counted directly. Therefore, Avogadro's number could represent 6.02×10^{23} of material, like the sugar particles on a powdered sugar donut or, in the field of chemistry, atoms. So 1g of carbon atoms contains the same number of atoms as 44g of carbon dioxide atoms. The mass of material in grams is equal to the atomic or formula weight and can now be expressed as a **mole** of that material. The number of atoms or molecules in a mole of material is Avogadro's number. A mole unit of any substance is a sample of proportions that can be seen, used, and manipulated in a laboratory. So the mole (abbreviated mol) is the formula weight in grams.

Examples of Moles:

1 Mole of H atoms weighs 1 gram and contains 6.02×10^{23} atoms.

1 Mole of C atoms weighs 12.0 grams and contains 6.02×10^{23} atoms.

1 Mole of CO weighs 28 g and contains 6.02×10^{23} atoms.

Moles can be expressed in multiples or in fractions. For example, the formula mass for water, H_2O, is 18.0, so 1 mol of H_2O weighs 18.0 g. Let's continue to use this example to see how we can manipulate the concept of a mole:

$$Moles = \frac{Mass\ of\ a\ substance\ (g)}{Formula\ weight\ (g/mole)\ of\ element\ or\ compound}$$

In 1.8 g of water, the number of moles $= \dfrac{1.8 \ \cancel{g}}{18 \ \cancel{g}/\text{mole}} = 0.10$ moles

In 36 g of water, the number of moles $= \dfrac{36 \ \cancel{g}}{18 \ \cancel{g}/\text{mole}} = 2.0$ moles

Also, be able to work through problems in which moles are given and you are asked to find the weight of a substance:

Example: How much does 4 moles of water weigh?

Answer: Weight (g) = Moles × Formula wt.

Water is H_2O, so the formula weight = 18g.

$$4 \ \cancel{\text{mol}} \times 18 \dfrac{\text{g}}{\cancel{\text{mol}}} = 72\text{g}$$

Knowing Avogadro's number lets you calculate the size and weight of a molecule and to approximate the number of molecules or atoms within a given sample:

Example: One mole of water weighs 18 g and occupies a volume of 18 cm^3. How many water molecules are in 1 cm^3?

Answer:
$$\text{Number of Moles} = \dfrac{1 \text{ mole}}{18 \text{ cm}^3} \times \left(6.02 \times 10^{23} \dfrac{\text{molecules}}{\text{mole}} \right)$$

$$= 0.33 \times 10^{23} \dfrac{\text{molecules}}{\text{cm}^3}$$

$$= 3.3 \times 10^{22} \dfrac{\text{molecules}}{\text{cm}^3}$$

Example: How many carbon atoms are in 3.00 g of carbon? (The atomic weight is 12.00.)

Answer: Conversion factor: $\dfrac{6.02 \times 10^{23} \text{ atoms C}}{12.0 \text{ g C}}$

Now multiply by 6.00 g C:

$$3.00 \text{ g\!\!\!/C} \times \dfrac{6.02 \times 10^{23} \text{ atoms C}}{12.0 \text{ g\!\!\!/C}}$$

$$= 1.51 \times 10^{23} \text{ atoms C}$$

The coefficients that we encountered earlier give us the proportion of substances in moles. So we read $2NaCl_2$ as, "For every 2 mol of Na that *reacts*, 1 mol of Cl_2 will also react, to give 2 mol of NaCl."

Working with the Mole

No, this does not involve bringing home the class pet for a week (besides, moles don't make good pets). In this section, we will use moles in the following areas:

a) Working with coefficients

b) Converting moles to grams

c) Converting grams to moles

Working with Coefficients

Example: How many moles of oxygen are needed to react with 0.600 mol of hydrogen in the reaction that produces water in the chemical equation that follows?

$$2H_2 + O_2 \rightarrow 2H_2O$$

Answer: The coefficients in this equation tell us that 2 mol of H_2 join with 1 mol of O_2. So the best conversion factor would be as follows:

$$0.600 \text{ mol H}_2 \times \dfrac{1 \text{ mol O}_2}{2 \text{ mol H}_2} = .300 \text{ mol O}_2$$

So .600 mol of H_2 needs .300 mol of O_2 for this reaction to occur.

Example: How many moles of hydrogen are needed to combine with 30 mol of carbon in the equation that follows?

$$C + 2H_2 \rightarrow CH_4 \text{ (process of making methane from coal)}$$

Answer: First decide on the conversion factor:

$$\frac{1 \text{ mol C}}{2 \text{ mol H}_2} \quad \text{OR} \quad \frac{2 \text{ mol H}_2}{1 \text{ mol C}}$$

The second conversion factor is the best choice:

$$30 \text{ mol C} \times \frac{2 \text{ mol H}_2}{1 \text{ mol C}} = 60 \text{ mol H}_2$$

Converting Moles to Grams

This converts moles into a useful, tangible unit that can be measured. If a chemist is given the moles of a substance, he or she would have to convert it to grams before the substance can be weighted. The formula unit will be used again but a bit differently: You will write g/mol (grams per mole) after the formula weight. This represents the **molar mass**. For example, the molar mass of carbon, which has an atomic weight of 12.0, is 12.0 g C/mol C.

Example: How many grams of Cl_2 are in .250 mol of Cl_2?

Answer: First, calculate the formula weight of Cl_2. (Remember, this is a diatomic molecule.) The atomic weight of chlorine is 35.5, which we multiply by 2 to determine the molar mass: $35.5 \times 2 = 71$ g Cl_2/mol Cl_2. To convert, choose the conversion factor that will allow you to cancel *mol* Cl_2 and leave you with *g* Cl_2.

$$.250 \text{ mol Cl}_2 \times \frac{71 \text{ g Cl}_2}{1 \text{ mol Cl}_2} = 17.75 \text{ g Cl}_2$$

Example: An experiment calls for 12 mol NaOH. How many grams is this?

Answer: Again, the first thing you want to do is calculate the formula weight. Na = 23.0, O = 16.0, and H = 1.0, for a formula weight of 40. So NaOH has a molar mass of 40g/mol NaOH. Next, choose the appropriate conversion factor:

$$\frac{40 \text{ g NaOH}}{1 \text{ mol NaOH}} \quad \text{OR} \quad \frac{1 \text{ mol NaOH}}{40 \text{ g NaOH}}$$

The first conversion factor is the best because it lets us cancel out the mol:

$$12 \text{ mol NaOH} = \frac{40 \text{ g NaOH}}{1 \text{ mol NaOH}} = 480 \text{ g NaOH}$$

Converting Grams to Moles

Example: You prepared 3.42 g of aspirin, $C_9H_8O_4$, in an experiment. How many moles is this?

Answer: With this problem, your conversion factor will be based on the grams per mole of aspirin as represented by its molar mass. Let's calculate the formula weight that will also give us the molar mass:

$$C \ (9 \times 12.0) \ + \ H \ (8 \times 1.0) \ + \ O \ (4 \times 16.0) = 180$$

$$1 \text{ mol } C_9H_8O_4 = 180 \text{ g } C_9H_8O_4$$

Now choose the best conversion factor:

$$\frac{1 \text{ mol } C_9H_8O_4}{180 \text{ g } C_9H_8O_4} \quad \text{OR} \quad \frac{180 \text{ g } C_9H_8O_4}{1 \text{ mol } C_9H_8O_4}$$

The first choice allows you to cancel grams and leave the mol unit:

$$3.42 \text{ g } C_9H_8O_4 \times \frac{1 \text{ mol } C_9H_8O_4}{180 \text{ g } C_9H_8O_4} = .019 \text{ mol } C_9H_8O_4$$

PERCENTAGE COMPOSITION

The percentage of each element in a compound can be useful in determining if the accurate percent of a given element is in the compound. It is also useful for determining how much of a compound needs to be decomposed to form the elements. For example, let's calculate the percentage of Cu, Cl, and O in $Cu(ClO_4)_2$:

(Make sure you balance the formula before doing the percentage calculation.)

atom × mass

Cu $1 \times 63.5 = 63.5$ amu $63.5/263 \times 100 = 24.1\%$

Cl $2 \times 35.5 = 71.0$ amu $71.0/263 \times 100 = 27.0\%$

O $8 \times 16.0 = 128.0$ amu $128/263 \times 100 = 48.7\%$

At other times a chemist must be able to identify a compound by knowing the mass of each element that makes up the compound or the percentage composition of the compound. This technique if determining a formula is called the empirical formula or simplest ratio of the atoms. There are two steps: 1) determine the number of moles and 2) divide by the smallest number of moles for each part of the compound.

For example, let's calculate the empirical formula of a compound with 65.2g of arsenic and 34.8g of oxygen:

Step 1

As moles = mass/formula mass = $65.2/74.9 = .870$ moles

O moles = $34.8/16 = 2.18$ moles

Step 2

.870m/.870m = $1 \times 2 = 2$ (multiply by 2 to get an even number of atoms)

2.18m/.870m = $2.5 \times 2 = 5$

Empirical Formula = As_2O_5

POP QUIZ

This brings us to the end of another section of chemistry. Did you survive? Try the problems below.

1. Balance the following equation: $ZnS + O_2 \rightarrow ZnO + SO_2$

   (A) $ZnS + 2O_2 \rightarrow ZnO + 2SO_2$

   (B) $2ZnS + 3O_2 \rightarrow 2ZnO + 2SO_2$

   (C) $3ZnS + 2O_2 \rightarrow ZnO + 2SO_2$

   (D) $2ZnS + 2O_2 \rightarrow ZnO + 3SO_2$

2. Calculate the formula weight of table sugar (sucrose), $C_{12}H_{22}O_{11}$.

   (A) 342 g

   (B) 256 g

   (C) 45 g

   (D) 29 g

3. A sample of silver weighs 2.00 g. How many moles is this?

   (A) 54 mol

   (B) 1.9 mol

   (C) 2 mol

   (D) .019 mol

4. Convert 1.76 mol of ascorbic acid (vitamin C), $C_6H_8O_6$, to grams.

   (A) 30.98 g

   (B) 3.98 g

   (C) 309.8 g

   (D) 100 g

Answers

1. **The correct answer is (B).** Find the equation with the same number of atoms on both sides of the equation. Choice (B) is the only balanced equation.

2. **The correct answer is (A).** To calculate the formula weight of sucrose, $C_{12}H_{22}O_{11}$, use the atomic weights of each element and multiply these weights by the appropriate subscript: C (12×12) + H (22×1.0) + O (11×16) = 342 g.

3. **The correct answer is (D).** Choice (A) is incorrect because it represents the wrong conversion factor (it divides the formula weight by the grams). Choice (B) is incorrect due to the misplacement of a decimal point. Choice (C) is wrong because it is just choice (B), only rounded up. Choice (D) represents the correct conversion factor, dividing the grams of silver (2.00) by the gram molar mass of silver (formula weight), which is 108 g.

4. **The correct answer is (C).** First calculate the formula weight, C(6×12.0) + H(1.0×8) + O(6×16.0) =176g $C_6H_8O_6$. Now to convert moles to grams, use a conversion factor, which will cancel out moles to leave the gram unit:

$$1.76 \; \cancel{\text{mol } C_6H_6O_6} = \frac{176 \text{ g } C_6H_8O_6}{1 \text{ mol } \cancel{C_6H_8O_6}}$$

Chemical Reactions: Gas Laws and Kinetic Theories

> The properties of air are also important to folks who hang-glide or ride hot air balloons since they must have a lot of confidence in the predictable nature of these properties.

Have you ever wondered why water droplets develop on an ice cold glass of water on a hot day? Or why the smell of a skunk or cheap perfume seems to linger for hours? This section explores properties of gases that explain these phenomena.

Some properties are found in all gases. For the most part, they can mix and diffuse, expand to fill containers, and are elastic, which means they can be compressed. Compressed gas causes a spring-like action due to the high amount of pressure it is under. For example, a cork in a champagne bottle shoots out when the bottle is opened because the volume is increased and the pressure is released (decreased). Rapidly expanding gas usually cools, which is the key principle behind a CO_2 fire extinguisher. Usually when compressed quickly, gases heat up. Try touching your bicycle pump as you rapidly fill your tire with air. The pump gets hot, and so does the tire. These and other properties have been tested and turned into a series of gas laws.

GAS LAWS

There are four important variables in describing the physical properties of gas:

- **pressure** (P)

- **temperature** (T) in kelvins

- **moles** (n), number of moles

- **volume** (V).

Measurements are covered on page 121.

Other important physical quantities are partial and standard pressure and temperature, or STP (273 K and 1 atm).

Pressure is defined as the force per unit area:

$$P = \frac{F}{A}$$

The units of measurement for pressure vary. The SI unit is the pascal, Pa, or kilopascal, which is a more useful measurement in terms of size. Other units include atmospheres (atm), millimeters mercury (mmHg), torr, and bar. These units are all interrelated:

1 atm = 760 mmHg = 760 torr = 1.01 bar = 101.325 kPa

Boyle's Law or Pressure-Volume Law

In 1661, Robert Boyle discovered that gas pressure is inverse to volume at a constant temperature. The mathematical representation of **Boyle's Law** is:

$$P_1 V_1 = P_2 V_2 \text{ or } PV = \text{constant}$$

This law describes the relationship between pressure and volume as long as the temperature and number of gas molecules remain constant. As the pressure increases, the volume decreases and temperature is constant.

Look at the container below. In part a, the container is filled with air and sealed with a lid that you can raise and lower. At the present height of the lid, the gas molecules are spread out. The nature of gas particles is such that they want to fill every possible space. So as gas particles move to occupy space, they collide into the sides of the container. This exerts a force onto the sides of the container, which represents the pressure created by the gas inside the container.

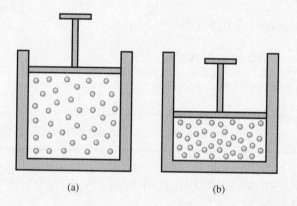

(a)   (b)

Now look at part b. As the lid is lowered, the gas particles are closely packed together. They are still moving and undergoing collisions at the same rate, but now they don't have far to travel before colliding with the sides of the container. So the shorter distance has increased the rate of collisions. The increase in collision enhances the internal pressure, which is inverse to the volume change (volume decreases as the lid moves down).

Charles's Law or Temperature-Volume Law

Jacques Charles discovered in 1787 that the volume of a fixed amount of gas at constant pressure is directly proportional to temperature in Kelvins. The mathematical representation of **Charles's Law** is:

$$\frac{V_1}{T_1} = \frac{V_2}{T_2}$$

This law goes into action when a hot air balloon rises. Balloonists heat the air inside the balloon. The heated air expands and becomes less dense than the surrounding air, allowing the balloon to lift and float.

Gay-Lussac's Law or Pressure-Temperature Law

Joseph Gay-Lussac furthered gas relationships by relating pressure and temperature. **Gay-Lussac's Law** states that the pressure of gas is directly proportional to temperature in Kelvins:

$$\frac{P_1}{T_1} = \frac{P_2}{T_2}$$

Gay-Lussac's Law is illustrated by the warning on aerosol cans. These cans are sealed, and even when the product is used up, residual gas remains inside the can. These gases are used as propellants, and most are under a high amount of pressure and are flammable. So you may see warnings concerning the temperature range at which the product can be stored as well as not placing the cans in an incinerator. The high heat in the incinerator will raise the temperature in the can, which in turn increases the pressure. Inevitably, the can will burst.

Avogadro's Law or the Volume-Mole Law

Yes, it's that famous Italian scientist again. In 1811, Avogadro theorized that equal volumes of gases have equal numbers of moles when compared at the same temperature and volume. It has been experimentally proven that at 273 K (0° C) and 1 atm, one mole of gas occupies 22.4 L. This set of conditions is referred to as the STP (standard temperature and pressure):

$$\frac{V}{n} = \text{constant}$$

By now, you may be wishing we could combine all these law into one equation instead of four separate equations. Well, your prayers are answered! Let's take what we've learned to make one giant "s'more" of a gas law, the combined gas law.

Combined Gas Law

The four laws are combined using all four variables: pressure, temperature, volume, and number of moles. The new formula is:

$$\frac{PV}{nT} = \text{constant} \rightarrow \frac{P_1 V_1}{n_1 T_1} = \frac{P_2 V_2}{n_2 T_2}$$

This form is easier to use to determine gas behavior under changing conditions.

In the combined gas law equation, the subscript 1 relates to the initial state of gas, and the subscript 2 relates to the final state. This equation can be manipulated according to the information given in a problem. For example, some problems will not use 'n' (number of moles), so this portion of the equation can be omitted. The same holds true if only pressure and volume are given, then temperature and number of moles can be omitted from the equation.

Example: A gas sample occupies 2.5 liters under a pressure of 3 atm at 300 K. Find its volume at 273 K and 1.5 atm.

> To keep all this information straight, write short-hand notes for units and values given: P_1= 3 atm; P_2 = 1.5 atm; V_1 =2.5 liters; V_2 = ? ; T_1=300 K; T_2 = 273 K

Answer: No value was given for *n*, so this variable will not be considered in our calculations.

Arrange your equation so you can solve for V_2. You have had practice changing equations around to solve for the missing portion in previous calculations:

$$V_2 = \frac{P_1 V_1 T_2}{P_2 T_1} = \frac{(3 \text{ atm})(2.5 \text{ liters})(273 \text{ K})}{(1.5 \text{ atm})(300 \text{ K})} = 4.6 \text{ liters}$$

Ideal Gas Law

The good news here is that the ideal gas law is not much different than the combined gas law. In fact, it is the simple form of the combined gas law set equal to a constant:

$$\frac{PV}{nT} = \text{constant}$$

Replace the constant with R, a value known as the ideal gas constant:

$$\frac{PV}{nT} = R, \text{ and } R = 0.0821 \text{ L-atm mol}^{-1}\text{K}^{-1}$$

Now rearrange the formula into a format similar to the combined gas law:

$$PV = nRT$$

Review conversions on page 121.

This formula can be used to determine the properties of any gas as long as the units for each variable given match the units of R (volume in liters, pressure in atmospheres, and temperature in kelvins). If the units don't match up, you may have to do a conversion.

Example: Aerosol cans such as those used to squirt Cheese Whiz use N_2 gas as a propellant. If Cheese Whiz occupies a volume 500 ml and weighs 4.67 g, calculate the pressure at 27 °C.

Answer: First, we have a few conversions:

Convert 500ml to liters = .5 liters

Convert 27 °C to Kelvins   K = (27 °C + 273) = 300 K

Convert N_2 to moles = 4.67 g / (28 g/mol) = 0.17 mol

Convert the formula to solve for P:

$$P = \frac{nRT}{V} = \frac{(0.17 \text{ mol})(0.0821 \text{ L} \cdot \text{atm mol}^{-1}\text{K}^{-1})300K}{.5 \text{ L}}$$

$$= 8.3 \text{ atm}$$

Chemistry

Law of Partial Pressures (Dalton's Law)

We have been considering properties and equations as they relate to a single sample of gas. However, many gas samples are a mixture of several gases. Air is a mixture of nitrogen (79 percent N_2), oxygen (21 percent O_2), and trace amounts of a few other gases. With altitude changes, the volume to volume ratios don't change, but each individual pressure of O_2 and N_2 does change. John Dalton, who came up with the atomic theory, was one of the first scientists to realize that partial pressures add up to the total pressure of a sample of a gas mixture. **Dalton's Law** states that the total pressures exerted by a mixture of gases is equal to the sum of the individual partial pressures:

$$P_t = P_a + P_b + P_c + \text{etc.} \quad P_t = \text{total pressure and}$$

$$P_a, P_b, P_c = \text{pressures of individual gases}$$

Example: N_2 has a pressure of 250 mmHg on the summit of a mountain. The atmospheric pressure is 387 mmHg. Ignoring any trace gases, assume N_2 and O_2 are the only constituents of air. What is the partial pressure of oxygen in mmHg on the mountain summit?

Answer: First, write down what you already know:

$$P_t = 387 \text{ mmHg}$$

$$P_a \text{ or } P_{N_2} = 250 \text{mmHg}$$

$$P_b \text{ or } P_{O_2} = ?$$

Now solve:

$$387 \text{ mmHg} - 250 \text{ mmHg} = P_b$$

$$137 \text{ mmHg} = P_b$$

KINETIC THEORY OF GASES

The physical behaviors of gases have led to a molecular theory that describes the nature of gases. This is commonly called the **Kinetic Theory of Gases,** and it is based on the gas laws we just reviewed. Here are some of the most important aspects of this theory:

- A gas is composed of very small molecules that are widely separated and are in a state of rapid, random motion.

- Gas molecules move in random straight-line paths in all directions and show a distribution of velocities. Some move fast, some move slow, but most move at a velocity close to average.

- The attractive and repulsive forces between molecules in a gas are negligible. Gas molecules move too fast and are too far apart to establish any force of attraction or repulsion.

- When gas molecules collide, the collisions are elastic. Elastic collisions result in gas molecules bouncing off one another and leaving a collision with the same amount of kinetic energy they had prior to a collision. Therefore, kinetic energy is conserved.

- The average kinetic energy of gas molecules is proportional to absolute temperature.

POP QUIZ

You've made it through another section! You know the drill by now. Try the Pop Quiz, and go back to your textbook and class notes if you need more review.

1. A gas occupies a volume of 3 liters at STP. What is its volume at a pressure .6 atm and a temperature of 540 K?

   (A) 8 L

   (B) 10 L

   (C) 12 L

   (D) 14 L

2. Which scientist discovered that gas pressure is inversely proportional to volume?

   (A) Boyle

   (B) Charles

   (C) Avogadro

   (D) Gay-Lussac

3. A gas cylinder has a pressure of 300atm at 293K. What would the pressure be if the temperature rises to 473 K but the volume of the cylinder remains the same?

(A) 200 atm

(B) 186 atm

(C) 150 atm

(D) 484 atm

4. A sealed container holds .5 L of carbon monoxide gas (CO) at STP. How many moles of CO does it contain?

(A) .0003 mol

(B) .002 mol

(C) .022 mol

(D) .2 mol

Answers

1. **The correct answer is (B).** First recall that STP (standard temperature and pressure) = 273K, 1 atm, and since the liters were given to you, the constant 22.4L was not needed. Using the combined gas law equation, rearrange it to solve for V_2:

$$V_2 = \frac{P_1 V_1 T_2}{T_1 P_2}$$

$$V_2 = \frac{(1atm)(3L)(540K)}{(273K)(.6atm)}$$

$$V_2 = \frac{1620L}{163.8}$$

$$= 9.9L, \text{ rounded to } 10L$$

2. **The correct answer is (A).** The law referred to here was discovered by Robert Boyle.

3. **The correct answer is (D).** The Guy-Lussac law is used to solve this problem. Note that the volume remains fixed and is not given, so this variable will not be considered in the formula. By rearranging the variables, you can solve for P_2:

$$P_2 = \frac{T_2\,P_1}{T_1}$$

$$= \frac{(300 \text{ atm})(293 \text{ K})}{473 \text{ K}}$$

$$= \frac{87900 \text{ atm}}{473}$$

$$= 186 \text{ atm}$$

4. **The correct answer is (C).** Here, the ideal gas law formula is used since there is no change in pressure, temperature, or volume given. By rearranging the equation to solve for *n*, you are able to cancel all units except moles. STP was also used, and since liters was given, we only needed the temperature (273 K) and pressure (1 atm):

$$n = \frac{PV}{RT}$$

$$= \frac{(1 \text{ atm})(.5\text{L})}{(0.0821 \text{ L} \times \text{atm mol } -1 \text{ K } -1)}$$

$$= .022 \text{ mol}$$

Water and Solutions

You may recall from chemistry or physical science class that water is the "universal solvent." This simply means that the properties of water give it the ability to dissolve many substances. In this section, we will review the properties of solutions in relation to solvents and solutes.

SOLUTIONS

A **solution** is a homogenous mixture of two or more substances. **Homogeneous** refers to the uniformity throughout a solution. **Heterogeneous** mixtures are not uniform throughout since they have separate phases. An example of a homogeneous mixture is salt water. This solution consists of NaCl and water—the two are indistinguishable. However, you could physically separate them by evaporating the water, leaving the salt behind. An example of a heterogeneous mixture would be strawberry Twizzlers coated in chocolate. Like the homogeneous mixture, you could separate these physically, but they have not chemically reacted. By melting off the chocolate (or nibbling it off!), you could separate the two.

The properties of a solution vary with the amounts of **solute** and **solvent** present. Think about lemonade. The lemonade is a solution. The solvent portion is water; solvents are substances that do the dissolving. The solutes are lemon juice and sugar; solutes, which can be liquids or solids, are the substances that are dissolved. The taste of the lemonade depends upon the strength or concentration of the solution.

Molarity

Forget how to calculate moles of a substance? Don't remember what a volumetric flask is? Go back to pages 124 and 161.

Molarity is the number of moles of solute per liter of solution. To make a 1 mol solution NaCl, you would weigh out 1 mole (58.5 g) of solid NaCl and add it to a 1.00 L volumetric flask. Then add enough water to fill the flask to exactly the 1 liter mark. To find the molarity of a solution, divide the moles of solute by liters of solution:

$$M = \frac{\text{Number of moles of solute}}{\text{liters of solution}}$$

Example: Prepare 1 L of solution of a 1 mole solution of AgCl (silver chloride).

Answer: Weigh out 1 mole, or (108 + 35.5 = 143 g), of AgCl. Then dissolve this in enough water to make 1L of solution.

Example: What is the molarity of a solution prepared by dissolving 26.8 g of AgCl in a total volume of 100 ml of solution?

Answer:

$$\text{Moles of AgCl} = \frac{26.8\text{g}}{179\text{ g/mole}} = 0.15\,\text{mole}$$

$$\text{Volume} = 100\text{ ml} = 0.100\text{ L}$$

$$\text{Molarity AgCl} = \frac{0.15\text{ mole}}{0.100\text{ L}} = 1.5\text{ M AgCl}$$

Molality

> Chemists use molality because it is a more precise measurement that is not affected by temperature change. Molarity changes with temperature because the volume of solution fluctuates with the temperature. Molality uses mass values that do not vary, whatever the temperature of the solution may be.

Molality is different than molarity, but they are often confused because they sound so much alike. **Molality** is the number of moles of solute per kilogram of solvent. The two measurements differ in two ways:

- With molality, you are measuring units of mass instead of units of volume.

- The *amount of solvent,* not the amount of solution, is used in the denominator when determining molality:

$$\text{Molality} = \frac{\text{number of moles of a solute}}{\text{kilograms of solution}}$$

Example: To obtain a 0.20 molal solution of .500 L (500g) glucose, how many grams of glucose must be added? The molecular weight of glucose, $C_6H_{12}O_6$, is 180 g/mole.

Answer: First, convert 500 g to .5 kg. Next, solve for the number of moles by rearranging the molality formula:

$$\text{\# moles of a solute} = \left(.2 \text{ mol/kg}\right)\left(.5 \text{ kg}\right)$$
$$= .1 \text{ mole}$$

Now it's just a matter converting moles to grams:

$$\text{mole} = \frac{\text{weight of substance}}{\text{formula weight}} = \left(.1 \text{ mole}\right)\left(180 \text{ g/mole}\right) = 18\text{g}$$

ELECTROLYTES

Many ionic compounds dissociate into **electrolytes** when they are dissolved in water. A solution of table salt mixed in water contains Na^+ ions and Cl^- ions, not a whole unit of NaCl. Except for a few covalently bonded substances, most do not dissociate into ions when dissolved in water. **Electrolytes** are derived from substances that, when dissolved in water, yield conducting solutions. Electrolytes can carry a current of electricity. Nonelectrolytes do not dissociate and retain their molecules in solution, so they can't conduct electricity.

This explains the warning on most blowdryers. To prevent electrocution, you are warned not to use blowdryers in or near a bathtub full of tap water. Ordinary tap water contains electrolytes that conduct electricity. If, as you were using the blowdryer, you dropped it while standing in a pool of water (such as a bathtub), the water would conduct the electrical current, which will then be directed into you!

Check out the figure on the following page. If the substance conducts electricity, then the bulb will light up (unshaded). If no electricity is conducted, then the bulb won't light up (shaded).

SPT/HSPA, FCAT, MEAP HST, GEE21, Regents Exams, SOL, NCCT, AHSGE, GHSGT, BST, BSA T, AHSGE, GHSGT, BST, BSAP, WASL, CAHSEE, TAAS, OGT, HSPT/HSP CAT, MEAP HST SPT/HSPA, FCAT, MEAP HST, GEE21, Regents Exams, SOL, NCCT, GHSGT, BST, BSA SGT, BST, BSAP, WASL, CAHSEE, TAAS, OGT, HSPT/HSPA, FCAT, MEAP HST, GEE21, R

CHAPTER

4

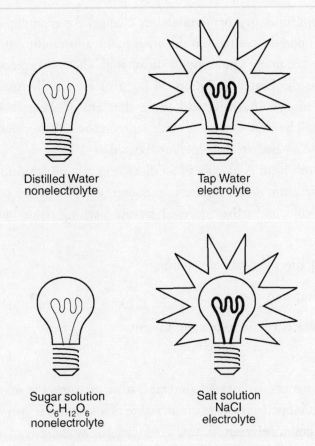

Distilled Water
nonelectrolyte

Tap Water
electrolyte

Sugar solution
$C_6H_{12}O_6$
nonelectrolyte

Salt solution
NaCl
electrolyte

SOLUBILITY

Have you ever dissolved powdered iced tea mix in water, but it doesn't taste right? Chances are that you either didn't have enough water or you had too much water. This illustrates **unsaturated** and **saturated** properties of a solution. **Unsaturated solutions** are solutions that can dissolve more solute. In the case of very little drink mix and lots of water, you could dissolve more drink mix into solution. By doing this, you have adjusted the concentration of solute (drink mix) to yield a better taste. In **saturated solutions**, a point has been reached in which no more material can be dissolved. In a **supersaturated solution**, there is more dissolved solute than the solution can actually hold. In a solution such as this, solids can reform from a solution or **precipitate** (come out of solution), provided they have something to form on. Supersaturated solutions are very unstable, so even a scratch in the container holding this solution can provide the "seed" on which crystals can precipitate out of solution and grow.

Some solutions result in a net temperature change. For example, calcium chloride releases heat upon dissolving. On the other hand, ammonium nitrate decreases in temperature, becoming cooler upon dissolving. These two reactions are known collectively as the **heat of solution,** H $_{solution}$ or H $_{soln}$. Chemical reactions that release heat are **exothermic,** and those that absorb heat (become cold) are **endothermic.** The heat associated with a process is called **enthalpy.** Exothermic reactions have a negative enthalpy, represented as $\Delta H_{soln} < 0$, and endothermic reactions absorb heat, $\Delta H_{soln} > 0$. So dissolving calcium chloride is exothermic, and dissolving ammonium nitrate is endothermic. This is the chemistry behind the hot and cold packs that are used to ease swelling tissue and soothe pulled muscles.

Three factors affect the rate of solubility:

- Temperature

- Natures of the solute and solvent

- Pressure

For most substances, an increase in temperature increases the solubility of a solid. For gases, solubility decreases as temperature of a solution increases. This explains why thermal pollution is significant in reducing the availability of oxygen. Changes in pressure have a very small effect on the solubility of a liquid or a solid, but for a gas pressure increases as solubility increases.

Polar vs. Nonpolar Solvents

Water, a polar molecule, is considered a universal solvent. However, water can only dissolve polar solutes. Oil is nonpolar—it cannot mix with water. When a liquid is insoluble with water, it is **immiscible.** Miscibility of solute to solvents follows the "like to like" rule. So gasoline, a nonpolar solvent, will dissolve oil, a nonpolar solute—they are **miscible.** Water, a polar solvent, dissolves salt, a polar solute.

> For your exit-level exam, a table of solubilities may be provided to assist you with questions related to solubility.

Temperature and pressure can also affect solubility. The effect that temperature has on a solvent is proportional to the properties of the solvent. For most solid solutes, an increase in temperature will lead to an increase in solubility. For gases, the effect of temperature is opposite. Gases become less soluble at higher temperatures. For this reason, carbonated drinks are served with ice to keep them cool longer. The cooler temperature decreases the formation of carbon dioxide bubbles. The bubbles represent carbon dioxide coming out of solution. So by keeping your soda cold, you can prolong that fresh, carbonated fizz!

EQUILIBRIUM

If excess, undissolved solute is present, a saturated solution sets up a system of **dynamic equilibrium.** If you add more solute to an already saturated solution, some dissolves and enters solution, and some reforms as the original solute. These two opposing activities result in no net change. If we have a saturated solution of NaCl and more NaCl crystals are added, some of those crystals will dissolve and the ions will enter solution and move around as the crystals become smaller. However, some of those dissolved ions will attach to a crystal surface and reform crystals that fall out of solution (reprecipitate). Eventually, the rates at which ions dissociate and leave the crystal and ions reform crystals become equal. Because these rates of crystal breakdown and formation are equal in this NaCl solution, there is no net change in the solution's concentration or in the mass of undissolved solute.

Once a saturated solution has reached dynamic equilibria, it can have both forward and reverse reaction:

$$solute_{undissolved} \rightleftharpoons solute_{dissolved}$$

Factors such as temperature, concentration, and pressure can upset equilibrium and shift it. The shift can be in favor of a forward reaction, producing more products, or backward, in favor of the solute. Henri Louis Le Chatelier predicted how stress will shift an equilibrium. **Le Chatelier's Principle** states that an equilibrium always responds to stress by shifting in whatever direction absorbs the stress.

The formation of ammonia from nitrogen and hydrogen can be used to illustrate this principle. By increasing the pressure and lowering the temperature, the amount of ammonia produced can increase.

N_2 (g) + $3H_2$ (g)	$\rightleftharpoons$	$2NH_3$ (g) + heat
Endothermic side		Exothermic side
More gas		Less gas
Likes low pressure		Likes high pressure
Likes high temperature		Likes low temperature

*Note: In chemical equations, abbreviations are used for gas (g), liquids (l), and aqueous (aq). These abbreviations are added after reactants or products.

POP QUIZ

This is the end of yet another section. Continue on to the Pop Quiz. Don't forget, it may be necessary to dust off that chemistry textbook for more review.

1. How many moles of solute are in a solution of 12 ml of 10 M hydrochloric acid, HCl?

    (A) .12 mol

    (B) 1.2 mol

    (C) 12 mol

    (D) 120 mol

2. What volume would be needed to prepare 0.300 moles of NaCl from a solution of 1.50 M NaCl?

    (A) 20 L

    (B) 2 L

    (C) 0.02 L

    (D) 0.200 L

3. Which would you expect to be a better solvent for oil, water or gasoline?

(A) Both water and gasoline would make good solvents.

(B) Neither water nor gasoline would make good solvents.

(C) Only gasoline

(D) Only water

4. What is the molality of a solution that contains 8.64 g of potassium chloride, KCl, in 400 g of water?

(A) .3 M

(B) .12 M

(C) 3 M

(D) .4 M

5. Two electrodes, connected to a wall socket and a light bulb, are submerged into Substance A. The bulb lights up. What can be said about Substance A?

(A) Substance A is a molecular substance.

(B) Substance A has high solubility.

(C) Substance A is an eletrolyte.

(D) Substance A lacks ions.

Answers

1. **The correct answer is (A).** Convert the molarity formula to solve for the number of moles of solutes. Make sure you also convert 12 ml in .012 L:

$$10M = \frac{x}{.012\ell}$$
$$= .12 \text{ moles}$$

2. **The correct answer is (D).**

$$1.5M = \frac{.300m}{volume}$$
$$= .2\ell$$

3. **The correct answer is (C).** Gasoline is a polar compound. It would serve as the better solvent for oil, also a polar compound. Remember, "like dissolves like."

4. **The correct answer is (A).** First, find the number of moles by dividing the grams of KCl by it formula weight (molar mass). Then plug this value into the molality formula. Also convert 400g = .4 Kg:

$$moles = \frac{8.64g}{74\,g\!\!\not{l}\!\!\not{m}\ of\ KC\ell}$$
$$= .12\ moles$$
$$400g = \frac{400ml}{1000}$$
$$= .40\ell$$
$$\frac{.12\,moles}{.40\ell} = .3M$$

5. **The correct answer is (C).** Choice (A) is incorrect, as molecules do not conduct electricity. Choice (B) is incorrect. A substance may have high solubility but no electrical conducting activity. Choice (D) is incorrect because electrolytes *are* dissociated ions in a solution.

Acids, Bases, and Salts

You've probably worked with small quantities of acids and bases in your science class. Acids and bases can be found outside the laboratory and in your home. The citric acid of a lemon and the acetic acid of vinegar are examples of household acids. **Acids** usually have a sour taste. They also have biological functions, such as in digestion—acids in the stomach help break down foods we eat. Certain cleaning products, such as household ammonia, are examples of bases. Bases are usually bitter and slippery in feel. Sodium hydroxide, or *lye*, is a basic solution used in hair straightening products. The table below outlines some major properties of acids and bases.

Major Properties of Acids and Bases

Acids	Bases
Turn blue litmus paper red	Turn red litmus paper blue
Neutralize bases	Neutralize acids
Provide hydrogen ions, H^+	Provide hydroxide ions, OH^-

ARRHENIUS DEFINITION OF ACIDS AND BASES

Svante Arrhenius proposed the earliest concept of an acid and base. His definitions are the most simplistic, but they describe the most commonly known acids and bases:

- **Arrhenius acids** are substances that, when dissolved in water solution, provide hydrogen ions (H^+):

    $$HCL\ (g) \rightarrow H^+\ (aq) + Cl^-\ (aq)$$

- **Arrhenius bases** are substances that, when dissolved in water solution, provide hydroxide ions (OH):

    $$KOH \rightarrow K^+ + OH^-$$

The Arrhenius model rates an acid or base by the degree of ionization. So an acid or base is considered strong if, when placed in water, it completely ionizes. Weak acids or bases are those that do not completely ionize. For example, HCl is considered a strong acid because it completely ionizes into H^+ and Cl^-. The table below outlines some strong and weak acids and bases.

Strong and Weak Acids and Bases

Strong Acids	Weak Acids	Strong Bases	Weak Base
Hydrochloric Acid (HCl)	Acetic Acid (CH_3COOH)	Potassium Hydroxide (KOH)	Ammonia (NH_3)
Nitric Acid (HNO_3)	Boric Acid $(HB(OH)_4)$	Sodium Hydroxide (NaOH)	
Sulfuric Acid (H_2SO_4)	Hydrocyanic Acid (HCN)	Calcium Hydroxide $(Ca(OH)_2)$	
	Carbonic Acid (H_2CO_3)		

BRØNSTED–LOWRY DEFINITION OF ACIDS AND BASES

The Arrhenius model is pretty simple. However, it does not give any information about the nature of a reaction between an acid or base and water. Also not all substances follow the rules of the Arrhenius model, but they can still be classified as an acid or base. For instance, sodium bicarbonate (Na_2CO_3) does not provide OH^- ions, yet it is a base in aqueous solution.

To address these issues, J.N. Brønsted and T.M . Lowry proposed a different way to define acids and bases:

- **Brønsted–Lowry acids** transfer a proton to another substance:

$$NH_3 \text{ (g)} + HCl \text{ (g)} \rightarrow NH_4Cl \text{ (s)}$$

- **Brønsted–Lowry bases** accept protons from another substance:

$$NH_3 \text{ (aq)} + H_2O \text{ (l)} \rightarrow NH_4^+ \text{ (aq)} + OH^- \text{ (aq)}$$

The Brønsted-Lowry model differs from the Arrhenius model in several aspects:

- Additional substances can be considered acids.

- Reactions can be considered that do not take place in aqueous solutions, as seen in the example of the acid. HCl and NH_3 are gases in this reaction.

- Bases need not always donate OH⁻ ions to increase the concentration of OH⁻ ions.

- Acids and bases need not always be molecular.

NEUTRALIZATION

When an acid and base come together, they **neutralize** one another. This reaction yields water and a salt:

$$\text{Acid} + \text{Base} \rightarrow \text{Water} + \text{Salt}$$
$$HCl + NaOH \rightarrow H_2O + NaCl \text{ (sodium chloride)}$$
$$HNO_3 + KOH \rightarrow H_2O + KNO_3 \text{ (potassium nitrate)}$$

If these solutions were boiled to remove the water, **salts** would remain. Salts taste salty and are electrolytes in aqueous solutions. Strong acids and bases form salts that, when in solution, are neutral.

THE pH SCALE

The pH is a way to indicate the acid or basic nature of a substance. We can also use the terms acidic or alkaline (basic). In particular, pH measures the power of the Hydrogen ion concentration in a solution. The scale for pH ranges in numerical value from 0 to 14. pH is calculated with the following equation:

$$pH = -\log[H^+]$$

A pH of 7 represents neutral solutions. In acidic solutions, the pH is less than seven, and in basic (alkaline) solutions, the pH is greater than 7. The following chart shows a pH scale with some common pH values:

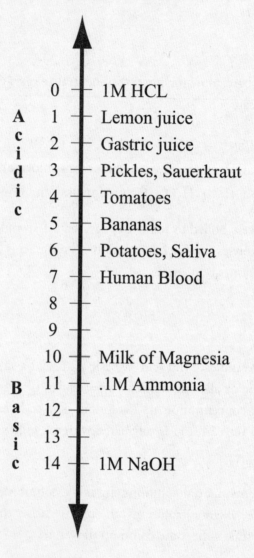

pH Scale and Values

	0	1M HCL
A	1	Lemon juice
c	2	Gastric juice
i	3	Pickles, Sauerkraut
d	4	Tomatoes
i	5	Bananas
c	6	Potatoes, Saliva
	7	Human Blood
	8	
	9	
	10	Milk of Magnesia
B	11	.1M Ammonia
a	12	
s	13	
i	14	1M NaOH
c		

In pure water, concentration of the hydroxyl ion and hydrogen ion are both $1 \cdot 10^{-7}$ molar. Pure water has a pH of 7.

$$[H^+] \times [OH^-] = 1 \cdot 10^{-14}$$

$$[1 \cdot 10^{-7}] \times [1 \cdot 10^{-7}] = 1 \cdot 10^{-14}$$

POP QUIZ

Guess what? You've reached the end of the Chemistry section! After you answer these questions, you have two options:

Option A: Proceed to the Earth Science section.

Option B: Take the section test on chemistry in Chapter 7.

1. A solution with a pH of 4.22 is

   (A) a base.

   (B) an alkaline.

   (C) neutral.

   (D) an acid.

2. A person was admitted to the hospital with a blood pH of 7.10. The normal range for the pH of blood is 7.35–7.45. An intravenous drip is administered in which a reagent is added to the blood to restore the pH to normal. Which one of the following reagents was most likely administered?

   (A) Sodium bicarbonate

   (B) Ammonium chloride

   (C) Water

   (D) Hydrochloric acid

3. In the following equation, identify the Brønsted-Lowry acid:

   $$NH_3 \text{ (aq)} + H_2O \text{ (l)} \rightleftharpoons NH_4^+ \text{ (aq)} + OH^- \text{ (aq)}$$

   (A) NH_3

   (B) H_2O

   (C) OH^-

   (D) NH_4^+

4. What is the pH of a solution with a H^+ concentration of $1 \cdot 10^{-3}$ M?

Answers

1. **The correct answer is (D).** Any pH less than 7 is considered to be in the acidic range.

2. **The correct answer is (A).** The person's blood is slightly lower than normal, thus moving in trend toward more acidity. By adding sodium bicarbonate, NaH_2CO_3, this person's blood can be made more alkaline and brought back to normal.

3. **The correct answer is (B).** By definition, a Brønsted–Lowry acid donates a proton, so the water in the equation fulfills this requirement.

4. $pH = -\log [H^+]$

   $pH = -\log [1.10^{-3} M]$

   $pH = 3$ (acidic)

CHAPTER 5

EARTH SCIENCE

The study of our planet and outer space encompasses many fields of science. Your exit-level exam will test you on several of these fields. Geology covers the composition of the Earth and past and present events (both interior and exterior) that have shaped it. Oceanography employs physics, biology, chemistry, and geology to study ocean-related processes. Meteorology is the study of the atmosphere, weather, and climate. Astronomy is the study of the universe and Earth's role in it.

Geology

Formation and History of the Earth

Outside of the realm of religion, scientists have developed many theories about how the Earth was first created. Today, many physicists believe in the **solar nebular theory**. This suggests that our solar system was born out of a rotating cloud of dust gas that flattened into a disk, rotated clockwise, and then contracted under the influence of gravity. No, you can't try this theory out on your little brother! Rather it is meant to explain how the planets' orbits came to lie in nearly the same plane as they move around the sun. This nebula did not happen all at once. Scientists think it took more than 1 billion years for gravity to cause the Earth's building blocks to settle and contract. Once this occurred, a sorting process called **differentiation** took place in which materials making up the forming proto-planets were sorted by densities. Materials with heavier densities sank to become the core material, and the lighter materials rose to the surface. The outer surface cooled and became the crust.

Based on radiometric evidence, the Earth is estimated to be 4.5 billion years old. Earth's history has been divided into **eras**. Some of these eras you may be familiar with—they have been the topic of some popular movies. Here are the four major geologic eras of Earth's history:

- **Precambrian:** Lasted about 4 billion years; no life on land; life flourished in the ocean, first with bacteria, then sponges, corals, jellyfish, and worms

- **Paleozoic:** From 545 to 245 million years ago; this era defined by the advent, evolution, and extinction of many life forms; life began moving from water to land as land emerged and formed; the first plants and amphibians emerged

- **Mesozoic:** From 245 to 66 million years ago (180 million years in duration); this era spans the Triassic, Jurassic, and Cretaceous periods; each period has unique characteristics, but one unifying element is dinosaurs, which first appeared in the Triassic period but experienced mass extinction by the end of the Cretaceous period

- **Cenozoic:** From 66 million years ago to the present; this is considered the most "modern" era; with massive evolution and processes of natural selection occurring, many distinct species began to form; hominids first began to develop in this era

FOSSILS

Much of what we know about past life forms and eras have been gathered from fossil evidence. **Fossils** represent the remains of living things preserved in layers of ancient rock, or **strata**. Fossils can be petrified when deposited minerals replace the original organism; petrified wood is one example. Other fossils are created when impressions form through compression, leaving a carbonaceous film of an organism. Sometimes an entire plant or organism is preserved, such as when a piece of amber (petrified tree sap) traps an insect.

Fossils provide proof that life forms have existed at different times in Earth's history. Geologists can use the strata samples to determine the age of rock layers. **Absolute dating** determines the age of specific strata through the **half-life** of radioactive elements. The half-life is a specific rate of decay, meaning the time required for 50 percent of a pure sample of a radioactive isotope to decay into other elements. The amount of a particular radioactive isotope in a sample can be measured and used to determine the age of the sample. However, some basic rules are used to establish geologic sequencing of events, including the **Law of Superposition**. This law states that rocks within strata that are closer to the surface of the Earth are younger than those rocks that lie beneath them. This means that layers of sediment that contain similar fossils are probably the same age.

COMPOSITION

Earth is quite rocky, with a diameter of about 12,750 km (7,900 miles) and a density that is 5.52 times greater than water. The Earth consists of several layers: the **crust**, the **mantle**, and the **core**:

- **Crust:** The outermost, thinnest layer; shows greatest degree of variation; the average thickness is 5 to 45 km (3 to 25 miles); composed of rocks enriched with silicon, potassium, and sodium; of the Earth's layers, the crust is the part we see and have contact with

High Stakes: Science

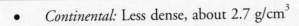
- *Continental:* Less dense, about 2.7 g/cm^3

- *Oceanic:* More dense, about 3.0 g/cm^3

- **Mantle:** The middle layer extends halfway to the Earth's center at a depth of 2,900 km or (1,800 miles); the largest of Earth's layers

  - Composed of silicate enriched with magnesium and iron

  - Density of 3.3 to 5.5 g/cm^3

  - High temperature and pressure cause the rocks in this layer to be fluid

- **Core:** The third innermost layer; diameter is larger than the entire planet of Mars

  - *Outer Core:* Mainly molten and comprised of nickel, iron, and sulfur; 2,270 km thick (1,400 miles); average density of 11.8 g/cm^3

  - *Inner Core:* Solid; comprised of iron and nickel; average density of 16.0 g/cm^3

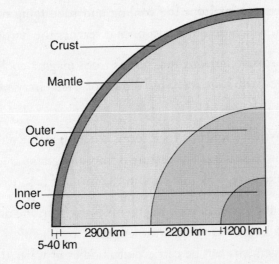

A great way to visualize the layers of the Earth is to think of it as a piece of hard candy covered in chocolate and coated with a candy shell. The hard candy at the center is the core, the chocolate is the liquid mantle, and the thin candy shell is the hard, thin crust.

ROCKS AND MINERALS

Rocks are hard substances comprised of combinations of different minerals.

There are three basic categories of rock: **igneous, sedimentary,** and **metamorphic.** Rocks form from the minerals of the Earth. As the Earth undergoes gradual changes, the rock groups are constantly transformed into one of the other groups in a continuous process called the **rock cycle.**

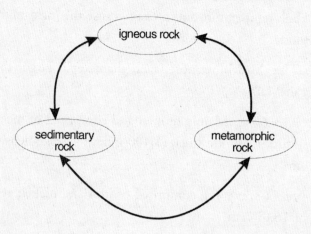

- **Igneous:** Forms from the cooling and solidifying of molten rock or **magma,** which becomes **lava** once it reaches the Earth's surface

  - **Intrusive igneous rock** forms from magma cooling slowly below the Earth's surface. This allows for a larger crystal size. **Granite** is an example.

  - **Extrusive igneous rock** forms when magma cools quickly on the Earth's surface. The texture is fine, and grains are not visible to the naked eye. Volcanic rock in the form of **basalt** is an example.

- **Sedimentary:** Small rock fragments form from the deposition of sediment caused by erosion, weathering, or by chemical processes. These small fragments can be carried into bodies of water (by wind or rain), where they sink to the bottom and deposit in layers.

  - **Clastic rocks** are formed by bits of previously existing rock. The pieces can be small and sand-like or larger pebbles. **Sandstone** is an example.

- **Organic rocks** are formed from previously living life forms.

- **Chemical rocks** are formed from dissolved minerals left from evaporated water. **Limestone** and **chalk** are examples.

- **Metamorphic:** This type of rock also forms from preexisting rock. However, the rocks are subjected to high temperatures and pressure, which chemically changes the original rock into something different. Metamorphic rock can be igneous, sedimentary, or metamorphic. **Marble** is an example.

LAND CHANGE: WEATHERING, SOIL FORMATION

Weathering

The process of weathering encompasses many mechanical and chemical events that slowly disintegrates and decomposes rocks. **Mechanical** events such as freezing water and thawing in the cracks of rocks can cause the rocks to expand and crack. Rocks can also be mechanically worn away by running water and wind. Have you ever been on the beach on a windy afternoon? The wind causes sand to blow around, and it doesn't feel all that great when it whips against your skin. Well, think about the same thing happening to rocks (with perhaps more force and over a longer period of time than an afternoon). The sand particles act as abrasives and wear the rock away over time. Water that flows continuously over rocks can also cause weathering. Rock particles scrape against each other in the flow of water in a lake or river, smoothing one another.

Chemical events, such as man-made pollutants like acid rain (H_2SO_4), can dissolve rocks. Acid rain occurs when pollutants in the atmosphere combine with rainwater and become acidic. The acid compounds that are formed, including sulfuric acid, can be strong enough to weather rocks.

Soil

Soil is created from weathered rocks. There are two main types of soil: **Residual soil** is found on top of the rock from which it formed. **Transported soil** has moved from its rock of origin, so it may not resemble the underlying rock. The undermost layer of rock that soil covers is called **bedrock** (like the name of the Flintstones' town!). Another type of soil, **humus**, is created from dead organisms such as animals and decayed plant matter. This form of soil is very important for plant growth. Several factors affect what type of soil is formed:

- Climate

- The type of rock from which it formed

- The biota of the soil (worms, insects, bacteria, and fungi)

So soil is actually a mixture of weathered rock and organic material. Soil can be damaged and degraded by improper care and misuse by humans.

Land Change: Forces of Erosion and Deposition

Erosion occurs when rocks and soil are moved from place to place and are ultimately deposited. There are several major forces at work here:

- Water

- Wind

- Gravity

- Glaciers

Erosion is a major force that is responsible for the gradually changing landscape of Earth.

Water

Running water produced as run-off by rain flows downhill, carrying particles with it as it moves. When the water moves onto land, it causes erosion by forming gullies. Arid regions that do not have much vegetation to hold down the soil (by roots) or to absorb the water experience even more erosion. The gullies can become deep enough to form streams that cause erosion by abrasion of sediments with rocks. Rapidly moving water can carry a huge amount of sediment, and over time it can completely change a landscape. Hillsides that lack any vegetation show the most pronounced effects of water erosion.

The Grand Canyon was formed over the course of thousands of years as billions of gallons of water flowed through the land and carved out the canyon.

Wind

Wind carries sediments many miles, and the abrasive effects of the sediments can create new sediments. The effect of wind erosion is more dramatic in some places than others.

Gravity

The force of gravity is a constant on Earth—and it plays a role in erosion. Just as we are pulled by gravity, so, too, are land masses. Gravity pulls on rocks and soil, sending them down slopes in an action called **mass wasting**. Rapid mass wasting occurs in the forms of landslides and mudslides. **Landslides** result when earthquakes loosen soil or when rain water pushes rocks down a slope. **Mudslides** occur after heavy rains or when volcanic eruptions cause snow to melt off the top of mountains.

Glaciers

The size of glaciers makes it easy to understand how they can cause erosion. **Glaciers** are like huge ice slugs slowly moving across a landscape and pushing large rocks on a layer of ice and mud. This results in heavy **glacial abrasion**. Glaciers also leave large boulders or foreign articles from different regions behind as they melt and move.

An example of glacial abrasion is Yosemite Valley in California.

Global Change: Plate Tectonics and Land Forms

Plate Tectonics

Approximately 225 million years ago, all of the continents were joined together as one major continent called **Pangea**. This land mass eventually broke up into several smaller land masses that drifted apart until they became today's continents. There are seven continents on the globe today. On a map or globe, they look as though they could fit together, like pieces of a jigsaw puzzle. This and other evidence gave birth to the **continental drift theory**. However, scientists are convinced that the continents are continuing to shift, driven by the interactions between tectonic plates or convection currents.

Plate tectonics theory states that the Earth's crust (both the bottom of the oceans and the continents) is a relatively thin layer that can be visualized as a bowl of soup with crackers floating on top. The soup is rock that flows under heat and pressure in the upper mantle, just beneath the crust. The crackers are the crust. The crust and upper mantle constantly shift against one another. There are about seven major plates and two dozen minor plates that make up the Earth's crust. This theory explains earthquakes, volcanic action, how mountain ranges are formed, and the locations of the continents.

Plates and Movement

The Earth's **lithosphere**, or outer shell, is made of the crust and upper mantle. Within the upper mantle, differences in temperature cause currents to form. Magma heated by the core rises toward the crust, while magma close to the crust cools off and sinks. This cycle causes **convection currents** to form that apply compression and tension forces on the lithosphere that pulls apart or compresses plates.

Faults are areas where two plates meet. The consequences of this can be dramatic and devastating. There are four basic types of movement that can occur between adjacent plates:

- **Convection currents** move molten to the surface, creating a gap that is filled with solidified molten material. **Mid-ocean ridges** were created in this manner.

- Plates can gradually slide past one another in a process called **shearing**. This movement can cause earthquakes. The **San Andreas Fault** is an example of this.

- One plate (the more dense of the two) slides under the less dense plate. This is called **subduction**. As the plate that is sliding under is forced down through the crust, it melts, and periodically it will erupt to the surface. **Mount Saint Helens**, a volcano that erupted in 1980 in Washington State, was induced when one plate off the Pacific Coast slid under the continental plate.

- Two plates can **collide** with one another at faults. This may produce earthquakes, but its more gradual effect is the formation of mountains. The compression forces cause the plates to lift up into mountains. An example of this is the **Himalayas**.

Land Forms

We've discussed some of the forces that can alter the topography of the Earth's surface. Let's review how two of these forces transform the Earth's surface:

- High internal temperatures and pressure create compression and tension forces, which cause the Earth's crust to fold and crumple.

- The forces of erosion smooth things out.

Mountains

- **Folded mountains** develop by the slow compression of sedimentary and/or volcanic rock layers. This results in mountains that are wavelike and look like a carpet that has been pushed together. Examples: the Appalachian, Alps, Himalayans, and Northern Rockies

- **Fault mountains** develop when tensile force is exerted along a crack in the crust. Over time, a mountain is formed, with one side bounded by a normal fault of a medium to high angle. The spreading of the crust segments by tensile force causes cracking, and the crust is lifted up. Example: Sierra Nevada of California

Volcanoes

Volcanoes are formed by igneous activity below the lithosphere. When the hot magma beneath the lithosphere is under great pressure and high temperatures, it erupts to the surface and forms a volcano. When the magma reaches the surface of the lithosphere, it is called **lava**. Not all volcanic activity is the same. Some eruptions are violent, while others are calm. Major volcanic eruptions and earthquakes occur in three major zones of the world where most of the Earth's plates meet.

Earthquakes

Earthquakes are also a result of pressures building up within the Earth. When the crust shifts and moves, vibrations of varying degree are created, causing earthquakes. To put it more technically, the tectonic plates move along boundaries or along faults. The movement can push together, pull apart, or slide the plates. This movement can reduce the tension and compression forces created by convection currents within the upper mantle, and the release results in an earthquake. Earthquakes that occur on the ocean floor are called **tsunami** and can produce waves more than 60 feet high!

If you've forgotten what a fault is, go back to page 202.

Earthquake waves are called **seismic**. They are divided into three types:

- **Primary waves** (P, or longitudinal, waves) are compressed waves that travel very fast, especially through denser materials of a solid, liquid, or gaseous nature. The damage they cause is moderate.

- **Secondary waves** (S, or transversal, waves) are side-to-side waves that travel at speeds slower than P waves. S waves only travel through solids and cause more damage than P waves. We know that the Earth's outer core is molten because these waves are lost in seismograph analysis.

- **Surface waves** (L, or Love and Rayleigh, waves) cause a shifting and shaking in the Earth's crust, both up and down and side to side. L waves are the slowest waves, but they cause the most extensive damage.

POP QUIZ

Great! You've completed the first Earth Sciences section. Let's see how much information you've retained:

1. Once magma reaches the Earth's surface, it is called

   (A) lava.

   (B) molten core.

   (C) a volcano.

   (D) the lithosphere.

2. The plate tectonics theory explains which of the following?

   I. Origin of the universe

   II. The sea floor spreading

   III. The current location of the continents

   (A) Both I and II

   (B) Both II and III

   (C) Both I and III

   (D) Only I

   (E) Only II

   (F) Only III

3. A geologist collects a rock and soil sample. From which layer did he collect these samples?

   (A) Stratosphere

   (B) Lithosphere

   (C) Biosphere

   (D) Hydrosphere

4. Which of the following statements is true?

    (A) The core of the Earth occupies three fourths of its volume.

    (B) The core of the Earth is three times as large as its mass.

    (C) The inner core of the Earth is liquid; the outer core is solid.

    (D) The most common and prevalent element found in the center of Earth's core is iron.

5. The plastic-like region beneath the Earth's crust is the

    (A) inner core of Earth.

    (B) atmosphere.

    (C) mantle.

    (D) plate.

6. Folded mountains develop when

    (A) tectonic plates push together.

    (B) tectonic plates pull apart.

    (C) tectonic plates slide past each other.

    (D) water erosion occurs.

7. Mass wasting includes

    (A) mudslides.

    (B) landslides.

    (C) rockslides.

    (D) all of the above.

8. The change of one rock type into another is known as

    (A) metamorphism.

    (B) the rock cycle.

    (C) petrification.

    (D) sedimentation.

ANSWERS

1. **The correct answer is (A).** Molten rock beneath the Earth's surface is called magma. When this rock flows onto the surface, it becomes a denser substance, lava.

2. **The correct answer is (B).** Plate tectonic theory is used to explain continental drift and the sea floor spreading. There are many theories that attempt to explain the origin of the universe, but this is not one of them.

3. **The correct answer is (B).** Rock and soils are gathered for the surface of the Earth's crust, the lithosphere. The stratosphere is the third level of the atmosphere; the biosphere consists of all the living plants and animals and those in states of decay; the hydrosphere refers to the Earth's waters.

4. **The correct answer is (D).**

5. **The correct answer is (C).** Choice (A) is incorrect because the inner core is solid iron. Choice (B) is incorrect since the atmosphere is above the Earth. Choice (D) is incorrect because plates are part of the lithosphere, Earth's crust.

6. **The correct answer is (A).**

7. **The correct answer is (D).**

8. **The correct answer is (B).** Choice (A) is incorrect; it refers to metamorphic rock, which is produced when high temperatures and pressures cause one rock type to change into another. The rock cycle refers to the gradual change occurring on Earth in which rock types change from one to another.

Oceanography

Most of the pictures we've seen of Earth from outer space look like a big light blue marble. This color comes from the vast amount of water found on our planet. In fact, oceans cover just about 71 percent of the Earth's surface. Oceans represent 97.2 percent of the planet's total water. Globally, the composition of ocean water includes ions such as:

- Chloride
- Sodium
- Sulfate
- Magnesium
- Calcium
- Potassium
- Bicarbonate

The average salinity of ocean water worldwide is 3.5 percent, with sodium chloride (NaCl) the major constituent.

> More than 80 percent of the Southern Hemisphere is comprised of ocean!

Oceans produce currents that have predictable patterns worldwide. These currents develop from global wind patterns and water temperature differences. The currents help control temperatures within the oceans as well as the atmosphere.

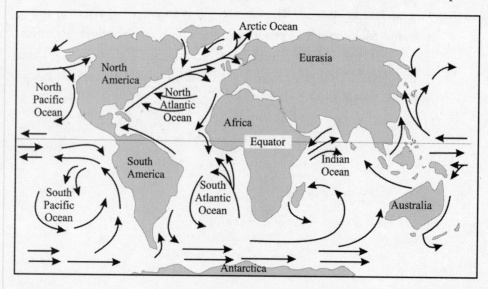

CONTINENTAL MARGINS

Continental margins are areas where the continents meet the oceans. Continental margins are made of continental shelves, which are submerged extensions of the continental crust beneath the oceans. The **continental shelf** projects outward from the coast to a depth of about 100 meters (325 feet). It is thought that the continental shelf may have been dry land at one time when oceans were smaller than their present sizes. The continental shelf gives way to the **continental slope,** which drops steeply to the ocean's bottom. The continental shelf then becomes the **abyssal plain** of the deep ocean floor. The abyssal plain is about 4000–5000 m below sea level. This distance beneath the surface does not make it a hot spot for sea life. In fact, the abyssal plain is like a barren desert. Most sea life and vegetation are clustered closer to shallow shore waters where sunlight is more abundant.

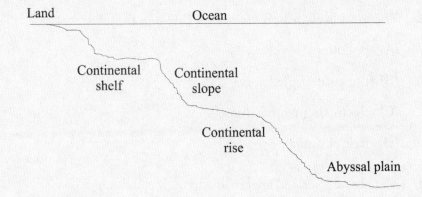

Let's take a look at some common features of the sea floor:

- **Seamounts** are submarine volcanic peaks. Above sea level, they form islands, such as Hawaii.

- **Mid-ocean ridges** are long linear chimneys that rise about 2.5 km (1.5 miles) above the surrounding ocean floor. These ridges represent pronounced seismic and volcanic activity. As the ocean floor spreads apart, new ocean crust is created at mid-ocean ridges.

- **Trenches** are narrow, curved depressions in the ocean floor that can reach depths of more than 11 km (7 miles). They can be found along continental margins, especially in the Pacific Ocean.

HIGH STAKES

Pop Quiz

Hey, another section finished! Try the review questions or check your class notes to clear up any points that didn't quite sink in.

1. The portion of the continental shelf that moves steeply towards the sea floor is

   (A) a trench.

   (B) a plain.

   (C) the continental slope.

   (D) a mid-ocean ridge.

2. The most likely reason life cannot thrive in the abyssal plain is

   (A) pollution.

   (B) presence of predators.

   (C) fluctuating temperatures.

   (D) lack of sunlight.

3. The Hawaiian island are classified as

   (A) trenches.

   (B) seamounts.

   (C) mid-ocean ridges.

   (D) an abyssal plain.

Answers

1. **The correct answer is (C).** As the continental shelf approaches the abyssal plain, it goes through a transition zone called the continental slope.

2. **The correct answer is (D).** Abyssal plains can be 4000–5000 m below sea level, which is too far for sunlight to penetrate and support producers. Since producers are the foundation of any food web, the likelihood of the presence of other life is very slim.

3. **The correct answer is (B).** From the text, the Hawaiian Islands are classified as seamounts.

Meteorology

The Earth's atmosphere not only sustains life, but it also acts as a shield that filters out harmful radiation and small meteors. The atmosphere is dominated by two major gases, nitrogen at 78 percent and oxygen at 21 percent. However, there are trace amounts of other gases in the atmosphere, such as argon.

One of these trace gases is carbon dioxide, CO_2. What this gas lacks in abundance (only about 0.035 percent of the total atmosphere), it makes up for in impact. Carbon dioxide, along with water vapor and methane, make up what are known as **greenhouse gases**, which are naturally occurring parts of the atmosphere. As radiant light from the sun enters our atmosphere, it is changed to heat energy or **infrared waves**. This infrared heat cannot pass out of the atmosphere because greenhouse gases trap it. The resulting global warmth, called the **greenhouse effect**, can effect weather, climate, and the ecosystem. In fact, without these gases, the Earth would be quite colder, about 35 °C (63 °F), making Earth an unsuitable, ice-cold planet.

However, too much of a good thing can greatly affect global temperatures. Pollution from cars, factories, and homes in the form of emissions has increased the amount of carbon dioxide in the atmosphere. Because carbon dioxide traps heat, many scientists believe that there is a direct cause-and-effect relationship between increased carbon dioxide and increased temperatures around the world. This phenomenon is called **global warming**. Current trends indicate that the temperature of the atmosphere is on the rise. This could have a significant impact on humans.

Humans, however, have encouraged the production of greenhouse gases by increased industrialization. Trees and plants absorb the abundant CO_2 during photosynthesis and produce oxygen. But the world's forests are being stripped, which means less plant life and more carbon dioxide production.

Ozone (O_3) depletion has occurred because of human-induced activities. It acts as a natural filter in the stratosphere, protecting life on Earth from overexposure to the Sun's harmful ultraviolet radiation. However, the concentration of the ozone has become compromised by human use of harmful chemicals, and it has become a pollutant in the lower atmosphere. One group of chemicals, chlorofluorocarbons (CFCs), which are used in refrigerants, foam, solvents, and propellants, have caused "holes" or extremely depleted areas to appear in the ozone. Several international treaties have been signed to limit and eliminate the use and production of CFCs.

OUR ATMOSPHERE

When you fly on an airplane and reach the cruising altitude of around 36,000 feet, the atmosphere doesn't appear uniform. If you have a window seat, you can see how the plane flies above the clouds in an area that is clear and blue. Both the air pressure and temperature have dropped at this altitude. The layering of the atmosphere is correlated to systematic changes in temperature and pressure that occur with distance from Earth.

There are four layers to the atmosphere, each of which has the suffix –*sphere* because they encircle the Earth, just like atmo*sphere*. The four layers are the **troposphere, stratosphere, mesosphere**, and **thermosphere**.

Troposphere

The **troposphere** is the lowest layer. It contains about 80 percent of the Earth's atmosphere. From ground level, it extends to an altitude that varies from 8 to 18 km. The troposphere is the main layer of atmospheric circulation. Most of Earth's weather is controlled by air circulation in the lowest portion of the troposphere. Most clouds form and stay in the troposphere. For this reason, planes fly in the uppermost portion of the troposphere to escape fluctuating weather conditions below.

Stratosphere

The **stratosphere** sits above the troposphere and extends about 50 km (30 miles). The temperature of the air remains constant and actually increases with altitude. The stratosphere contains 90 percent of all atmospheric ozone, including the ozone layer.

Mesosphere

The **mesosphere** lies above the stratosphere and is the layer where meteors first start to burn upon entering the atmosphere. The boundary between the mesosphere and stratosphere is called the **stratopause,** and at this point, the temperature once again drops as altitude increases. This change is due to the diminishing effects of the ozone.

Thermosphere

Above the mesosphere, at about 100 km (62 mi), resides the **thermosphere**. The air is thin and highly reactive to incoming solar radiation. Within this layer, temperatures rise again as the air molecules absorb short-wave radiation produced by **solar wind**. Solar wind is a stream of ionized gases blown from the Sun at supersonic velocities. During periods of peak velocity, the temperature in the thermosphere can reach temperatures in the staggering range of 1225 °C (2237 °F). During periods of low solar wind activity, temperatures can fall as low as 225 °C (437 °F). These temperature fluctuations are due to the thin nature of air in the thermosphere—there are few molecules present to absorb and distribute heat. The thermosphere is also called the **ionosphere** due to its electrical properties.

WEATHER

Weather is a description of many atmospheric conditions at any one place in a given timeframe. Energy from the Sun in the form of electromagnetic waves determines weather, climate, and, at times, environmental problems. **Radiant heat or radiation** is the transfer of heat from the sun. The light rays providing heat travel through space and reach Earth. The clouds reflect some of the radiant energy, but much of it enters our atmosphere and warms. As the atmosphere traps this energy, it redistributes it through radiation, conduction, and convection.

- **Radiation** is the transfer of heat energy by the Sun's electromagnetic waves.

- **Conduction** is the direct transfer of energy from a region of higher temperature to one of lower temperature.

- **Convection** is the transfer of heat in a fluid; most of the Sun's energy is transferred in this manner. As Earth is heated, the air around Earth is heated. Warm air rises (less dense) and cool air falls (more dense) closer to Earth. As the cool air comes close to Earth, it is heated and rises. This cycle accounts for much of our weather.

Although the Sun hits the Earth everywhere, the solar energy is stronger in the equator and weaker in the poles. This is because some regions of the globe receive slanted light rays (the poles), while others receive it directly (the equator) due to the tilt of the Earth's axis. So air circulates in an attempt to equalize temperatures. This initiates what we call **weather**.

Air Pressure

The Earth's atmosphere has a mass of five thousand million tons. Most of this lies within 18 km (11 mi) of the planet's surface. Gravity maintains this mass in an envelope surrounding the Earth. The downward push of gravity gives the atmosphere a pressure, or **atmospheric pressure**. As we've seen in other substances, density can affect atmospheric pressure. More dense air exerts greater pressure on Earth's surface than less dense air. Factors such as temperature, water vapor, air masses, and elevation contribute to the total atmospheric pressure. Warm temperatures produce less dense air and lower air pressure. Believe it or not, moist air is less dense than dry air, so moist air has a lower pressure. Also, as altitude increase, air density decreases because there are fewer particles to exert pressure. Barometers are instruments used to measure air pressure and predict weather patterns.

Air Mass

Air masses are large bodies of air with two constant features: temperature and humidity. Air masses develop due to local conditions in their place of origin. For instance, if an air mass develops over the tropics, it is going to warm. If an air mass develops over the poles, it will be cold. What happens if these two air masses meet? When two air masses of different characteristics collide and mix, fluctuating and usually awful weather conditions is the result. This meeting of two air masses is called a **front**. Two major types of fronts can form:

- **Cold fronts** develop when cold air pushes under warmer air, forcing the warmer air up. This causes violent storms.

- **Warm fronts** develop when warm air pushes cold air out.

Other front types include a **stationary front** (when air masses move parallel to one another without mixing) and **occluded fronts** (when a fast-moving cold front overtakes a warm front). When a warm front meets a cold front and nimbostratus clouds form, rainstorms and snowstorms result. When a cold front collides with a warm front, thunderstorms develop. Air masses tend to rise and fall in columns that have low- and high-pressure centers. A column of air mass having low-pressure centers results in a **cyclone**.

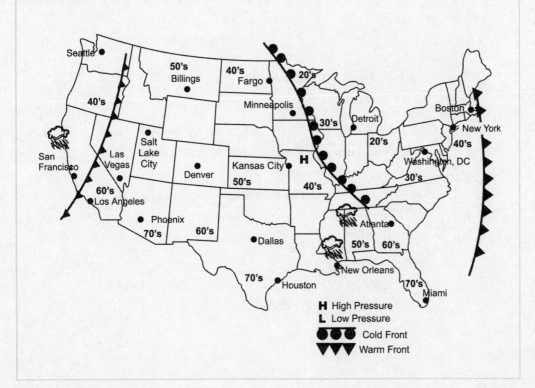

Humidity

We all know humid days are uncomfortable. Muggy, moist, and foggy days can be miserable, and for many people, it makes breathing a real chore. But how does humidity relate to weather? Humidity forms when the Sun's energy warms up a body of water. The resulting water vapor converts to gas upon entering the atmosphere. At any given temperature, the air can only hold a limited amount of moisture. Once the moisture surpasses the limit, the water vapor returns back to Earth in the form of rain or snow.

Humidity is described as **relative humidity**. Relative humidity is the relationship between the air temperature and the amount of water vapor in the air. Water vapor condenses at **dew point.** Dew point signifies the temperature at which vapor condenses and turns to liquid. Cold air cannot hold much water, so it becomes saturated more quickly than warm air. In this manner, water is continuously recycled. Water moves to the atmosphere by evaporation in the form of water vapor. If the air is warmer, it rises through the atmosphere, where it is cooled. Condensation occurs when this cooled air is saturated and the water vapor condenses into water droplets or ice particles. Under favored atmospheric conditions, the droplets or ice return to Earth's surface as precipitation. All of this can be summed up with a diagram of a water cycle:

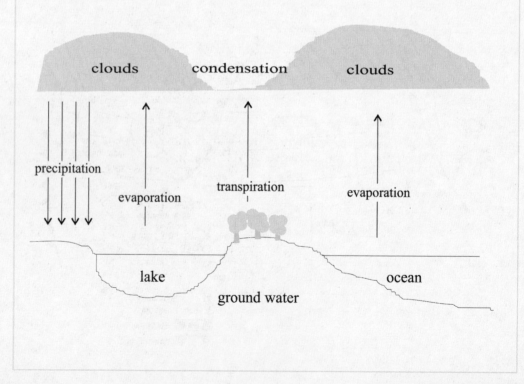

Cloud Formation

Clouds form when warm air rises and cools down. This cool air then condenses, forming water vapor that turns into cloud formations. They represent evidence of colliding air masses. Certain clouds are associated with weather fronts and can be used to assess the movement of these fronts:

- **Cirrus** clouds are wispy and are composed mainly of ice crystals.

- **Cumulus** clouds are puffy and may indicate unstable weather conditions.

- **Stratus** clouds are relatively flat and occur in moist, stable air; these clouds are composed of water droplets.

The suffix *–nimbus* is added to describe a certain type of storm cloud. For instance, cumulonimbus clouds are thunderclouds that can indicate violent thunderstorms.

Wind

Winds illustrate variations in atmospheric pressure. A pressure gradient generates wind. For example, if you've walked into the mall on a hot summer day, the rush of air or wind you experience when you open the door is caused by the pressure differences between the air-conditioned mall and the atmospheric air pressure outside.

The two basic wind types, **local** and **global** winds, follow patterns based on differences in air pressure. High-pressure regions evolve when cooler air moves toward the surface and spreads outward. Low-pressure regions are created when the warmed air rises up toward the troposphere. **Local winds** move over shorter distances, such as a sea breeze blowing on to shore. **Global winds** are a result of solar energy and move over longer distances. As we've established, air is warmer at the equator than the poles. As the air above the equator rises, the cooler air from the poles will replace it. In this way, a cycle of air currents is created where the cool air from the poles moves to the warm equator. However, the tilt of Earth's axis produces circulations of air north of the equator that curve toward the east and air south of the equator that curves to the west. The **doldrums** refer to calm areas generated by bands of low pressure around the equator.

Climate

Typically it requires at least thirty years for a general weather pattern to be established in a geographical area. During this time, trends in temperature and precipitation are noted. This is what is called **climate**. Depending on where you live, seasonal changes are illustrated in different ways and are used to describe **climate belts.** Climates in different parts of the world vary greatly:

- Regions closer to the equator experience continuous warmth and high rainfall and are virtually seasonless.

- Regions above and below the equator become more seasonal, with warm to hot summers and cool to cold winters.

- As the poles are approached, winters become increasingly longer, until a perpetual state of winter exists at the poles.

Elevation also affects the climate. It is not uncommon to see a number of beautiful snow-capped mountains in regions near the equator. The higher the mountain is elevated, the more likely its peak will be subjected to thin air, which does not hold heat well. This results in low temperatures at higher elevations in temperate zones.

Regions near the ocean have climates that are affected by the ocean's current. The temperature of the water that an ocean carries, warm or cold, can affect the temperature of the air above the water. If a body of water is warm, the air above it will be warm. This warm air raises land temperatures near the body of water. It's interesting to notice that two land regions with the same altitude and latitude can have different climates as a result of water. On average, land near water (coastal regions) experience more moderate temperatures than inland regions. Global air circulation can affect climate, as previously mentioned in reference to winds.

Pop Quiz

Yes! You've reached the end of another section.

1. The most prevalent gas in the atmosphere is
   (A) nitrogen.
   (B) oxygen.
   (C) carbon dioxide.
   (D) hydrogen.

2. The relationship between the air temperature and the amount of water vapor in the air is
   (A) relative humidity.
   (B) absolute humidity.
   (C) air mass.
   (D) air temperature.

3. Which of the following factor does not represent a feature of weather?
   (A) Temperature
   (B) Wind direction
   (C) Ozone concentration
   (D) Precipitation

4. All of the following are greenhouse gases EXCEPT
   (A) water vapor.
   (B) carbon dioxide.
   (C) methane.
   (D) sulfur dioxide.

5. The appearance of cumulonimbus clouds could predict

(A) a warm front resulting in a thunderstorm.

(B) a cold front resulting in a thunderstorm.

(C) a cyclone.

(D) the doldrums.

6. Which of the following statements is true?

(A) Storm clouds have a high holding capacity for water vapor.

(B) Air at lower latitudes tends to cool and fall downward, creating heavy precipitation.

(C) Rapidly cooling air loses its holding capacity to retain water vapor, resulting in thunderstorms.

(D) Lightening always accompanies rainfall.

ANSWERS

1. **The correct answer is (A).** Nitrogen is the most abundant gas in our atmosphere, with oxygen coming in second. Carbon dioxide and hydrogen are trace gases.

2. **The correct answer is (A).** Relative humidity refers to the amount of water in the air in comparison with the amount it can hold.

3. **The correct answer is (C).** Choices (A), (B), and (D) are all factors of weather. Ozone is a layer of the atmosphere.

4. **The correct answer is (D).** Choices (A), (B), and (C) are greenhouse gases. Sulfur dioxide is produced when pollution in the atmosphere mixes with rainwater. This causes acid rain.

5. **The correct answer is (B).** Cumulonimbus clouds result from cold air that pushes under warmer air, forcing the warmer air up. As the warmer air rises, it expands and cools due to falling temperatures. Provided the temperature is low enough and there is adequate moisture, clouds form. If these processes occur very rapidly, cumulonimbus clouds result, which usually indicate a thunderstorm.

6. **The correct answer is (C).** See the answer to question 5, above.

SCIENCE

Astronomy

Through centuries of scientific investigation, humans have tried to understand how our universe came to be. Other questions, such as the order to the universe and the quest to find life forms similar to ourselves, soon followed. With the accumulated information we have now, we know that planet Earth belongs to a solar system made of nine planets that orbit a star, the Sun. However, our solar system represents just one system, in one galaxy, the Milky Way. The universe contains billions of galaxies, and each galaxy has millions of stars. The study of space and the prospect of discovering new galaxies, new planets, and perhaps extraterrestrial life have led to advances in space science that years ago were thought to be "science fiction."

The early Greeks realized that the sky contained different celestial objects. They called these objects "planets" after the Greek word for wanderer. It appeared to them that these planets moved across the sky in relation to stars such as Polaris (north star), which seemed to be fixed. These early Greek investigators thought that the Earth remained stationary while the heavens rotated around it. This became formalized into the **geocentric theory** (earth centered). This theory remained until the 1543, when Polish astronomer **Nicolaus Copernicus** challenged this theory. Copernicus stated that all planets, including Earth, traveled in regular, circular paths called **orbits** around the Sun. This theory became known as the **Copernican** or **heliocentric** theory. A German astronomer, **Johannes Kepler**, modified this theory by asserting that planets moved in oval-shaped elliptical orbits.

In 1609, Italian scientist **Galileo Galilei** made several significant discoveries with the telescope. He discovered four of Jupiter's sixteen moons and demonstrated for the first time that not all bodies revolve around Earth. Galileo also discovered the changing illuminations, or phases, of Venus. This discovery was consistent with the proposed orbital motion around the Sun as stated in the heliocentric theory. Galileo supported this theory so strongly, in fact, that in 1616, the Catholic Church dismissed his work because it did not support the Church's dogma that man was at the center of the universe. Late in life, Galileo was placed under house arrest and forced to renounce his work.

SPACESHIP EARTH

Earth exhibits two kinds of movement:

- **Rotation** describes the spinning action of Earth on its axis, an imaginary line extending from pole to pole. The Earth rotates once every 24-hour period. This produces daily cycles of daylight and night. Day and night exist because only half the planet can face the Sun at any one time. When the side of the Earth facing the Sun is illuminated, the other side experiences darkness.

- **Revolution** is the movement of Earth around the Sun. It takes Earth about 365 days to complete one revolution around the Sun at a distance of 150 million km (93 million miles). This orbit is in an elliptical pattern. Planets closer to the Sun take less time to revolve around it than planets further away. For example, Mercury takes only 88 "Earth days" to orbit the Sun and Jupiter takes about 12 "Earth years" to orbit the Sun.

Term	Definition	Diagram
rotation	the spinning of a body on its axis, like a top	axis
revolution	the movement of a body around another body	earth sun

With all this spinning, you may be wondering what keeps planets in their orbits and not flying off into space. The answer is **gravity**. The Sun's gravitational pull keeps the planets within their orbital paths and keeps us firmly on the Earth.

Tilt

Ever wonder why we experience seasonal variations? This is mainly due to rotational tilt. The rotation of the Earth around the sun does not occur in perfect vertical axes because the Earth's axis is not perpendicular to the elliptical orbit it makes around the Sun. The Earth's axis is inclined at a tilt of about 23° from the perpendicular. This tilt causes some parts of Earth to receive more sunlight and other parts to receive less. This accounts for the different seasons.

The Moon

The moon is a natural satellite that orbits the Earth. All of the planets in our solar system have satellites, except Mercury and Venus. The moon is about 384,400 km (238,300 miles) from Earth. It orbits Earth once every 28 days. The gravity on the Moon is about 1/6 that of Earth. The Moon completes one rotation each time it revolves once around the Earth. This means we only see one side of the Moon from Earth. The "dark side" of the moon always faces into space.

> The gravity on the moon accounts for the popular 80's dance, the "moonwalk," which imitated how astronauts walk on the moon.

The Moon does not emit its own light—it reflects light from the Sun. As the Moon orbits, it goes through several phases because it passes in and out of Earth's shadow; this affects the reflection we see at night. On nights when the Moon is completely in Earth's shadow, the side of the Moon facing the planet is completely dark. This is called a **new moon**.

As the Moon moves out of Earth's shadow, more and more of it becomes visible as a crescent shape. This process is called **waxing**. Once the entire Moon is visible again, it is known as a **full moon**. After this, the Moon continues its revolutions, and during the second half of the month, we again begin to see less and less of it, or it **wanes**. Once it is hidden again, the cycle renews with the new Moon.

Eclipse

There are two types of eclipses:

- A **solar eclipse** occurs when the Moon is positioned between the Sun and the Earth.

- A **lunar eclipse** occurs when the Earth is positioned between the Sun and the Moon and the Earth's shadow is cast upon the Moon.

THE SOLAR SYSTEM

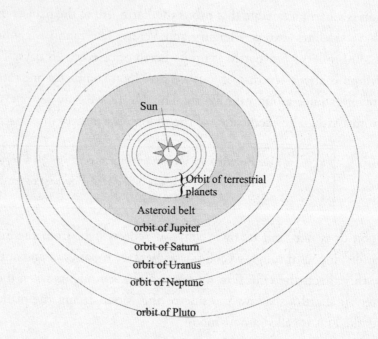

There are nine planets in our Solar System. Moving away from the Sun, they are:

- Mercury
- Venus
- Earth
- Mars
- Jupiter
- Saturn
- Uranus
- Neptune
- Pluto

The planets can be divided into two categories based on physical characteristics. The **terrestrial planets** include Mercury, Venus, Earth, and Mars. They share rock materials in common with Earth (hence the name "terrestrial"). The **Jovian** (Jupiterlike) planets are Jupiter, Saturn, Uranus, and Neptune. They are made mostly of gases such as hydrogen, helium, and methane. Due to its position on the edge of our universe and its small size, Pluto is difficult to categorize as a planet. Some scientists wonder if Pluto is really even a planet. Generally speaking, planets vary in characteristics because of their size and distance from the Sun.

The terrestrial planets are much smaller than the Jovian planets. Terrestrial planets also have high densities and consist mainly of a solid mineral crust with metals, with some gases and ice. The Jovian planets have lower densities and consist mainly of gaseous emission and varying degrees of ice. Because the Jovian planets are composed mainly of gases, their densities are extremely low compared to terrestrial planets. Terrestrial planets have thinner atmospheres. Gravity is also another area in which the two types of planets differ. Terrestrial planets have weaker gravitational fields than Jovian planets, which accounts for their lighter atmospheres.

THE SUN AND STARS

The Sun is at the center of our solar system. The glowing orb that we see during the day is the result of fusion gases burning at temperatures reaching 14 million K at the Sun's core (15 million degrees Celsius). The core is the Sun's hottest region. The Sun appears quite large to us, but when it is compared to other stars, it is actually a medium-sized star. Its relative closeness to Earth (if you want to call 93 millions miles close) makes it seem larger. In our solar system, however, the Sun is the largest body—about 1 million times larger than Earth! The Sun is 90 percent hydrogen and 10 percent helium, with trace amounts of metals. The energy the Sun generates is produced by nuclear fusion, a reaction that takes four hydrogen nuclei and converts them into one helium nucleus. This reaction produces a staggering amount of energy.

It is hard to imagine the distance of stars from Earth as we gaze into the night sky. The Sun is the closest star to Earth, with the next closest star being light years away. It is believed that all stars have properties similar to the Sun, which can be measured and analyzed to distinguish one star type from another:

- Stellar brightness (magnitude)

- Color

- Mass

- Temperature

- Size

The relationship of temperature, color, and magnitude is summarized in the **Hertzsprung-Russel** (H-R) diagram. Stars are plotted by their luminosity and temperature on this diagram.

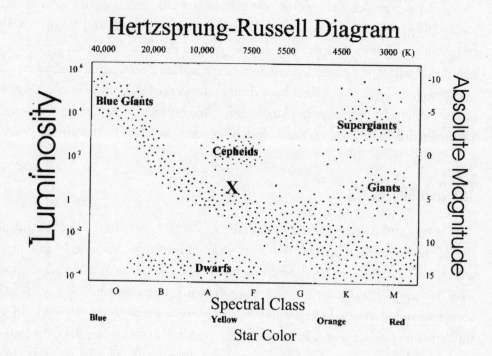

The brightest stars are also the hottest in the main sequence. Those that are less bright are cooler. Most stars follow this relationship and are classified as **main sequence**. In this H-R diagram, the stars that are main sequence appear from the upper left to the lower right. Earth's sun is a yellow main sequence star and is marked by X on the diagram, showing its relative location. Let's classify some of the other stars seen on the H-R diagram by looking at a brief life cycle of stars.

Life Cycle of Stars

Using the main sequence trend, stars that plot in the upper right are **giants**. Stars that plot in the lower left are red or white **dwarf** neutron stars. The life of a star is sustained by the thermonuclear reactions in its core. The energy produced by these reactions prevents gravitational collapse of the core onto its own center. However, as a star increases in age, the nuclear fuel of the core runs low, and the star is no longer able to maintain its size. Let's use a mid-sized star as an example to illustrate what happens when a star begins to "fade." As a star depletes its hydrogen energy, it can enter one of three paths depending on its stellar mass:

1. Low-mass red main sequence stars continue to burn until all fuel is used. They then collapse into hot **white dwarfs**.

2. Medium-mass yellow stars temporarily expand into **red giants** as their gravitational energy is converted to heat. Once the red giant has exhausted its remaining energy, it will also shrink into a white dwarf. Sometimes the gas released as a red giant collapses creates a glowing sphere of gas called a **planetary nebula.**

3. Stars whose masses are three time larger than the Sun are called **blue giants.** The collapse of these massive stars releases a tremendous amount of energy. This creates a rapid expansion as the star becomes a **super-giant**, and it dies in a spectacular explosion known as a **supernova.**

Pop Quiz

You are done with the Earth Sciences review! Go on and knock out these review questions and then proceed to Physics.

1. Arrange the following main sequence stars in order.

  I.   White main-sequence

  II. Yellow main-sequence

  III. Red main sequence

  (A) I, II, III

  (B) II, I, III

  (C) I, III, II

  (D) III, II, I

  (E) II, III, I

2. Imagine you took a space exhibition to Jupiter and then traveled back to Earth. On which planet would you weigh more?

   (A) You would weigh more on Earth.

   (B) You would weigh more on Jupiter.

   (C) You weigh the same on both Earth and Jupiter.

   (D) You are more massive on Jupiter.

3. The seasons on Earth are due to

   (A) the rotation of Earth.

   (B) tectonic plates.

   (C) the tilt of Earth's axis.

   (D) a high-pressure atmosphere.

4. The Moon doesn't actually shine on its own. It _____ light from the _____.

   (A) reflects; Sun

   (B) reflects; Earth

   (C) refracts; Sun

   (D) polarizes; atmosphere

5. The heliocentric theory was first established by

   (A) Ptolemy.

   (B) Galileo.

   (C) Kepler.

   (D) Copernicus.

6. The Earth rotates _____ every 24 hours.

   (A) four times

   (B) once

   (C) two times

   (D) three times

ANSWERS

1. **The correct answer is** (E). As mid-sized stars "die," they move from a yellow color to a red dwarf and culminate as a white dwarf.

2. **The correct answer is** (B). Remember that weight is a measure of the force of gravity. More massive objects exert more gravitational force. Jupiter is more massive than Earth, so you would weigh more on Jupiter than Earth. Choice (D) is incorrect because weight changes on different planets, but mass does not.

3. **The correct answer is** (C). Choices (B) and (D) have no effect on seasons, and choice (A) does not describe season formation. Without the tilt on the axis, there would be relatively little seasonal variation.

4. **The correct answer is** (A).

5. **The correct answer is** (D). Choices (B) and (C) refer to later investigators who embellished on the original theory put forth by Copernicus. Choice (A) refers to the originator of the geocentric theory.

6. **The correct answer is** (B).

CHAPTER 6

PHYSICS

Physics deals with the fundamental laws of the universe. It is closely related to the other subjects we have reviewed in this book. The living systems of biology are made up of fundamental particles that follow the same laws as the laws of physics. Chemistry explores how atoms interact to form molecules. Geology studies the Earth's physics, while astronomy deals with the physics of the stars and outer space. Physics explores properties such as temperature, pressure, and motion and can be used to describe any process involving energy and matter.

Motion, Energy, and Work

Review the rotation of the Earth on page 222.

Our universe is filled with objects in motion. Cars speeding down the highway, kids running to catch their school bus, and soaring birds. Even the Earth rotates. Motion is an integral part of our life on Earth, and it is described in terms of speed, velocity, and acceleration.

Motion	Approximate Speed
Automobile on a highway	55 to 65 mph
Race car	160 to 220 mph
Person walking	3 to 5 mph
Person running	8 to 15 mph
Airplane	400 to 500 mph
Earth's revolution	66,500 mph

Average speed is $\text{Velocity} = \dfrac{\text{Distance}}{\text{Time}}$. If you walk a distance of 50 miles in 10 hours, your speed would be 5 miles per hour. The units for speed are expressed in many ways:

- mph (miles per hour)
- km/h (kilometers per hour)
- cm/s (centimeters per second)
- ft/s (feet per second)
- m/s (meters per second)

Instantaneous speed is the speed at any one instant. The speedometer of a car measures instantaneous speed, which helps you stay within the speed limit when driving. A pedometer is useful when running or walking to determine how many miles you've covered as you move at a particular speed.

Velocity is speed in a given direction. In the previous example, when you traveled 5 miles per hour, no consideration was given to the direction in which you were walking. You know your speed, but the velocity is unknown. Velocity can change if either speed or direction changes. So if you were to walk 5 miles per hour east, then your velocity is given as 5 miles per hour east. To find velocity, we use the same units as speed.

Acceleration, (a), is the rate at which velocity changes. Acceleration is found by dividing the change in velocity by the change in time:

$$a = \frac{\Delta V}{\Delta t}$$

The units for acceleration include:

- mph/s
- cm/s^2
- ft/s^2
- m/s^2

Momentum

Momentum is based on mass and velocity. To change the momentum of an object, a force is required. The product of the force and time is called the impulse. Impulse causes a change in momentum. The law of conservation of momentum states that the momentum before collision is equal to the momentum after collision in a closed system. Here are some examples:

A 110-kg football player runs at 4 m/sec. What is the momentum?

Momentum = mass × velocity

(110 kg)(4 m/sec) = 440 kg m/sec

A car of 1000 kg is moving at 20 m/sec. What breaking force is needed to stop the car in 10 seconds?

(Force)(time) = (mass)(velocity)

(F)(10 sec) = (1000 kg)(20 m/sec)

F= 2000 N

Free-fall

Objects in motion under the influence of gravity are in **free-fall**. Objects released from rest, thrown upward or downward, are in free-fall once released. All objects in a near-vacuum fall at the same rate of 9.8 m/sec^2. In 1971, astronaut David Scott proved on the moon that regardless of the mass, objects fall at the same rate.

An astronaut drops an object from 1.2 m above the surface of the moon. The acceleration of gravity is 1.6 m/sec^2. How long does it take the object to hit the ground?

$d = \frac{1}{2}gt^2$

$1.2m - \frac{1}{2}(1.6 \text{ m/sec})(t^2)$

$t = 1.2$ seconds

The graphs below illustrate how motion can be shown graphically. The graph on the left shows a person walking at a constant rate from 5 m. The graph on the right shows a person walking at a constant rate:

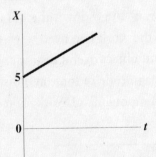
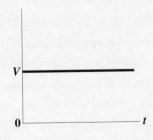

Energy and Work

Energy

Motion does not occur in a vacuum. It not only changes over time, but it also requires **energy**, or the ability to do work. There are two major types of energy, both of which are scalar quantities:

- **Potential energy** is stored energy. Imagine that you are on a skateboard at the top of the hill. You and the skateboard have potential energy (the potential to move down the hill). The formula for potential energy is **PE** = *mgh*, where *m* equals mass, *g* equals gravity, and *h* equals height.

- **Kinetic energy** is the energy of motion. Its formula is $KE = \frac{1}{2}mv^2$, where *m* equals mass and *v* equals velocity. This formula relates both mass and velocity to kinetic energy. So if you and your little sister both skateboard down the hill, you, with more mass, will have more kinetic energy. However, if your little sister moves at a faster rate (increased velocity), her kinetic energy will be greater.

Work

Let's stick with the skateboard and the hill. When you descend the hill, you experience the most acceleration at the initial decline. If you want to stop, you have to physically move the skateboard in such a way as to break the momentum, and you use your feet to slow yourself down. If you want to go down the hill again, you have to walk back up it. This action provides the work you need to go down the hill again. **Work** is the applied force to move an object over a distance. Work is a scalar quantity defined as the product of the magnitude of force and distance: W = Force × Distance. When you separate the components of work, Force and Distance, you have potential energy.

Pushing your lawn mower across the lawn, lifting a pile of books into your locker, or pulling open the refrigerator door are all examples of work.

For work to take place, a force must be applied that causes an object to move. In some instances, you can exert a force, but no work is done on the object. For example, pushing on a stationary wall results in no work because the wall doesn't move.

The SI unit of work is defined as the *newton-meter* (N.m), although most scientists prefer to use the unit **joule** (j) when referring to the newton-meter. Work and energy are measured in joules. The rate at which work is done is called **power**. The unit for power is the watt, W. One watt is equal to 1 J/s.

$$\text{Power} = \frac{\text{Work}}{\text{Time}}$$

THE LAW OF CONSERVATION OF ENERGY

Potential energy can be transferred to kinetic energy. When you and your sister were on your skateboards, you had potential energy as you stood at the top of the hill. Moving down the hill, you converted your potential energy to kinetic energy. At the bottom of the hill (provided you didn't wipe out), you stopped and reached maximum kinetic energy. The **Law of Conservation of Energy** can be applied here. This law states that energy cannot be created or destroyed but rather it can be changed into different forms. So as you and your sister descended the hill, no energy was lost or gained, it just changed forms. These forms include light, heat, chemical, mechanical, and electrical.

POP QUIZ

That was pretty easy, huh? Let's take a Pop Quiz and see what you know.

1. A hang-glider at the edge of a cliff has

    (A) kinetic energy.

    (B) potential energy.

    (C) neither potential nor kinetic energy.

    (D) more kinetic than potential energy.

2. A car is accelerating from 0 to 60 mph in 10 seconds. What is the acceleration?

    (A) 60 mph

    (B) 10 mph

    (C) 6 mph

    (D) 6 mph/s

For Questions 3 and 4, refer to the following graph.

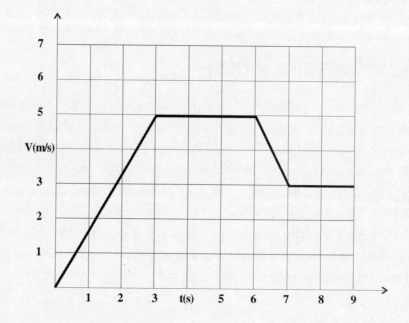

This graph shows a track team member running along a straight track. The velocity as a function of time is illustrated for the first 9 seconds for the runner.

3. What is the runner's velocity at 8 seconds?

    (A) 3 m/s

    (B) 5 m/s

    (C) 2 m/s

    (D) 4 m/s

4. What is the instantaneous velocity of the runner at 3 s?

(A) 2 m/s

(B) 3 m/s

(C) 5 m/s

(D) 4 m/s

Answers

1. **The correct answer is (B).** At the edge of the cliff, the hang-glider has stored potential energy but is not actually moving yet, so no kinetic energy can be seen.

2. **The correct answer is (D).** Acceleration $= \dfrac{\Delta V}{\Delta t} = \dfrac{60 \text{ mph}}{10 \text{ s}} = 6$ mph/s

3. **The correct answer is (A).** This information is taken from the graph.

4. **The correct answer is (C).** This information is taken from the graph.

Force and Laws of Motion

> Force occurs when you lift a can of soda to your mouth, when you slam a door shut, or when you push the wheels of your inline skates against the ground to gain momentum.

A **force** is needed to cause an object to accelerate or decelerate. If your dog is pulling on one end of a rope, you are pulling on the other end, and you are both pulling with the same force but in opposite directions, the **net force** is zero. No motion occurs. Motion only occurs when there is a net force, which means either you or your dog will have to exert a greater force than the other for the rope. The force of gravity causes objects to fall; in fact, force is a part of our daily lives. Force can be described as a push or pull that starts, stops, or changes the direction in which an object may be travelling. It is measured in Newtons.

Sir Isaac Newton, a seventeenth-century English physicist, discovered some fundamental rules concerning movement—reportedly as a result of having an apple fall on his head while lounging under a tree. Don't worry! You won't need to be hit on the head with an apple to understand **Newton's Three Laws of Motion**.

1. **Newton's First Law of Motion** states that objects at rest and objects in uniform motion will remain at rest or in uniform motion unless acted on by an outside force. **Inertia** is the tendency for an object to remain in rest or motion. So this first law is also known as the **Law of Inertia**. Mass is the quantitative measure of inertia of an object.

2. **Newton's Second Law of Motion** states that the net force acting on an object is equal to its mass times its acceleration, or **F = ma**. This is also called the **Law of Force**. The **F** and **a** are vectors with magnitude (size) and direction. The mass, or **m**, is a scalar quantity with no direction, only magnitude.

   • Weight (W) is not to be confused with mass. It is the force of gravity acting on mass, or W = mg where g is the acceleration due to gravity, and a constant, 9.8 m/s^2. Weight is also a vector quantity.

   • The unit of force is known as a **newton**. It is defined as 1 kg m/s^2.

3. **Newton's Third Law of Motion** states that when one object subjects a force on a second object, the second object exerts an equal force on the first in an opposing direction. This is also called the **Law of Action and Reaction**. An example is a tennis ball hitting a tennis racket. The ball is forced forward while in contact with the racket, while the ball exerts a backward force on the racket.

Friction

Friction is a unique type of force. It resists motion of an object due to surface rubbing. Friction always works in the opposite direction of motion and occurs whenever surfaces move past each other. When you rub your hands together, they warm up as a result of friction.

POP QUIZ

Another section down! On to the Quiz!

1. What force (in newtons) must a baseball bat exert on a baseball of a mass 0.143 kg to give it an acceleration of 8,500 meters per second squared? *Neglect the weight of the ball.*

   (A) 59,441 N

   (B) 1.68×10^{-5} N

   (C) 1215.5 N

   (D) 1.4 N

2. What is the weight in newtons of a 2.5 kg bag of sugar?

   (A) 24.5 N

   (B) 49 N

   (C) .51 N

   (D) 1.96 N

3. The Law of Inertia is also known as

   (A) Newton's Second Law of Motion.

   (B) Newton's Third Law of Motion.

   (C) the Law of Action and Reaction.

   (D) Newton's First Law of Motion.

Answers

1. The correct answer is (C). Use the equation F = ma: (0.143 kg) (8500 m/s^2) = 1215.5 N

2. The correct answer is (A). Applying Newton's second law, use the equation w = mg:

   w = (2.5 kg) (9.8 m/s^2) = 24.5 N

3. The correct answer is (D). If you answered this incorrectly, go back to the laws of motion.

Heat It Up!

Heat represents the energy that flows when a body of higher temperature interacts with a body of lower temperature until thermal equilibrium is reached. Heat can also be used to do work. Heat energy is produced by the vibration or movement of molecules. More vibrations equal more heat. It is determined by the mass of substance, specific heat, and change in temperature. To raise the temperature of a system, we heat it. The unit of heat is the **calorie**, and it is defined as the amount of heat required to increase the temperature of 1 gram of water by 1° Celsius. Another calorie, the food calorie, is defined as 1,000 calories. The standard unit of measurement of heat is the joule: one calorie equals 4.186 J.

Heat can be transferred in three ways:

1. **Conduction**—The transfer of heat by a solid material

2. **Convection**—The transfer of heat from hot to cold through a fluid medium (liquid or gas)

3. **Radiation**—The transfer of heat by electromagnetic waves (microwaves use radiant energy to cook your food; sunbathers use the Sun's infrared energy to tan themselves)

The study of heat transfer is called **thermodynamics**. There are two very important laws derived from thermodynamics:

- **The First Law of Thermodynamics:** Heat energy cannot be created or destroyed, it just changes form. If you mixed two glasses of water of unequal temperatures together, the cooler body becomes warmer and the warmer body becomes cooler. It is also called the Law of Conservation of Energy.

- **The Second Law of Thermodynamics:** As energy is transferred, some is converted to thermal energy, and its availability to do work is lost. The heat generated from a car engine due to friction of rubbing parts and any dissipated heat is not available to power the engine itself. This is called entropy.

Specific Heat

Not all substances absorb heat in the same way because their properties differ. The amount of heat needed to heat 1 kg of lead, iron, or aluminum will vary. **Specific heat** is defined as the amount of heat required to raise the temperature of 1 g of a substance 1°C. The specific heat of water is 1 calorie per gram. The specific heat of iron is .11. So 1 gram of iron would require .11 calories to increase in temperature by 1°C. The specific heat of water is higher than that of iron, so if the same amount of heat is applied to equal quantities of water and iron, the iron will feel hotter.

Heat = (mass)(specific heat)(change in temperature)

Latent Heat of Fusion and Vaporization

The latent heats of fusion and vaporization are applied in converting a solid to a liquid to a gaseous state. When heat is added or removed, a phase change occurs but the temperature does not change.

Latent heat of fusion for water = 3.34×10^5 J/kg

Latent heat of vaporization for water = 2.26×10^6 J/kg

High Stakes: Science

POP QUIZ

It's quiz time again.

1. A steel spoon and a silver spoon are put in a cup of coffee at the same time. The silver spoon rapidly approaches the temperature of the coffee, while the iron spoon only changes its temperature slightly. How does this relate to specific heat?

    (A) The silver spoon has a lower specific heat.

    (B) The iron spoon has a lower specific heat.

    (C) The silver spoon has a higher specific heat.

    (D) There is no net difference in specific heats.

2. Heat transfer occurs from regions of

    (A) cold to hot.

    (B) hot to cold.

    (C) hot to hot and cold to cold.

    (D) Heat does not transfer.

3. Energy transferred from your body and clothes to the surrounding air is an example of

    (A) radiation.

    (B) conduction.

    (C) ventilation.

    (D) convection.

4. Calculate the heat (energy) needed to raise the temperature of 50 g of water from 4.5°C to 8.3°C.

5. A 100 kg mass of an element at 100°C is placed in .200 kg of water at 20°C. The mixture reaches equilibrium at 21.6°C. Calculate the specific heat of the element. (Heat loss = Heat gain)

Answers

1. **The correct answer is (A).** The silver spoon has a lower specific heat, so it takes fewer calories to raise its temperature than the steel spoon that has a higher specific heat.

2. **The correct answer is (B).** This reflects the Second Law of Thermodynamics.

3. **The correct answer is (D).** Air currents can carry heat produced by the body into the surrounding air.

4. Heat = (mass)(specific heat)(change in temp.)

   = (50 g)(4.18 J/gC°)(8.3 − 4.5°C)

   = 794.2 J

5. Heat loss = Heat gain

   (mass)(spec. heat)(change in temp.) = (mass)(spec. heat)(change in temp.)
   (.100 kg)(x)(100 − 21.6°C) = (.200 kg)(4180 J/kgC°)(21.6 − 20°C)
   Specific heat = 171 J/kgC°

Waves, Magnetism, and Electricity

Waves

The word wave may get you thinking of water or the ocean, and you wouldn't be far off track. Waves occur not only in water but also in light and sound. Think of a **wave** as a displacement or disturbance occurring in all states of matter. Waves also have some specific characteristics. See the diagram below for the important parts of a wave.

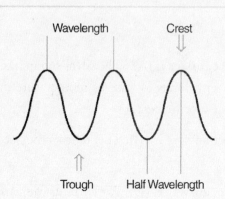

Referring to the diagram, the **crest** of a wave is at the top, and the **trough** of the wave is at the bottom. The **wavelength** is the distance between consecutive crests. The number of crests passing a certain point per unit time is the **frequency** of a wave. The higher the frequency, the shorter the wavelength. Wavelength is measured in meters, frequency in hertz.

Light Waves

Light also travels in waves. The variations of colors we see are a result of different frequency ranges of light. Humans can see color only within a particular range called the **visible spectrum**. The visible spectrum range for humans ranges from low-frequency waves like red to high-frequency waves like violet. Electromagnetic waves are part of the eletromagnetic spectrum. They vary in wavelength and frequency, but in a vacuum they all travel at the speed of light, which is $3 \cdot 10^8$ m/sec.

This spectrum ranges from long waves like radio waves to short rays called gamma waves. The invisible spectrum is composed of many different rays such as infrared rays, which are detectable through heat. X-rays travel through matter and are used to view structures beneath the skin. Ultraviolet rays from the sun can damage skin, and gamma rays—the shortest rays—originate from radioactive substances.

Light normally moves along a straight line called a **ray**. When a ray of light hits a surface such as a mirror, the light is reflected back. The light ray moving toward the mirror is the **incident ray**. The ray of light bouncing back is the **reflected ray**. The angle of the incident ray and the angle of the reflected ray are equal; this is known as the **Law of Reflection**. Check out the figure below for an illustration of this point.

r

e

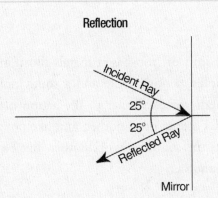

Reflection

When light rays pass through different mediums, such as air and water, they can be bent. The bending of light rays is called **refraction**. At some point, you may have noticed that objects immersed in water or some other liquid seem bent or broken at the point where they enter the liquid. The colors of a rainbow illustrate refraction.

Sound Waves

Sound is also a form of energy. It is a wave that occurs in high- and low-frequency ranges and that needs a medium to travel through. A high-frequency sound like a dog whistle has many waves per second. A low-frequency sound has fewer waves per second. The frequency of a sound wave is measured in **hertz,** which equals one wave per second. Ultrasound technology uses a very high frequency (10^6 Hz) while a dog can hear a frequency of 50,000 Hz. The normal range for human hearing is between 20 to 20,000 hertz.

A variation in the apparent sound frequency due to motion of the sound source is called the **doppler effect.** For example, one hears a difference in frequency as a train or race car approaches or moves away from an observer or another moving object. The doppler radar can help a meteorologist predict storms, such as tornadoes. The doppler red shift has shown that the galaxies in the universe are moving away from one another.

The speed of sound is dependent on air pressure and temperature. It measures .6 m/sec for every 1°C.

$$V = \text{frequency} \times \text{wavelength}$$

MAGNETISM

Materials attracted to iron or iron-based metals illustrate **magnetism**. Magnets have two **magnetic poles**, a north pole and a south pole. The poles represent regions of high magnetic force. Similar to the action of protons and electrons, opposite magnetic poles attract one another, and like poles repel. The north pole of one magnet attracts the south pole of another, but two north poles and two south poles repel one another.

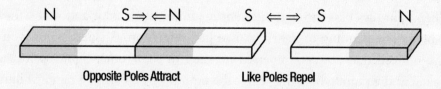

Opposite Poles Attract   Like Poles Repel

The space around the magnetic body is the **magnetic field**. The poles create the force of this field. To demonstrate magnetic field, iron filings can be sprinkled on a piece of paper under which a magnet has been placed. The filings, depending on the arrangement of the magnets, align themselves in the area of the field.

ELECTRICAL CIRCUITS

Electricity is the most widely used source of energy. The movement of electrons between atoms creates the electrical currents we know as electricity. Electricity exits in two forms: **static** and **electric current**. You're familiar with static electricity, especially if you've ever shuffled across a carpet in you socks and then touched something. This form of electricity is called "static" because it is electric charge **resting** on an object.

Coulomb's Law for static charges states that the force between two charged objects is proportional to the magnitude of the charge and inversely proportional to the distance. A **coulomb** is a very large unit. Static charges, which often occur in the home, are measured in microcoulombs. This law is used to calculate the force between protons or electrons in an atom:

$$F = k \frac{(\text{coulomb})(\text{coulomb})}{\text{distance}^2}$$

$$k = \frac{9 \cdot 10^9 \ \text{Nm}^2}{\text{coulomb}^2}; \text{this is constant.}$$

Electric current occurs when electrons **flow**. Electrons can move through all three states of matter (solids, liquids, and gases). Solids (such as metal) and liquids (such as water) act as **conductors** because they allow electrons to flow easily. Voltage is the energy that moves the charge through the conductor. It is measured in Joules per coulomb (J/coulomb). Other solids, like glass, plastic, and wood, act as **insulators** because they do not conduct electricity. The measure of the strength of an electric current is called **amperes** (amps). Amperes measure the flow of electric charge past a certain point in one second (coulomb/sec). Resistance is the opposition to a current; it is measured in ohms (Ω).

Electric current may be direct or alternating. Direct current flows in one direction (for example, a battery). Alternating current reverses direction at a frequency of 60Hz (for example, nuclear and coal energy at power plants goes to our homes, schools, and offices).

Electric Circuits

A circuit is a closed path for electrons to flow along. Circuits provide usable electricity to power your television or laptop computer. The following lists the parts of a circuit:

- Power: supply, such as a battery

- Wires: for electrons to flow through

- Resistance: the parts that use the energy, like a radio

- Switch: opens and closes the path

These parts create a circle in which the circuit operates. If there is a block in this circuit, the current won't pass through the circle and the electricity won't flow. Electrical resistance is measured in **ohms**. Substances such as metals make good conductors because they have low resistance.

The basic law of circuits is Ohms Law:

$$\text{Current} = \frac{\text{voltage}}{\text{Resistance}}, \text{ or I (current)} = \frac{\text{E (voltage)}}{\text{R(Resistance)}}$$

Types of Circuits—There are two types of circuits, **series** and **parallel**.

- **Series circuit:** A circuit in which the current must pass through every resistor in order to return to power

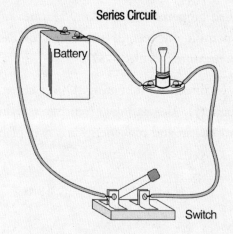

Series Circuit

When more than one resistor is in a series circuit, the value of each resistor is added together to give the total resistance:

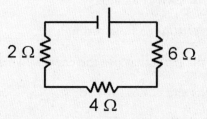

$R_t = R_1 + R_2 + R_3 + ...$

$R_t = 2\Omega + 4\Omega + 6\Omega$

$R_t = 12\Omega$

- **Parallel circuit:** A circuit in which the main current is divided into individual pathways; if there is a block or break in any part of the path, the electrons are still permitted to flow through.

AHSGE, GHSGT, BST, BSAP, WASL, CAHSEE, TAAS, OGT, HSPT/... CAT, MEAP HST, ... SPT/HSPA, FCAT, MEAP HST, GEE21, Regents Exams, SOL, NCCT, A... GHSGT, BST, BSA...

CHAPTER

6

Parallel Circuit

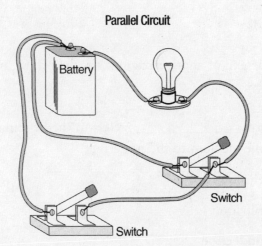

The total resistance of a set of parallel resistors is found in the following manner:

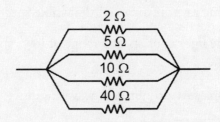

$$\frac{1}{R_t} = \frac{1}{R_1} + \frac{1}{R_2} + \frac{1}{R_3} + \ldots$$

$$\frac{1}{R_t} \quad \frac{1}{2\Omega} \quad \frac{1}{5\Omega} \quad \frac{1}{10\Omega} \quad \frac{1}{40\Omega}$$

$$\frac{1}{R_t} = .825$$

$$R_t = 1.21\Omega$$

Pop Quiz

You've reached the end of another section. Try the review questions to follow or go back and review.

1. The term _____ refers to the bending of light as it passes from one medium to the next.

   (A) reflection

   (B) reduction

   (C) conduction

   (D) refraction

2. Choose the statement that is true about the electromagnetic spectrum.

   (A) Gamma rays are a part of the visible spectrum.

   (B) Visible light consists of a range of low- and high-frequency wave lengths.

   (C) Gamma rays do not have wavelengths.

   (D) Microwaves are not a part of the electromagnetic spectrum.

3. A hertz measures

   (A) the crest of a wave.

   (B) the speed of light.

   (C) reflection.

   (D) the frequency of a sound wave.

4. Two magnets are placed together, yet as you try to make them touch, they repel one another strongly. What can account for this repulsion?

   (A) You are trying to force together two like poles, which naturally repel one another.

   (B) You are trying to force together two opposite poles, which naturally repel one another.

(C) You are not pushing the magnets hard enough.

(D) The electricity from your hands is causing them to repel.

5. You pull a woolen sweater over your head and hear a crackling sound. Later, you notice that strands of your hair are sticking straight out. Which of the following terms best describes this phenomenon?

(A) Convection

(B) Magnetism

(C) Static electricity

(D) Conduction

6. How much current flows through a device that has a resistance of 60Ω when 12 V is supplied?

7. Two objects have the identical charge of 1 coulomb and are separated by a distance of 1000 meters. Calculate the force between them.

8. A ray of light passes from air into water at an angle of 30°. Find its angle of reflection if $n_1 = 1$ for water and $n_2 = 1.33$ for air.

9. AM radiowaves are broadcast at frequencies between 550 kHz and 1600 kHz. Find the wavelengths.

10. In the following, elements of both the series circuit and the parallel circuit are combined.

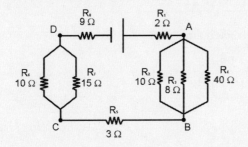

a. Find the total resistance for the circuit.

b. Use Ohm's Law to find the total current in the circuit.

ANSWERS

1. **The correct answer is (D).** Choice (A) is the bouncing back of an incident ray. Choice (B) is not a process related with light. Choice (C) refers to the ability to carry heat or a current.

2. **The correct answer is (B).** Based on the text information, choices (A), (C), and (D) are all false.

3. **The correct answer is (D).**

4. **The correct answer is (A).** The opposite poles (north and south) attract one another and the like poles (north to north or south to south) repel one another on a magnet.

5. **The correct answer is (C).**

6. $I = \dfrac{E}{R}$

   $I = \dfrac{12V}{60\Omega}$

   $I = .2A$

7. $F = \dfrac{9 \cdot 10^9 Nm^2}{coul^2}$

   $F = \dfrac{(1 \ coul)(1 \ coul)}{(1000m)^2}$

   $F = 9 \cdot 10^3 \ Nm$

8. According to Snell's Law, the incident angle equals the refracted angle.

   incident angle = refracted angle

   $n \sin\theta = n^2 \sin\theta$

   $(1)(\sin 30°) = (1.33)(\sin\theta)$

   angle = $22°$

9. $$\text{velocity} = \text{frequency} \times \text{wavelength}$$

$$3 \cdot 10^8 \,{}^{m}\!\!\big/\!_{\text{sec}} = (550 \cdot 10^3 \text{Hz})(x)$$

$$x = 550\text{m}$$

$$3 \cdot 10^8 \,{}^{m}\!\!\big/\!_{\text{sec}} = (1600 \cdot 10^3 \text{Hz})(x)$$

$$x = 190\text{m}$$

10a. The first step is to find the resistance for the $R_2 - R_3 - R_4$ parallel set of resistors:

$$\frac{1}{R_t} = \frac{1}{10\Omega} + \frac{1}{8\Omega} + \frac{1}{4\Omega}$$

$$\frac{1}{R_t} = .25\Omega$$

$$R_t = 4\Omega$$

Next, find the resistance for the $R_6 - R_7$ pair:

$$\frac{1}{R_t} = \frac{1}{10\Omega} + \frac{1}{15\Omega}$$

$$\frac{1}{R_t} = .1667$$

$$R_t = 6\Omega$$

Finally, add the two parallel values to R_1, R_5, and R_8:

$$R_t = 2\Omega + 4\Omega + 3\Omega + 6\Omega + 9\Omega$$

$$R_2 = 24\Omega$$

10b. $V = IR$

$$I = \frac{V}{R}$$

$$I = \frac{24V}{24\Omega}$$

$$I = 1A$$

Simple Machines

The mechanical devices that allow us to perform everyday tasks are called **machines.** The principle behind a door knob, a zipper, and a pair of scissors are all based on mechanical principals. All machines are composed of variations of numbers and arrangements of simple machines. There are six designs of machines that you are likely to see on your assessment exams:

- Lever

- Pulley

- Inclined plane

- Screw

- Wheel and axle

- Wedge

THE LEVER

The **lever** consists of a rod or pole that rests on an object at a fixed point called a **fulcrum.** The object to be lifted is referred to as the **resistance** and may be placed at various places with respect to the fulcrum. There are three types of levers based on fulcrum placement:

- **First-class levers** have a centrally located fulcrum between the load (what is being lifted) and the force (the work applied to do the lifting). Examples: seesaw, scissors, and pliers

- **Second-class levers** have the fulcrum located at one end, you at the other end (the force), and the load in the middle. Example: wheelbarrow

- **Third-class levers** have the fulcrum and force on one end and the load on the other. Examples: tongs, hammer, shovel

Pulley

The basic **pulley** consists of a wheel with a belt, chain, or rope wrapped around the wheel. With pulleys, the load (resistance) can be moved slowly and with less effort than would otherwise be needed. There are two pulley types:

- **Fixed pulleys** alter the direction in which the force moves the object so the load moves upward as the force is applied downward. Work must still be done to cause the movement, and if the load is greater than the force applied, the pulley won't be effective.

- **Moveable pulleys** provide more of a mechanical advantage. You can lift heavier objects by altering the amount of work needed.

> Pulleys are found throughout the home. Take a look at sliding draperies or your garage door.

The Inclined Plane

An **inclined plane** is a ramp that connects two levers. Heavy objects are moved by pushing them up a ramp as opposed to trying to lift them. The steepness of the slant on the ramp may make it increasingly difficult to move objects up, especially if the objects are heavy. So the length of the ramp can be made longer and the angle reduced to facilitate moving heavier objects.

> Examples of inclined planes are a sloping driveway, a staircase, and a treadmill.

Screw

A **screw** is an inclined plane, but it is in a circular form. It has fewer frictional forces, so the efficiency is high. This makes it ideal to drive through solid wood.

Wheel and Axle

Another simple machine, the **wheel** and **axle** consists of circular parts that vary in size. The wheel is usually larger and moves in a greater circular path than the axle. Some examples are an ice cream maker, a rotating can opener, a door knob, bicycle pedals, a steering wheel, and a screwdriver.

Wedge

This is another special type of inclined plane, but the **wedge** moves. This machine is commonly metal, and it consists of two inclined planes facing away from each other, back to back. Examples of this are a letter opener, a knife, an axe, and a zipper.

Pop Quiz

Guess what? This is the last Pop Quiz in the book! Once you finish it, go back and review anything you had trouble with, or jump to the Physics test in the last chapter.

1. A garage door illustrates what type of simple machine?

    (A) An inclined plane

    (B) A pulley

    (C) A wheel and axle

    (D) A lever

2. You are a member of the road crew for a musician. You need to get a grand piano up on a stage that is about 14 feet off the ground. Which of the following simple machines would be the best choice to move the piano?

    (A) Lever

    (B) Wheel and axle

    (C) Fixed pulley

    (D) Movable pulley

3. A fulcrum is found in a

    (A) lever.

    (B) pulley.

    (C) screw.

    (D) wedge.

4. The wedge and the screw are both special types of

    (A) pulley.

    (B) lever.

    (C) wheel and axle.

    (D) inclined plane.

Answers

1. **The correct answer is (B).**

2. **The correct answer is (D).** Choice (A) would not be the appropriate tool nor would it be effective at lifting a heavy piano to the height of 14 feet. Choice (B) is useless because no rotary movement is needed to lift the piano. Choice (C) is the correct principle but wrong model, as it is meant for objects of lesser weight; the force required to use a single pulley to lift a piano would be inefficient. Movable pulleys are needed to lift a load of this size.

3. **The correct answer is (A).**

4. **The correct answer is (D).** The screw presents a spiral inclined plane, and the wedge illustrates a two-sided incline plane.

PART

III

EXERCISES

CHAPTER 7

THE FINAL REVIEW

Most of the questions that you will encounter on your exit-level science exam will be multiple choice. However, there probably will be a few open-response questions thrown in, too. With these questions, you won't get to choose an answer from a list of choices, like in multiple-choice questions. Instead, this is your chance to "show what you know." You will have to demonstrate that you understand scientific facts, concepts, and procedures; you can correctly use scientific terms; and you can think "scientifically."

After you have completed each section review below, check your responses against the answer key, and then read the explanations to the questions you got wrong. If you still don't feel comfortable with any concepts, go back to the chapter review and study them again (use the index at the end of the book to find the right page) or crack open your textbooks and class notes.

Biology

1. The difference between chromatin material and chromosomes is

   (A) their form.

   (B) the kind of atoms that they contain.

   (C) where you find them.

   (D) that one is a gas and the other is a liquid.

2. A nucleus is found in

   (A) bacteria.

   (B) eukaryotic cells.

   (C) blue-green algae.

   (D) All of these answers are true.

3. A carrier molecule is required for

   (A) osmosis and active transport.

   (B) active transport and facilitated diffusion.

   (C) osmosis and diffusion.

   (D) facilitated diffusion and endocytosis.

4. Antibiotics interfere with a

   (A) prokaryotic cell's vacuole.

   (B) eukaryotic cell's metabolism.

   (C) eukaryotic cell's vacuole.

   (D) eukaryotic cell's membrane.

5. The direct intake of a liquid, such as an oil, into a cell is called

   (A) osmosis.

   (B) phagocytosis.

   (C) induction.

   (D) pinocytosis.

6. A cell that is 98 percent water is placed in a solution containing 3 percent salt. This cell is now _____ compared to its surroundings.

   (A) isotonic.

   (B) hypertonic.

   (C) hypotonic.

   (D) hydrophilic.

7. Most plant cells differ from animal cells in that they

   (A) possess nucleoli.

   (B) lack nucleoli.

   (C) contain mitochondria.

   (D) lack centrioles.

8. Some people get repeated fungal infections because they cannot destroy these microbes after their white blood cells phagocytize them. This most likely means that these people have _____ that do not work properly.

   (A) robosomes

   (B) lysosomes

   (C) mitochondria

   (D) microtubules

9. When you boil an egg white (albumin is protein), you have

   (A) inhibited the protein.

   (B) denatured the protein.

   (C) competed with the protein.

   (D) optimized the protein.

10. The substrate is

    (A) the material changed by an enzyme.

    (B) a coenzyme.

    (C) the material formed by an enzyme.

    (D) always a protein.

11. The enzyme salivary amylase in the mouth breaks down starch into the simple sugar glucose. The mouth has a pH of 7. Salivary amylase will

    (A) also break down starch in the stomach, which has a pH of 2.

    (B) be able to break down proteins to amino acids in the stomach.

    (C) be able to break down starch in a test tube. It doesn't need to be in the mouth.

    (D) only work at body temperature.

12. Before you dump an enzyme-active presoak into the washing machine, be sure to _____ so it will do a better job.

    (A) rub it into the stained area to increase enzyme-substrate contact

    (B) turn up the water temperature to boiling to get the enzyme molecules moving faster

    (C) add chlorine bleach to the enzyme

    (D) dilute the enzyme with water

13. Aerobic respiration requires the use of

    (A) N2.

    (B) O2.

    (C) H2.

    (D) H_2O.

14. Which of the following statements concerning photosynthesis and cellular respiration is false?

    (A) Both are biochemical pathways.

    (B) Both involve many enzyme-controlled reactions that are linked together.

    (C) Both involve the transfer of energy.

    (D) Photosynthesis occurs exclusively in plants, and cellular respiration occurs exclusively in animals.

15. The end product of glycolysis is

    (A) ketone.

    (B) alcohol.

    (C) pyruvic acid.

    (D) lactic acid.

16. A correct equation for photosynthesis is

    (A) $SUN + 6O_2 + 6CO_2 \rightarrow C_6H_{12}O_6 + 6H_2O$

    (B) $SUN + C_6H_{12}O_6 + 6O_2 \rightarrow 6CO_2 + 6H_2O$

    (C) $SUN + 6CO_2 + 6H_2O \rightarrow C_6H_{12}O_6 + 6O_2$

    (D) $SUN + 6CO_2 \rightarrow 6H_2O + C_6H_{12}O_6 + 6O_2$

17. In fermentation, yeast produces

    (A) ethyl alcohol.

    (B) oxygen.

    (C) hydrogen.

    (D) All of these answers are true.

18. After exercising at an increased rate, your muscles become sore. Which statement best describes what's happening in muscle cells?

    (A) The muscle cells have shifted into metabolism, and you are making lactic acid that causes them to ache.

    (B) You are producing lactic acid. Once you slow down, it will make its way back to your liver, where it will be converted into glucose.

    (C) You need to get more O_2 to your muscle cells.

    (D) All of these answers are true.

19. Which one of the following does NOT apply to RNA?

    (A) Single strand

    (B) Uracil base

    (C) Deoxyribose sugar

    (D) Involved in translation and transcription

20. A nucleotide is composed of molecules arranged in the following order:

    (A) three amino acids covalently bonded in a series.

    (B) three fatty acids individually bonded to three different places on glycerol.

    (C) a base bonded to a sugar bonded to a phosphate.

    (D) mRNA bonded to tRNA bonded to an amino acid.

21. The backbone of a double helix is

    (A) sugar-phosphate.

    (B) hydrogen bonds.

    (C) base-pairing.

    (D) All of these answers are true.

22. In DNA replication,

    (A) a new cover is made for the gene.

    (B) a new gene is made for the cover.

    (C) Both of these occur.

    (D) None of these occur.

23. A single strand, twisted back on itself like a hairpin, best describes

    (A) DNA.

    (B) mRNA.

    (C) tRNA.

    (D) ribosome.

24. If the sequence of bases in mRNA is U–C–A, the sequence of bases in DNA is

    (A) A–G–U.

    (B) A–G–T.

    (C) A–C–A.

    (D) T–G–U.

25. In translation, a cytosine in tRNA pairs opposite

    (A) uracil.

    (B) guanine.

    (C) thymine.

    (D) adenine.

PT/HSPA, FCAT, MEAP HST, GEE21, Regents Exams, SOL, NCCT, AHSGE, GHSGT, BST, BSAP
AHSGE, GHSGT, BST, BSAP, WASL, CAHSEE, TAAS, OGT, HSPT/H... CAT, MEAP HST, M
PT/HSPA, FCAT, MEAP HST, GEE21, Regents Exams, SOL, NCCT, AHSGE, GHSGT, BST, BSAP

CHAPTER
7

26. A codon calls for the placement of an individual

(A) protein.

(B) rRNA.

(C) amino acid.

(D) mRNA.

27. Which of the following is the correct sequence of events in protein synthesis?

(A) DNA > tRNA > mRNA > Protein

(B) mRNA > tRNA > Ribosome > Protein

(C) DNA > mRNA > tRNA > Ribosome > Protein

(D) tRNA > mRNA > DNA > Protein

28. If a drug interferes with the function of ribosomes, which one of the following is likely to occur?

(A) DNA will NOT be able to make copies of itself.

(B) Proteins will NOT be able to be produced.

(C) Mutations will occur to the DNA.

(D) Messenger RNA will not be able to be manufactured.

29. If every cell in a patient's body has undergone the same genetic change, it is most likely that

(A) he acquired this change from one of his parents.

(B) he was exposed to mutagenic agents.

(C) his mother was the only source of the mutant gene.

(D) All the above are true.

30. In a human, the 46 chromosomes would be at the equator during

    (A) interphase.

    (B) prophase.

    (C) anaphase.

    (D) metaphase.

31. A cell that contains eight chromosomes and is undergoing mitosis will produce _____ daughter cell (s); each daughter cell will contain ____ chromosomes.

    (A) two; eight

    (B) two; four

    (C) four; four

    (D) one; eight

32. Which one of the following techniques would be useful in controlling cancer once it has formed an abnormal growth?

    (A) Prevent mutations from occurring in the cancer cells

    (B) Treat the cancer with drugs or other therapies that kill dividing cells

    (C) Increase the mutation rate to kill the cancer cells

    (D) Increase the rate of mitosis in the cancer cells

33. When the pairs of chromosomes are at the equator of the cell, it is in

    (A) metaphase.

    (B) metaphase I.

    (C) metaphase II.

    (D) Any of these stages

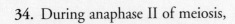
34. During anaphase II of meiosis,

    (A) the cell plate forms.

    (B) daughter cells form.

    (C) chromosomes move to the poles.

    (D) chromatid exchange.

35. If an organism proceeds through meiosis and produces sex cells with 32 chromosomes, the cells of the organism's stomach will each contain ____ chromosomes.

    (A) 32

    (B) 16

    (C) 64

    (D) 128

36. A condition when a diploid organism has different allelic forms of a particular gene is the definition of

    (A) homozygous.

    (B) phenotype.

    (C) genotype.

    (D) heterozygous.

37. In humans, normal vision dominates color blindness and both are sex-linked (the genes are located on the X chromosome). A color-blind male marries a woman who is heterozygous for normal vision. If they have a boy, the chance that he will be color blind is

    (A) 100 percent.

    (B) 0 percent.

    (C) 75 percent.

    (D) 50 percent.

38. The probability of parents with the genotypes Aa × aa having an offspring with the genotype (aa) is

   (A) 1/2.

   (B) 1/4.

   (C) 3/8.

   (D) 0.

39. In the cross AaBb × AaBb, _____ of the offspring will express _____.

   (A) 1/16; both dominant traits

   (B) 3/16; one dominant and one recessive trait

   (C) 6/16; one dominant and one recessive trait

   (D) 3/16; both recessive traits

40. "She is a carrier of the cystic fibrosis trait." This statement acknowledges that this person

   (A) is homozygous for the trait.

   (B) is heterozygous for the trait.

   (C) is trisomic.

   (D) has two recessive alleles.

41. Most of the oxygen carried by the blood

   (A) is dissolved in the plasma.

   (B) is bound to hemoglobin molecules.

   (C) is present as tiny bubbles in the blood.

   (D) is part of sugar molecules.

42. The function unit of the kidney is called

   (A) Bowman's capsule.

   (B) a collecting duct.

   (C) a nephron.

   (D) a loop of Henle.

43. Which is the normal direction in which the nerve impulse flows?

   (A) axon—soma—dendrite

   (B) dendrite—soma—axon

   (C) soma—dendrite—axon

   (D) dendrite—synapse—axon

44. The nervous system is most similar to which of the following?

   (A) A radio broadcast system

   (B) A motor

   (C) A computer

   (D) A chemical reaction

45. Which of the following endocrine glands produces the largest number of different kinds of hormones?

   (A) The pancreas

   (B) The testes

   (C) The thyroid

   (D) The pituitary

46. Skeletal muscle contractions are under the control of

   (A) exocrine glands.

   (B) the endocrine system.

   (C) the endocrine and exocrine systems.

   (D) the nervous system.

47. The embryo develops into a fetus while it is in the

    (A) ovary.

    (B) cervix.

    (C) vagina.

    (D) uterus.

48. In humans, egg production (oogenesis) differs from sperm production (spermatogenesis) in that oogenesis

    (A) produces many more cells than spermatogenesis.

    (B) usually results in fertilization.

    (C) produces polar bodies.

    (D) occurs for the majority of a person's life.

49. Alternation of generations is a characteristic of

    (A) mycetae.

    (B) prokaryotae.

    (C) animalia.

    (D) plantae.

50. A host provides the means of reproduction for

    (A) plantae.

    (B) mycetae.

    (C) algae.

    (D) viruses.

51. A kingdom of eukaryotic, one-celled organisms is the

    (A) prokaryotae.

    (B) protista.

    (C) plantae.

    (D) animalia.

52. Which of the following correctly shows the organisms' sizes from largest to smallest?

   (A) prokaryotic cell → eukaryotic cell → virus

   (B) eukaryotic cell → prokaaryotic cell → virus

   (C) eukaryotic cell →virus → prokaryotic cell

   (D) virus → eukaryotic cell → prokaryotic cell

53. _____ viruses are called retroviruses because their genetic material is RNA.

   (A) DNA

   (B) Small

   (C) RNA

   (D) Protein

54. The style and the stigma are both parts of the

   (A) stamen.

   (B) ovary.

   (C) seed.

   (D) pistil.

55. An insect-pollinated plant would be likely to have

   (A) no petals and no odor.

   (B) colorless petals and no odor.

   (C) reduced petals and a fragrant odor.

   (D) showy petals and fragrant odor.

56. Gymnosperms, angiosperms, and ferns are alike in that they all

    (A) produce seeds.

    (B) have well-developed vascular tissue.

    (C) have flowers during some part of their life cycles.

    (D) lack a gametophyte generation.

57. You observe a pine with two distinctly different types of cones. The best explanation for this is

    (A) the tree was produced by graphing.

    (B) a mutation has occurred in this plant.

    (C) one cone is the male reproductive structure, and the other is the female reproductive structure.

    (D) one cone is a gameophyte, and the other is a sporophyte.

58. A kind of vascular tissue, called _____, carries manufactured food from leaves to stems and roots.

    (A) zylem

    (B) phloem

    (C) cambium

    (D) stroma

59. Animals with backbone are

    (A) vertebrates.

    (B) chordates.

    (C) colonial.

    (D) invertebrates.

60. Members of this group of animals have the following characteristics: spines on surface; radial symmetry; live in marine habitats only; tube feet; and water vascular system.

(A) Mollusca

(B) Annelida

(C) Echinodermata

(D) Arthropoda

61. What is the difference between a renewable resource and a nonrenewable resource? Provide examples of each.

_____

_____

_____

_____

62. What is a neuron, and how does it work?

_____

_____

_____

63. Give an example of an animal from each of the following phyla:

(A) Porifera

(B) Chordata

(C) Annelida

(D) Cnidaria

(E) Arthropoda

STOP. Go to page **309** to check your answers

Chemistry

1. Which is true about the characteristics of a neutron?

   (A) It has no charge and no mass.

   (B) It has no charge and a mass of 1 amu.

   (C) It has a charge of +1 and no mass.

   (D) It has a charge of +1 and a mass of 1 amu.

2. Which energy level can hold a maximum of 2 electrons?

   (A) 1

   (B) 2

   (C) 3

   (D) 4

3. Which equation is correctly balanced?

   (A) $H_2 + O_2 \rightarrow H_2O$

   (B) $Ca + Cl_2 \rightarrow CaCl$

   (C) $2H_2 + O_2 \rightarrow 2H2O$

   (D) $Ca + Cl_2 \rightarrow Ca_2Cl$

4. Which of these elements has an atom with the most stable outer electron configuration?

   (A) Ne

   (B) Cl

   (C) Ca

   (D) Na

5. What is the total number of moles of solute in 250 milliliters of a 1.0 M solution of NaCl?

   (A) 1.0 mole

   (B) 0.25 mole

   (C) 0.50 mole

   (D) 42 moles

6. A student dissolves a substance in water. When he tests the resulting solution, he observes that red litmus paper turns blue. Based on this result, the solution is

   (A) organic.

   (B) inorganic.

   (C) basic.

   (D) acidic.

7. Given the following reaction $HSO_4^- + NH_3 \rightleftarrows SO_4^{2-} + NH_4^+$ at equilibrium, what are the two Brønsted-Lowery acids?

   (A) NH_3 and NH_4^+

   (B) NH_3 and SO_4^{2-}

   (C) HSO_4^- and SO_4^{2-}

   (D) HSO_4^- and NH_4^+

8. Identify the reaction when an equal concentration of H^+ and OH^- are mixed.

   (A) Oxidation

   (B) Reduction

   (C) Hydrolysis

   (D) Neutralization

9. Given the reaction Ag(s) + 2HCl(aq) → AgCl (aq) + H$_2$ (G), the oxidation number of Ag(s) increases because it

   (A) loses electrons.

   (B) gains electrons.

   (C) loses protons.

   (D) gains protons.

10. If the temperature of sample gas A increases at constant pressure, the volume of the gas

    (A) decreases.

    (B) increases.

    (C) remains the same.

11. Which is the smallest particle sucrose (table sugar) that still has all the properties of sugar?

    (A) Atom

    (B) Proton

    (C) Isotope

    (D) Molecule

12. An electron cloud is defined as

    (A) a space around the nucleus where electrons are found.

    (B) the first two energy levels of electrons in an atom where electron density is greatest.

    (C) a more specific term for the entire atom, since all chemical properties are determined by the electrons.

    (D) an atmosphere cloud in which electrons have been stripped from atoms and molecules and are free in the cloud.

13. Melting can be defined as a

    (A) chemical change.

    (B) phase change of solid to liquid.

    (C) substance undergoing sublimation.

    (D) change from solid to gas only in the presence of a high temperature.

14. Which represents a chemical change in matter?

    (A) Carbon dioxide undergoing sublimation

    (B) Water dissolving salt to form a solution

    (C) Water undergoing condensation

    (D) Metal fence beginning to rust

15. Tang drink mix is prepared for breakfast by stirring the crystals into water. Water is the

    (A) solute.

    (B) solvent.

    (C) compounding agent.

    (D) heterogeneous agent.

16. Today, your lab work involves working with acids. Which types of safety equipment are you most likely to need?

    (A) Gloves and safety glasses

    (B) Safety glasses and litmus paper

    (C) Fire extinguisher and blanket

    (D) Litmus paper and an apron

17. Which group contains elements that are monatomic gases at STP?

    (A) 1

    (B) 2

    (C) 17

    (D) 18

18. Which property is characteristic of nonmetals?

    (A) They have a high electronegativity.

    (B) They lose electrons easily.

    (C) They have a low first ionization energy.

    (D) They are good conductors of electricity.

19. Which element is an alkali metal?

    (A) Hydrogen

    (B) Calcium

    (C) Sodium

    (D) Zinc

20. A sample of an unknown gas at STP has a density of 1.25 grams per liter. What is the gram-molecular mass of this gas?

    (A) 28.0 g

    (B) 44.0 g

    (C) 64.0 g

    (D) 80.0 g

SCIENCE

21. According to the Brønsted-Lowry theory of an acid, it is a substance that

    (A) releases hydroxide ions into solution.

    (B) releases oxide ions into solution.

    (C) donates protons to another species.

    (D) accepts protons from another species.

22. Matter is anything that

    (A) has mass and occupies space.

    (B) has the capacity to do work.

    (C) can be changed in form.

    (D) can produce change.

    (E) can be conserved.

23. N_2 and O_2 are examples of

    (A) compounds consisting of two different elements.

    (B) elements consisting of a compound and an ion.

    (C) molecules consisting of two elements of the same compound.

    (D) molecules consisting of two atoms of the same element.

    (E) molecules consisting of two ions of the same element.

24. Protons, neutrons, and electrons are all

    (A) forms of energy.

    (B) equal in mass.

    (C) subatomic particles.

    (D) negative ions.

    (E) positively charged.

25. The volume of an atom is mostly

    (A) electrons.

    (B) protons.

    (C) neutrons.

    (D) ions.

    (E) free space.

26. Each of the vertical columns of the periodic table of elements is called a

    (A) metal group.

    (B) nonmetal period.

    (C) metalloid column.

    (D) period.

    (E) group.

27. Which of the following characterizes metal?

    (A) They are found in the upper right of the periodic table.

    (B) Examples of metals include hydrogen and carbon.

    (C) They usually conduct electricity.

    (D) They are not usually shiny.

    (E) They usually form covalent bonds.

28. All of the following are among the six elements that make up the vast majority of the atoms of all living things EXCEPT

    (A) hydrogen.

    (B) nitrogen.

    (C) sulfur.

    (D) carbon.

    (E) sodium.

29. Forces of attraction between water molecules are called

    (A) ionic bonds.

    (B) hydrogen bonds.

    (C) covalent bonds.

    (D) nonmetal-nonmetal bonds.

    (E) metal-nonmetal bonds.

30. H_2O and NaCl are

    (A) elements.

    (B) mixtures.

    (C) inorganic compounds.

    (D) organic compounds.

    (E) usually liquids.

31. A teacher and a kindergartner spent a half hour picking up all the toys and placing them on the shelves and in the drawers. The next evening, most of the toys were back on the floor. The concept that best describes this observation is

    (A) conservation of matter.

    (B) conservation of energy.

    (C) entropy.

    (D) kinetic energy.

    (E) potential energy.

32. In the expression $C_6H_{12}O_6 \rightarrow 2C_2H_5OH + 2CO_2$, the products are

    (A) $C_6H_{12}O6$.

    (B) $C_6H_{12}O_6$ + zymase.

    (C) zymase + $2C_2H_5OH + 2CO2$.

    (D) $2C_2H_5OH + 2CO2$.

33. If a particular atoms has 14 electrons, 14 protons, and 12 neutrons, its mass number would be

(A) 12

(B) 14

(C) 26

(D) 28

34. $AgNO_3 + NaCl \rightarrow AgCl + NaNO_3$. The $AgNO_3$ in the equation is called

(A) a reactant.

(B) an acid.

(C) a product.

(D) a base.

35. A solution with a high concentration of hydrogen ions could have a pH of

(A) 2

(B) 6

(C) 9

(D) 11

36. If an atom has an atomic number of 10, which orbital will be filled with electrons?

(A) $1s, 2s, 2px, 2py, 2pz$

(B) $2s, 2px, 2py, 3s$

(C) $1s, 2s, 2p, 3s$

(D) $1s, 2sx, 2sy, 2sz$

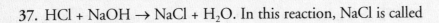

37. HCl + NaOH → NaCl + H_2O. In this reaction, NaCl is called

   (A) a product.

   (B) an acid.

   (C) a molecule.

   (D) All of these answers are true.

38. One molecule of sodium nitrate ($NaNO_3$) contains _____ atoms.

   (A) 6

   (B) 5

   (C) 4

   (D) 3

39. The pH of a strong base is

   (A) 2

   (B) 6

   (C) 9

   (D) 12

40. Which reaction produces a salt?

   (A) KOH + H_2O → K^+ + OH^- + H_2O

   (B) $HC_2H_3O_2$ + H_2O → $C_2H_3O_2$- + H^+ + H_2O

   (C) HCl + NaOH → NaCl + H_2O

   (D) $C_6H_{12}O_6$ + $C_6H_{12}O_6$ → $C_{12}H_{22}O_{11}$ + H_2O

41. Which combination is MOST likely to undergo chemical reaction based on its elements' positions in the Periodic Table of the Elements?

    (A) Na and Cl

    (B) Na and Mg

    (C) F and Me

    (D) All of the above would react.

42. Which of the following is a base or alkaline material?

    (A) NaOH

    (B) HCl

    (C) H_2SO_4

    (D) NaCl

For questions 43–47, refer to the Periodic Table at the back of the book.

43. The element that has the atomic number of 6 is

    (A) sodium.

    (B) oxygen.

    (C) fluoride.

    (D) carbon.

44. Find the carbon family. What do these elements have in common?

    (A) They are in the same period.

    (B) They are metals.

    (C) They have the same number of electrons.

    (D) They have four electrons in their outer shell.

45. The noble gases belong to

(A) Group O.

(B) Group VIIA.

(C) Group IA.

(D) Group IIA.

46. How many electrons are in the outside level of an atom of iodine?

(A) 5

(B) 4

(C) 7

(D) 2

47. Calculate the formula weight of $CaCO_3$.

(A) 50

(B) 68

(C) 100

(D) 124

48. _____ involves a chemical reaction.

(A) Burning a match

(B) Breaking a pencil

(C) Freezing water

(D) Dropping a ball

49. Determine the volume of 4.50 moles of an unknown gas that exerts 7.50 atm pressure at 350 K.

(A) 28L

(B) 17.2L

(C) 1.72L

(D) 46.7L

50. The scientist who discovered the volume of gas is inversely proportional to pressure is

(A) Avogadro.

(B) Charles.

(C) Pascal.

(D) Boyle.

51. Describe the difference between the chemical and physical properties of matter.

_____

_____

_____

_____

52. Name 2 ways in which you can speed up a chemical reaction.

_____

_____

_____

_____

STOP. Go to page **315** to check your answers.

Earth Science

1. The thin gaseous layer of air around the planet is called the

    (A) atmosphere.

    (B) lithosphere.

    (C) stratosphere.

    (D) hydrosphere.

    (E) troposphere.

2. Fossil fuels and minerals are found in the

    (A) atmosphere.

    (B) lithosphere.

    (C) biosphere.

    (D) hydrosphere.

    (E) troposphere.

3. The sun is composed primarily of

    (A) hydrogen.

    (B) helium.

    (C) heavy metals.

    (D) ions.

    (E) neutrons.

4. When incoming solar radiation is converted to heat, it is least likely to be trapped in the atmosphere by

    (A) water vapor.

    (B) carbon dioxide.

    (C) methane.

    (D) nitrogen gas.

    (E) ozone.

HIGH STAKES

5. Humans are most likely to alter the Earth's thermostat through their impact on the compound

  (A) carbon dioxide.

  (B) nitrogen gas.

  (C) phosphate.

  (D) hydrogen sulfide.

  (E) carbohydrate.

6. Computer models suggest that adding carbon dioxide to the atmosphere could

  (A) enhance the natural greenhouse effect.

  (B) disrupt food production.

  (C) raise sea levels.

  (D) alter climate patterns.

  (E) All of the above

  (F) None of the above. The Earth can maintain balance no matter what we do.

7. The most common gas in the atmosphere is

  (A) nitrogen.

  (B) carbon dioxide.

  (C) oxygen.

  (D) hydrogen.

  (E) water vapor.

8. Features of weather include all of the following EXCEPT

  (A) temperature.

  (B) barometric pressure.

  (C) wind direction.

  (D) ozone concentration.

  (E) precipitation.

9. You glance up at the sky and observe a giant thunderhead. You predict the arrival of a

    (A) warm front.

    (B) cold front.

    (C) hurricane.

    (D) typhoon.

    (E) cyclone.

10. You turn on the news. The weather reporter predicts the arrival of a high-pressure air mass. You are most likely to

    (A) stay home.

    (B) wear a raincoat and boots.

    (C) wear a jacket that suits the temperature.

    (D) put on a down jacket with ear muffs and mittens.

    (E) buy a snow blower.

11. Climate is influenced by

    (A) global air circulation.

    (B) topography.

    (C) atmospheric composition.

    (D) ocean currents.

    (E) All of the above

12. The term "greenhouse effect"

   (A) describes occupational diseases of florist.

   (B) describes the trapping of heat energy in the troposphere by certain gaseous molecules.

   (C) describes the trapping of heat energy in the stratosphere by nitrogen.

   (D) describes effort by the White House to support environmental legislation.

   (E) makes Earth uninhabitable.

13. Ozone

   (A) in the stratosphere is a pollutant.

   (B) is formed in the stratosphere through the interaction of infrared radiation and molecular oxygen.

   (C) filters out all harmful ultraviolet radiation.

   (D) in the stratosphere forms a thermal cap that is important in determining the average temperature of the troposphere.

   (E) All of the above

14. Oceans cover about _____ percent of the Earth's surface.

   (A) 50

   (B) 60

   (C) 70

   (D) 80

   (E) 90

15. Earth's interior concentric zones include

    (A) the shell.

    (B) the crust.

    (C) the mantle.

    (D) the core.

    (E) All of the above

    (F) Choices (B), (C), and (D)

16. Which of the following comparisons of Earth's processes to other pro-
    cesses does not make sense?

    (A) Convection cells resemble a pot of boiling soup.

    (B) A mantle plume is like smoke coming from a chimney on a cold,
        calm morning.

    (C) Tectonic plates are like large pieces of ice floating on the surface
        of a lake during the spring breakup.

    (D) Chemical weathering is like smashing a candy cane with a
        hammer.

    (E) The speed of movement of lithospheric plates is similar to the
        speed of fingernail growth.

17. The majority of earthquakes and volcanoes occur

    (A) in the interior of continents.

    (B) on oceanic islands.

    (C) along the edge of continents.

    (D) in the open ocean.

    (E) at the poles.

HIGH STAKES

18. The theory of plate tectonic explains

   (A) the occurrence of earthquakes.

   (B) the occurrence of volcanoes.

   (C) continental drift.

   (D) the movement of Earth's plates.

   (E) All of the above

19. Folded mountains form at the boundary of

   (A) Earth's crust and the mantle.

   (B) Earth's mantle and the core.

   (C) the asthenosphere and the lithosphere.

   (D) two converging tectonic plates.

   (E) two diverging tectonic plates.

20. Earthquakes can be triggered when

   (A) Earth's crust and mantle collide.

   (B) the asthenosphere solidifies.

   (C) tectonic plates move in opposite but parallel directions along a fault.

   (D) tectonic plates move away from each other.

   (E) tectonic plates collide with each other.

   (F) Choices (C), (D), and (E)

21. Mass wasting includes

   (A) mudflows.

   (B) slumps.

   (C) rockslides.

   (D) earthflows.

   (E) All of the above

22. All of the following are broad classes of rock EXCEPT

    (A) sedimentary.

    (B) igneous.

    (C) metamorphic.

    (D) crystal.

    (E) None of the above; all four are broad classes of rock.

23. Lava is an example of _____ rock.

    (A) metamorphic

    (B) igneous

    (C) sedimentary

    (D) plasticized

    (E) None of the above

24. The most abundant type of rock is

    (A) metamorphic.

    (B) igneous.

    (C) sedimentary.

    (D) gemstones.

    (E) None of the above

25. Which of the following rocks is most likely to be formed from com-
    pacted plant remains?

    (A) Coal

    (B) Limestone

    (C) Rock salt

    (D) Marble

    (E) Granite

26. The strength of an earthquake is measured on the ____ scale.

    (A) Richter

    (B) Miller

    (C) Zambini

    (D) Geiger

    (E) pH

27. Tsunamis are

    (A) underground caves.

    (B) large ocean waves.

    (C) atolls formed by South Pacific volcanoes.

    (D) sites of meteor impacts.

    (E) hurricanes.

28. A positive result of volcanic activity is

    (A) the creation of majestic mountains and lakes.

    (B) the production of geysers and hot springs.

    (C) the generation of fertile soil.

    (D) geothermal energy.

    (E) All of the above

29. Explain the relative positions of the Earth, the Moon, and the Sun during a lunar eclipse.

    _____

    _____

    _____

    _____

30. Carbon dioxide is important to life on Earth. However, international measures have been taken to reduce the emissions of this gas from the burning of fossil fuels as well as other sources. Identify two negative effects of increased carbon dioxide in Earth's atmosphere.

_____

_____

_____

_____

31. Which object orbits Earth in both the Earth-centered (geocentric) and Sun-centered (heliocentric) models of our solar system?

   (A) The Moon

   (B) Venus

   (C) The Sun

   (D) Polaris

32. The two most abundant elements (by mass) found in Earth's crust are

   (A) aluminum and iron.

   (B) sodium and chlorine.

   (C) calcium and carbon.

   (D) oxygen and silicon.

33. A blue giant is

   (A) a small cool star.

   (B) the core of the Sun.

   (C) a large hot star.

   (D) a star cluster.

For questions 34 and 35, refer to the following illustration:

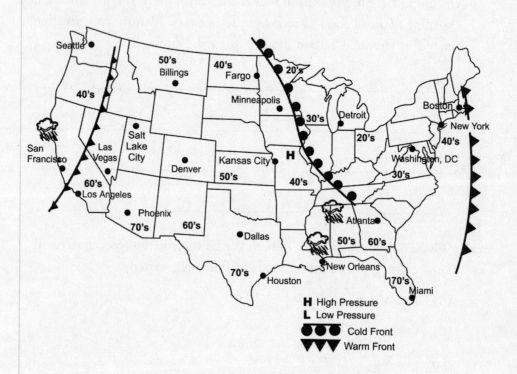

34. According to the illustrated weather map, in which city is it raining?

    (A) Miami

    (B) Dallas

    (C) Minneapolis

    (D) San Francisco

35. Which city on the weather map is experiencing a warm front with temperatures in the 60s?

    (A) Washington

    (B) Los Angeles

    (C) Denver

    (D) Atlanta

36. Which of the following natural changes would be considered gradual rather than catastrophic?

    (A) Drought

    (B) Landslide

    (C) Climate change

    (D) Fire

    (E) Volcanic eruption

37. A meteorologist collecting data in the field is least likely to use

    (A) a computer model.

    (B) aircraft.

    (C) satellites.

    (D) radar.

    (E) weather balloons.

38. Which of the following statements is false?

    (A) The amount of solar energy reaching Earth's surface is dependent on latitude.

    (B) Hot air rises.

    (C) Air at the lower latitudes tends to cool and fall or sink downward.

    (D) Cool air is denser than warm air.

    (E) Air is heated much more at the equator than at the poles.

    (F) None of the above

39. The deepest part of the ocean is

    (A) abyssal zone.

    (B) euphotic zone.

    (C) estuary zone.

    (D) bathyal zone.

    (E) estuarine zone.

40. If you were studying Earth's internal crust changes, which of the following time frames would be most appropriate to use?

(A) Minutes to hours

(B) Hours to decades

(C) Decades to centuries

(D) Thousands of years to millions of years

(E) Millions of years to billions of years

41. What is erosion? Discuss five ways in which it occurs.

_____

_____

_____

_____

STOP. Go to page **319** to check your answers

Physics

1. If one tuning fork has a higher frequency than the other, it also has

    (A) less volume.

    (B) a higher pitch.

    (C) greater amplitude.

    (D) a lower Hertz value.

2. For a science experiment, you submerge your hand into a large dish of water. The heat transfers from your skin to the water. This transfer of heat is an example of

    (A) radiation.

    (B) induction.

    (C) convection.

    (D) evaporation.

3. An astronaut weighs 500 newtons on Earth and 25 newtons on asteroid X. What is the gravity on asteroid X?

    (A) 1 m/s^2

    (B) 2 m/s^2

    (C) 0.2 m/s^2

    (D) 0.5 m/s^2

4. Which graph best represents the motion of an object whose speed is increasing at a constant rate?

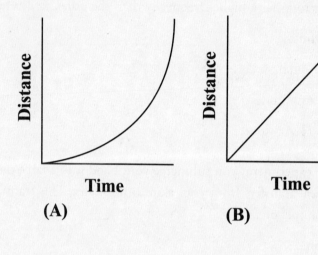

(A)

(B)

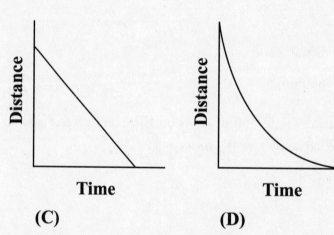

(C)

(D)

SCIENCE

5. The graph below shows a car traveling over a 4-hour period. Between hours 2 and 3, the best description about what is happening to the car is

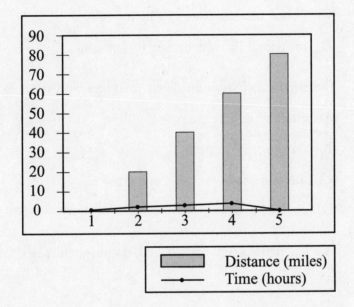

Distance (miles)
Time (hours)

(A) the car is stopped.

(B) the car is moving at a constant speed of 30 miles per hour.

(C) the car is accelerating.

(D) the car is decelerating.

6. A vase falling off a table and on to the floor illustrates

(A) potential energy converted to kinetic energy.

(B) kinetic energy converted to potential energy.

(C) energy being destroyed.

(D) force.

7. A mirage is caused by

   (A) reflection of light rays off the sand creating a false image.

   (B) refraction of light rays off the sand creating a false image.

   (C) virtual images created by light.

   (D) incidental light illuminated from sand.

8. The electrical circuit most likely used in a blow dryer is

   (A) alternating current.

   (B) transformed current.

   (C) direct current.

   (D) circuit breakers.

9. As a magnetic pole is approached, the magnetic force

   (A) decreases.

   (B) increases.

   (C) remains the same.

   (D) fluxuates.

10. Which of the following is the best example of a pulley?

    (A) The human forearm

    (B) A chain hoist

    (C) A round water faucet

    (D) A staircase

11. Which of the following would not be a form of energy?

    (A) Heat

    (B) Chemical

    (C) Light

    (D) All of the above are forms of energy.

12. Sound waves move faster in _____ as a result of density.

(A) air

(B) liquids

(C) liquids and solids

(D) vacuums

13. Energy can be formally defined as

(A) the randomness of molecules.

(B) the ability to do work and transfer heat.

(C) a force that is exerted over some distance.

(D) the movement of molecules.

14. Energy is classified as being either

(A) chemical or physical.

(B) kinetic or mechanical.

(C) potential or mechanical.

(D) potential or kinetic.

15. All of the following are examples of kinetic energy EXCEPT

(A) a speeding bullet.

(B) a stick of dynamic.

(C) a falling rock.

(D) a waterfall.

16. A chair is pushed across a floor at a constant force and velocity, on a friction-free horizontal surface. In this manner,

(A) mechanical energy is converted into electrical energy.

(B) mechanical energy is converted into heat.

(C) heat is transferred from the chair to the surface.

(D) kinetic energy is conserved.

17. Appliances come equipped with electric cords consisting of two pieces of copper wire wrapped with a plastic cover. Explain the functions of the copper and the plastic.

_____

_____

_____

_____

18. A spoon used to stir a glass of tea appears bent through the water, but upon removal, it is straight again. Explain the property at work causing the spoon to appear bent in the water.

_____

_____

_____

_____

19. Light and sound share the property of

(A) pitch.

(B) dispersion.

(C) waves.

(D) diffraction.

20. In which of the following scenarios is the most work being done?

(A) A cashier ringing up a purchase

(B) A student carrying a backpack full of books down a flight of stairs

(C) A teacher grading papers

(D) A group of men pushing a stalled car that won't move

21. What is the amount of work done as a 100-pound force is applied to slide a barrel 5 feet along a level surface?

    (A) 500 ft./lb

    (B) 20 ft./lb

    (C) .05 ft./lb

    (D) 25 ft./lb

22. Calculate the potential energy of a vehicle with a mass of 3500kg that is resting on a hydraulic lift 3 meters above the floor of an auto body shop.

    (A) 10,290 J

    (B) 10,500 J

    (C) 1029 J

    (D) 102,900 J

23. When you weigh a quantity of fruit in the produce section, the scales used work on the principle of what simple machine?

    (A) Wheel and axle

    (B) Pulley

    (C) Lever

    (D) Incline

24. A child swinging back and forth on a swing illustrates

    (A) the First Law of Thermodynamics.

    (B) the Law of Definite Proportions.

    (C) the Law of Conservation of Energy.

    (D) the Law of Inertia.

25. Based on the specific heats of the following materials, which one would be the best choice to make pots and pans out of?
Aluminum = .22; Iron = .11

(A) Iron

(B) Aluminum

(C) Neither

(D) Iron coated with Aluminum

26. Calculate the gravitational force between Jupiter and the Sun using the data below.

$G = 6.67 \times 10^{-11} \text{ Nm}^2/\text{kg}^2$

$M_J = 2 \times 10^{30} \text{ kg}$

$M_S = 2 \times 10^{27} \text{ kg}$

$d = 7.78 \times 10_{11}\text{m}$

27. A 5.2 kg object is accelerated from rest to a velocity of 12 m/sec as the object covers 5m of approach before being released. What is the force exerted on the object during this time?

28. A 2575 kg van runs into the back of an 825 kg car at rest. The vehicles travel after collision as one mass at 8.5 m/sec. Find the initial velocity of the van.

29. A student drops an object from a cliff to a lake 12.0 m below. Calculate the velocity before the rock strikes the water.

Answers and Explanations

Biology

1. **The correct answer is (A).** Chromatin is the unorganized DNA that has not been coiled into chromosomes.

2. **The correct answer is (B).** Choices (A) and (C) refer to organisms that are prokaryotic. Prokaryotes do not have a nucleus.

3. **The correct answer is (B).** Active and facilitated transport require a protein mediator to move larger molecules into a cell or to work against a concentration gradient.

4. **The correct answer is (B).** Antibiotics can disrupt important metabolic pathways of bacteria, preventing their growth and spread.

5. **The correct answer is (D).** Choice (A) refers to the movement of water. Choice (B) refers to the cellular ingestion of particles. Choice (C) is not a biological process; it refers to how certain metals can be made into magnets.

6. **The correct answer is (C).** The solution is 97 percent water with 3 percent salt. The cell has a higher concentration of water but a lower solute concentration, making it hypotonic to the solution's solute concentration.

7. **The correct answer is (A).** Centrioles are organelles found in animal cells but not in plant cells. For mitosis, plants use a system of microtubules to separate chromosomes.

8. **The correct answer is (B).** Phagocytosis is marked by lysosomal activity performed on ingested material.

9. **The correct answer is (B).** Choices (A) and (B) refer to actions associated with an enzyme. Choice (D) is not a process.

10. **The correct answer is (A).** Choice (B) is a substance that assists the action of an enzyme. Choice (C) is a definition for a *product*. Choice (D) is incorrect because a substrate can be any substance acted upon by an enzyme.

11. **The correct answer is (C).** Salivary amylase, as with most enzymes, will perform hydrolysis to an extent outside of its optimal conditions. However, if the enzyme is put in extremes outside of its optimal conditions for factors like pH and temperature, it will cease to be functional. The test tube can be calibrated to mimic those conditions found in the mouth that cause the amylase to hydrolyze its substrate.

12. **The correct answer is (A).** Choices (B), (C), and (D) will either denature the enzyme or make the concentration of the enzyme too weak to be effective at catalyzing a reaction.

13. **The correct answer is (B).** Aerobic respiration requires sugar and oxygen in the presence of enzymes to start its reaction.

14. **The correct answer is (D).** Some bacterial cells are photosynthetic, and mitochondria are found in plant cells.

15. **The correct answer is (C).** Choice (A) is an organic molecule not used in glycolysis. Choices (B) and (C) are the end products of some forms of fermentation.

16. **The correct answer is (C).** This equation is balanced and shows the appropriate building blocks for photosynthesis.

17. **The correct answer is (A).** Choices (B) and (C) are incorrect, as they are not molecules produced separately during fermentation. Ethyl alcohol and carbon dioxide are the products of fermentation.

18. **The correct answer is (D).** All the statements listed are true of strenuous exercise. As you increase your movement, your heart rate and respiratory rate also increase. However, your skeletal muscle is using up the available oxygen faster than you can supply it. So to continue producing contraction, skeletal muscle switches to lactate fermentation, in which energy can be used without the need for oxygen. As your muscles move deeper into lactate fermentation, the lactic acid build-up produced is an irritant to skeletal muscle, causing them to ache.

19. **The correct answer is (D).** Deoxyribose sugar is found in DNA.

20. **The correct answer is (C).** Choice (A) is incorrect, as amino acids make proteins. Choice (B) describes a triglyceride lipid molecule. Choice (D) describes processes that occur during protein synthesis.

21. **The correct answer is (A).** Choices (B) and (C) occur within the double helix.

22. **The correct answer is (C).** DNA replication creates "replicas" off of opened DNA helices. This creates new yet identical copies of itself, which also means new genes.

23. **The correct answer is (C).** tRNA is often described as having "hooks" for amino acid attachments that resemble the loop of a hairpin.

24. **The correct answer is (B).** mRNA uses the base uracil in place of thymine, so when it base pairs with DNA, the *u* for uracil base pairs with the *t* for thymine in DNA. The cytosine to guanine base pairing remains the same.

25. **The correct answer is (B).** Except for uracil, all the other RNA bases retain the same base pair configurations found in DNA.

26. **The correct answer is (C).** Choice (A) is incorrect because proteins are assembled only after the correct amino acid sequence is organized by the tRNA and polymerized by ribosomes.

27. **The correct answer is (C).**

28. **The correct answer is (B).** Protein synthesis occurs on ribosomes.

29. **The correct answer is (A).** For a genetic change to occur in all of a person's cells, there must be an inherited precursor gene. Mutations will only affect those cells in which the mutagenic agents have altered

30. **The correct answer is (D).** This is seen in mitosis.

31. **The correct answer is (A).** Mitosis produces two cells that are genetically identical.

32. **The correct answer is (B).** Choices (A), (C), and (D) would have no effect on cancerous growth. In fact, choices (C) and (D) would increase the spread of the cancerous cells.

33. **The correct answer is (B).** The operative word here is *pairs*. Homologous pairs align along the equator in metaphase of meiosis II, or metaphase II.

34. **The correct answer is (C).** Choice (A) refers to a process occurring in plant cells. Choice (B) occurs at the end of telophase. Choice (D) is an incorrect allusion to crossing over.

35. **The correct answer is (C).** Cells produced by meiosis contain half of the genetic complement. These are sex cells. A stomach cell is a body cell that undergoes mitotic divisions. Therefore, it has a full genetic complement of 64 chromosomes.

36. **The correct answer is (D).** This is the basic genetic concept of heterozygosity; one dominant and one recessive gene. Each codes for the same trait, but the way in which they code is different.

37. **The correct answer is (D).** This is a sex-linkage problem, so remember to use XX for women and XY for men. Attach the genes to these. By working through the Punnet square for this cross: $X^H X^h \times X^h Y$, where H=normal and h=hemophilia. The result when considering only males is 50 percent.

38. **The correct answer is (B).** The cross AA × aa results in ¼ AA; ½ Aa; and ¼ aa.

39. **The correct answer is (C).** This is a dihybrid cross, so your Punnet square should have 16 squares. Be careful when you count the gene combinations. One mistake could throw off your whole square.

40. **The correct answer is (B).** Choices (A) and (D) denote the same genes: both dominant and both recessive, or homozygosity. Choice (C) is a term used to describe mutations resulting in three copies of a chromosome.

41. **The correct answer is (B).** Red blood cells contain carrier molecules called hemoglobin that bind oxygen.

42. **The correct answer is (C).** Choices (A), (B), and (D) are all parts of the nephron.

43. **The correct answer is (B).** Between adjacent neurons, an impulse moves from the axonal terminals of the presynaptic neuron across the synaptic cleft and then to the dendrites of the postsynaptic neuron.

44. **The correct answer is (C).** Choice (A) describes the action of hormones. Choice (B) is not related, and choice (D) is much too small of a scale for comparison.

45. **The correct answer is (D).** The pituitary is sometimes called the "master gland" for the numerous hormones it releases that affect other glands and organ.

46. **The correct answer is (D).** Skeletal muscle contracts by nervous impulses directing the fibers of muscle.

47. **The correct answer is (D).** Choices (A), (B), and (C) cannot hold, nor do they function in maintaining a fetus.

48. **The correct answer is (C).** This is the only true statement.

49. **The correct answer is (D).** The process of alternating sporophyte and gametophyte generations is exclusively seen in the plant kingdom.

50. **The correct answer is (D).** Choices (A), (B), and (C) do not need hosts to reproduce.

51. **The correct answer is (B).** Choice (A) is unicellular bacteria, and choices (C) and (D) are muliticellular.

52. **The correct answer is (B).**

53. **The correct answer is (C).** Choice (A) uses the term "DNA," which should tip you off that this is not the choice because the question tells you that the genetic material is RNA.

54. **The correct answer is (D).** The stigma, style, and ovary are all parts of the pistil.

55. **The correct answer is (D).** Insects are attracted to the ornate petals and aromatic fragrances; plants use these characteristics to increase their chances of pollination.

56. **The correct answer is (B).** Choice (A) is incorrect because ferns produce spores, not seeds. Choice (C) is incorrect because gymnosperms and ferns do not produce plants. Choice (D) is incorrect because all have a gametophyte phase.

57. **The correct answer is (C).** Pine trees contain both male and female cones.

58. **The correct answer is (B).** Choice (A) carries water and minerals for the plant. Choice (C) is a part of bark structure. Choice (D) is found in chloroplasts of plant cells.

59. **The correct answer is (A).** Choice (B) is incorrect because although vertebrates are a subphyllum of Phylum Chordata, this phylum also includes invertebrates. So it is not specific enough.

60. **The correct answer is (D).** Choices (A), (B), and (C) do not fit the characteristics given.

61. A renewable resource can be regenerated or repaired, such as hydropower. As long as a body of water (a river or waterfall) continues to flow beneath a hydropower plant, energy can be made. A nonrenewable resource cannot be regenerated or repaired. Continual consumption of a nonrenewable resource, such as oil, will eventually lead to its depletion.

62. Neurons are the nerve cells that transmit information throughout the body. Each neuron has its own job, and together they allow our bodies to be aware of everything we see, hear, taste, and feel. The neuron sends and receives electrical signals through a process of chemical exchange or a mechanical stimulus. These signals or messages are channeled through the brain. Sensory neurons are responsible for transmitting messages to the brain and the spinal chord. Motor neurons carry commands from the brain and spinal cord to the muscles and glands. Interneurons send signals back and forth between the brain and spinal cord to other parts of the body. The process of sending messages takes only a fraction of a second.

63. Possible answers:

    A. Sponge

    B. Shark, frog, snake, eagle, gorilla

    C. Leech, earthworm

    D. Jellyfish, coral, sea anemone

    E. Spider, fly, lobster, millipede

CHEMISTRY

1. **The correct answer is (B).** Both protons and neutrons have a mass of 1 amu.

2. **The correct answer is (A).**

3. **The correct answer is (C).** By counting the number of atoms for each element, you equalize the number of atoms on either side of the equation with coefficients.

4. **The correct answer is (A).** This is a noble gas, and these gases have stable outer shells.

5. **The correct answer is (B).** By using the molarity formula, you can rearrange it to solve for the volume.

$$M = \frac{\text{Number of moles of solute}}{\text{Liters of solution}}$$

$$1M = \frac{x}{.250\ell}$$

$$x = 0.25 \text{ moles}$$

6. **The correct answer is (C).** Litmus is red in acids and blue in bases.

7. **The correct answer is (D).** Brønsted-Lowry acids donate protons.

8. **The correct answer is (D).** This reaction is an acid-base neutralization.

9. **The correct answer is (A).** Oxidation numbers indicate the number of electrons lost through oxidation.

10. **The correct answer is (B).** Temperature and volume are directly related at constant temperature.

11. **The correct answer is (D).** Sugar is a molecular compound made of many different elements. Choice (A) is incorrect for this reason. Choices (B) and (C) are parts of an atom.

12. **The correct answer is (A).** This is a relatively modern theory explaining the electron's position in relation to the nucleus.

13. **The correct answer is (B).** Melting is a physical phase change.

14. **The correct answer is (D).** Choice (A) is incorrect because only solids undergo sublimation. Choice (B) is incorrect because the salt could be separated physically from water by evaporating the water. Choice (C) is a phase change.

15. **The correct answer is (B).**

16. **The correct answer is (A).** Choice (B) lacks gloves, and choices (C) and (D) lack any personal protective equipment.

17. **The correct answer is (D).** Group 0 are noble gases that fit the description of being monatomic at standard temperature and pressure.

18. **The correct answer is (A).** Choices (B), (C), and (D) are all properties of metals.

19. **The correct answer is (C).** Group IA are the Alkali Earth metals, to which sodium belongs.

20. **The correct answer is (A).** The Ideal Gas Law is rearranged to solve for n, which is the number of moles. The units can then be cancelled to leave 28 g.

$$PV = nR7$$
$$n = (1\,atm)(273\,k)(0.0821\,L - atm\,mol^{-1}K^{-1})(1.25g/\ell)$$
$$n = 28g$$

21. **The correct answer is (C).**

22. **The correct answer is (A).**

23. **The correct answer is (D).** These are "diatomic" elements.

24. **The correct answer is (C).**

25. **The correct answer is (E).** This characteristic was discovered by Lord Rutherford.

26. **The correct answer is (E).** This is the general definition for a group or family of elements.

27. **The correct answer is (C).** Choice (A) gives the location of some noble gases. Choice (B) is incorrect. Hydrogen is a gas, and carbon is a nonmetal. Choices (D) and (E) give characteristics of nonmetals also.

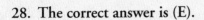
28. **The correct answer is (E).**

29. **The correct answer is (B).**

30. **The correct answer is (C).** Compounds consist of two or more elements chemically bound together. Choice (B) is not a chemically bound substance. Choice (D) refers to substance containing carbon. Choice (E) is false.

31. **The correct answer is (C).** Entropy is the degree of randomness or disorder in a system.

32. **The correct answer is (D).** Products are found on the right side of a chemical equation.

33. **The correct answer is (C).** Atomic Mass = Protons + Neutrons = 14 +12 = 26.

34. **The correct answer is (A).** Reactants are found on the right side of the equation.

35. **The correct answer is (A).** A high proton concentration is indicative of an acid. Acids have a low pH.

36. **The correct answer is (A).** The $1s$ level holds only two electrons. The 2 level is divided into $2s$, $2px$, $2py$, $2pz$, and each holds to electrons for a total of eight.

37. **The correct answer is (A).** NaCl is on the product side of this equation.

38. **The correct answer is (B).** Na is one atom, N is another, and there are three O atoms, for a total of five.

39. **The correct answer is (D).** Bases have a high pH.

40. **The correct answer is (C).** This is the only reaction that produces a salt.

41. **The correct answer is (A).**

42. **The correct answer is (A).** Alkaline implies a base, and classical Arrhenius bases contain OH⁻ ions.

43. **The correct answer is (D).**

44. **The correct answer is (D).** This information is given from the atomic # = protons = electrons. Knowing the electron number, you can figure out the configurations.

45. **The correct answer is (A).**

46. **The correct answer is (C).** This information is given by the group number to which iodine belongs, Group VII A.

47. **The correct answer is (C).** Ca = 40 + C = 12 + O_3 (3 × 16 = 48) = 100

48. **The correct answer is (A).** Choices (B), (C), and (D) are physical changes.

49 **The correct answer is (B).** Use the Ideal Gas Law equation and rearrange it to solve for V. Make sure all units cancel except liters.

$$Pv = nRT$$
$$(7.5\,\text{atm})(x) = (.45\text{m})(.082)(350\text{k})$$
$$x = 17.2\ell$$

50. **The correct answer is (D).**

51. Chemical properties are properties that, if changed, result in the formation of a different kind of matter. Flammability is an example of a chemical property. When a piece of wood burns, it becomes ash. Physical properties are qualities that, if changed, do not fundamentally change the type of matter. An example would be viscosity, or resistance to flow. Honey flows more slowly than gasoline, so honey has a higher viscosity. If you heat the honey, its viscosity decreases. However, it is still honey.

52. 1. Make the size of the reactant smaller to increase its surface area.

    2. Increase the temperature.

    3. Increase the concentration of your reactants if they are in a solution.

    4. Add a catalyst.

EARTH SCIENCE

1. **The correct answer is (A).** Choice (B) is part of the earth. Choices (C), (D), and (E) are subdivisions of the atmosphere.

2. **The correct answer is (B).** Choice (A) is not logical. Choice (D) refers to the Earth's waters above and below ground. Choice (E) is a part of the atmosphere.

3. **The correct answer is (A).** Hydrogen gas fuels the fusion reactions that generate the Sun's energy.

4. **The correct answer is (D).** Choices (A), (B), and, (C) are greenhouse gases that trap solar radiation.

5. **The correct answer is (A).** As a result of rapid industrialization and negative, wasteful handling of the environment, excess carbon dioxide becomes trapped in the atmosphere.

6. **The correct answer is (E).**

7. **The correct answer is (A).** Our atmosphere is 78 percent N and 21 percent O, with a few trace gases.

8. **The correct answer is (D).**

9. **The correct answer is (B).** When warm air is forced upward over a cold air mass, the contact zone between the two air masses is called a cold front. When this movement occurs rapidly, cumulonimbus clouds form. These are also called thunderheads.

10. **The correct answer is (C).** When air masses meet, weather is created. So until you are told what effect this high pressure air mass will have on the existing air mass, you should adjust your clothing accordingly.

11. **The correct answer is (E).**

12. **The correct answer is (B).** All the other choices are fictitious.

13. **The correct answer is (C).**

14. **The correct answer is (C).** It is true that the earth consists of 90 percent water; only 70 percent of this is found in the world's oceans.

15. **The correct answer is (F).** Choice (A) is the uppermost portion of the Earth's lithosphere.

16. **The correct answer is (E).**

17. **The correct answer is (C).** The point where continents meet are areas of where movements occur that can cause geological stresses like earthquakes or volcanoes.

18. **The correct answer is (E).**

19. **The correct answer is (D).** Converging plates over time crumple upward, creating mountains.

20. **The correct answer is (F).** Choice (A) is incorrect; the crust overlies the mantle. They don't collide. Choice (B) is incorrect since it contains plastic-like molten rock.

21. **The correct answer is (E).**

22. **The correct answer is (D).**

23. **The correct answer is (B).** Igneous rocks result from the cooling of hot magma and lava.

24. **The correct answer is (B).**

25. **The correct answer is (A).** Coal is classified as a biogenic sedimentary rock, formed by the accumulation and compaction of plant matter.

26. **The correct answer is (A).**

27. **The correct answer is (B).** Ocean earthquakes create tsunamis.

28. **The correct answer is (E).**

29. A lunar eclipse occurs when the plane of the Moon's orbit is a few degrees away from Earth. When the Moon's orbit and the Earth's orbit intersect, the line of intersection includes the Moon, the Earth, and the Sun, in this order.

30. Increased carbon dioxide increases the greenhouse gases that prevent radiation in the form of heat from leaving Earth's atmosphere. This causes a gradual global warming that causes polar ice caps to melt,

which in turn causes mass flooding. Vegetation that is not productive in higher temperatures will die. Air quality will deteriorate as increased particulate matter creates a persistent pollution dome in the immediate atmosphere.

31. **The correct answer is (A).** The Moon is Earth's satellite. Its orbit is not affected by the belief of either model.

32. **The correct answer is (D).** From the text, these two elements are in the highest concentration in the Earth's crust.

33. **The correct answer is (C).** Choice (A) is a red dwarf.

34. **The correct answer is (D).**

35. **The correct answer is (B).**

36. **The correct answer is (C).** Choices (A), (B), (D), and (E) can all be catastrophic.

37. **The correct answer is (A).** Typically when a meteorologist is collecting "field data," this implies actual data from the environment. This data can then be analyzed by a computer.

38. **The correct answer is (C).** At lower latitudes, air is warmed by nearby bodies of water.

39. **The correct answer is (A).**

40. **The correct answer is (E).**

41. Erosion is a process by which rock and soil is moved on the surface of the earth. There are five basic ways that erosion can take place. 1) Weathering takes place when the climate of an area affects the land. Hot or cold weather can expand or contract rocks and minerals. Rainy weather can have the effect of leaching the soil of minerals. 2) Wind erosion causes particles of soil and sand to be moved, especially in arid climates. Sand dunes are created by the wind blowing. 3) Glacial erosion occurs over a long period of time and removes rock as the glacier melts. 4) Coastal erosion occurs because of the waves of the ocean. It is particularly severe during storms. 5) Water erosion occurs when the ground is saturated with moisture. Excess water runs off, carrying with it loose soil.

PHYSICS

1. **The correct answer is (B).** High-frequency sounds produce high pitch. Pitch refers to the position of a musical note on a scale. It is determined by the frequency of the sound impulses produced.

2. **The correct answer is (C).** Convection, in this sense, is the transfer of energy from your hand into the water.

3. **The correct answer is (B).** By dividing 500N by 25N, you get a factor of 20. Divide 20 by $9.8 m/s^2$ to get $2 m/s^2$.

4. **The correct answer is (B).**

5. **The correct answer is (C).**

6. **The correct answer is (A).** While on the table, the vase had only potential energy. When it fell, this energy was converted to kinetic. This illustrates the Law of Conservation.

7. **The correct answer is (B).**

8. **The correct answer is (A).** Electricity is supplied to homes and commercial businesses by alternating current.

9. **The correct answer is (B).** The magnetic poles show the strongest magnetic strength.

10. **The correct answer is (B).** Choice (A) is an example of a lever. Choice (C) is an example of a wheel and axle. Choice (D) is a special inclined plane.

11. **The correct answer is (D).**

12. **The correct answer is (C).** Sound is greater in liquids and solids because of the greater "stiffness" or density. For example, sound waves travel 4.5 times faster in water than air.

13. **The correct answer is (B).** Choice (C) is the definition of work. Choice (D) refers to kinetic energy.

14. **The correct answer is (D).** These are the two major classifications of energy.

15. **The correct answer is (B).** Energy stored in a stick of dynamite, although chemical in nature, is classified as potential.

16. **The correct answer is (B).** Friction results in the conversion of mechanical energy into heat. No electrical energy results. Work has occurred since a force (you) has acted on the chair over a distance.

17. Copper is a good conductive metal that will allow electrons to flow with ease to create an electrical current within the circuit. The wires are covered in plastic for insulation purposes. The current would not make it to its destination if something interfered with the transfer of electrons. It also acts as a protection mechanism that prevents electrocution when someone touches exposed wires.

18. The property that causes the spoon to appear like it does in water is called **refraction**. This phenomenon is created by the bending of light rays as they pass through the water. The refracted rays occur if light rays strike the boundary between the two materials at an angle other than 90 degrees.

19. **The correct answer is (C).** Choice (A) is a property of sound only. Choice (B) is the process of separating white light into colors. Choice (D) is a property of light also.

20. **The correct answer is (B).** $W = F \times D$. The student is carrying a load of books and moving. Choices (A) and (C) have negligible force and distance. Choice (D) shows force, but the car isn't moving.

21. **The correct answer is (A).** The amount of work is calculated by using the equation $W = \text{force} \times \text{distance}$.

$W = fd$
$W = (100 \text{ lb})(5 \text{ ft})$
$W = 500 \text{ ft}$

22. **The correct answer is (D).** Using the equation P.E. = mgh, you get 102900 kg m²/s² units, also synonymous with Newton-meters, which is also Joules.

PE = mgh
PE = (3500 kg)(9.8 m/sec)(3m)
PE = 102,900 J

23. **The correct answer is (B).**

24. **The correct answer is (C).** As the child swings, the energy converts from potential to kinetic in a continuous fashion. No energy has been created or destroyed, it's just changed in form.

25. **The correct answer is (A).** The lower specific heat of iron means it will heat faster and quickly transfer this energy to food.

26. $F = G\dfrac{m_1 m_2}{d_2}$

$F = (6.67 \cdot 10^{-11}\,\mathrm{Nm^2}\big/\mathrm{kg^2})\left(\dfrac{(2 \cdot 10^{30}\,\mathrm{kg})(2 \cdot 10^{27}\,\mathrm{kg})}{(7.78 \cdot 10^{11}\,\mathrm{m})^2}\right)$

$F = 4.2 \cdot 10^{23}\,\mathrm{N}$

27. $vf^2 = v_{i^2} + 2ad$

$(12\,{}^{m}\!/_{sec})^2 = 0 + 2(a)(5m)$

$a = 14.4\,{}^{m}\!/_{sec^2}$

$F = ma$

$F = (5.2\mathrm{kg})(14.4\,{}^{m}\!/_{sec^2})$

$F = 75\,\mathrm{N}$

28. $(mass)(velocity) + (mass)(velocity) = (mass_{total})(velocity)$

$(2575kg)(x) + (825kg)(0) = (2575 + 825kg)(8.5\,{}^{m}\!/_{sec})$

$v = 11.2\,{}^{m}\!/_{sec}$

29. $vf^2 = v_i^2 + 2gd$

$vf^2 = O + 2 = (9.8 \, {}^m\!/_{sec^2})(12m)$

$vf = 15.3 \, {}^m\!/_{sec}$

That's the End!

You did it! You've completed the four basic science disciplines that will be covered on your exit-level exam. What's next? You can go back and review any really difficult parts in your textbooks or class notes before you take the real exam. **Good luck!**

INDEX

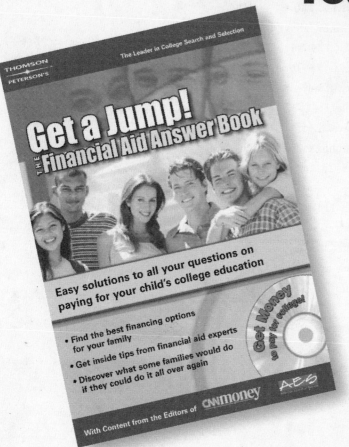